Negotiating Culture

Negotiating Culture

Heritage, Ownership,

and

Intellectual Property

EDITED BY

Laetitia La Follette

University of Massachusetts Press

AMHERST AND BOSTON

ISBN 978-1-62534-008-5 (paper); 007-8 (hardcover)

Designed by Sally Nichols
Set in Adobe Caslon Pro
Printed and bound by Thomson-Shore, Inc.

Library of Congress Cataloging-in-Publication Data
A catalog record for this book is available from the Library of Congress.

British Library Cataloguing in Publication Data
A catalogue record for this book is available from the British Library.

Cover: Roman statue of the goddess Peace (1st century CE), excavated at Palombara Sabina in Latium, one of the long-term loans made to American museums in exchange for the return of contested antiquities. Photo: Museum of Fine Arts, Boston, courtesy of Dr. Zaccaria Mari, Soprintendenza per I Beni Archeologici del Lazio. Reproduced by permission.

CONTENTS

Negotiating Culture

---⚬⚬⚬---

NEGOTIATING OWNERSHIP CLAIMS
Changing Attitudes toward Cultural Property

———— ∞∞∞ ————

Laetitia La Follette

R IVAL CLAIMS IN the realm of culture represent some of the most contentious issues in the world today, appearing in the news on a weekly if not daily basis. Some of the highest-profile cases have involved disputes over material objects—Native American remains, Greek and Roman antiquities, works of art looted by the Nazis—with important repercussions for museums as well as the disciplines of anthropology, archaeology, and art history. But debates over the ownership and control of nontangible cultural property are also shaping fields as diverse as economics, history, genetic studies, linguistics, and philosophy. The results are changing attitudes toward ownership, calling attention to the need for dialogue, negotiation, and collaboration over contested cultural property.

The burgeoning interest in cultural ownership is also reflected in the proliferation of college courses and university master's-degree programs devoted to aspects of this topic. While coverage by the media tends to stress the opposing sides of a given conflict, often further inflaming passions rather than suggesting a path to resolution, much of the academic literature on cultural heritage has become highly specialized, with significant bibliography in anthropology, cultural heritage management, legal studies, museum studies, and public art issues, but little dialogue across these areas.[1]

The aim of this book is to offer both a broader and a deeper approach, allowing the reader—interested layperson, advanced undergraduate, engaged graduate student, or even the professional somewhat familiar with some of these issues—the chance to pursue the subject of owning culture in a variety of contexts. It brings together a series of case studies by preeminent scholars, each focusing on a particular example of cultural ownership—from contests over tangible artifacts to those over more abstract forms of culture, such as language and oral traditions, to current studies of DNA and genes that combine nature and culture, to new nonproprietary economic and political models. In time and space, the material discussed extends from prehistoric North America to fascist and Republican Spain, from the Greco-Roman Mediterranean to Vedic India, from discrete Indigenous communities to the contemporary technological revolutions of global cyberspace. Each essay sets the debate in question in its historical and disciplinary context to illustrate the arena(s) in which such disputes arise, show how they have been approached, and suggest ways in which these approaches are changing or should change.

Intended as a tool with which to begin, or continue, exploration into the very timely issues of cultural heritage and intellectual property, *Negotiating Culture* stresses the importance of dialogue and careful listening as prerequisites to the negotiations and collaborations such disputes entail. One of the most innovative aspects of the volume is the way each author recognizes the social dimensions of group ownership and demonstrates the need for renegotiation and new models. Taken as a whole, the collection challenges the reader to reevaluate traditional ways of thinking about cultural ownership, such as those that focus solely on legal aspects, and stresses the importance of the broader social contexts within which negotiation over the ownership of culture is taking place.

The unusual interdisciplinary nature of this volume owes its origins to a sustained series of conversations on the topic of cultural ownership hosted by the Interdisciplinary Seminar in the Humanities and Fine Arts (ISHA) at the University of Massachusetts Amherst in 2006–2007. The diversity of contributors to the initial seminar made its discussions an exercise in interdisciplinary practice, and the collaborative nature of the enterprise has had lasting effect on the composition and contents of the final volume. Two essays, one by Margaret Speas on Navajo language revitalization and the other by Joe Watkins on Native American remains, were invited to supplement the chapters contributed by members of the original seminar, to showcase in particular the way thinking about Indigenous cultural property is changing. Many of the authors address the way academic boundaries are constructed and how we negotiate and interact across them. This includes the recognition that while different kinds of knowledge have their own authority, the exchanges that take place between such diverse forms of knowledge can be both rewarding and fruitful. Although each essay is grounded in disciplinary practice, the topics have far-reaching consequences beyond the academy.

The chapters have been grouped into three parts. Part I, Contested Physical Culture, deals with disputes over material objects. The studies focus on controversies over Native American human remains, Greco-Roman antiquities in American collections, and cultural documents seized by the fascist government of Spain in the late 1930s. One of three essays with a Native American focus, chapter 1, "The Politics of Archaeology: Heritage, Ownership, and Repatriation," by Joe Watkins (an Indigenous archaeologist and a member of the Choctaw Nation of Oklahoma), examines disputes over the repatriation of sensitive American Indian material in the wake of the Native American Graves Protection and Repatriation Act of 1990 (NAGPRA). This legislation set up the mechanism whereby federally recognized Indian tribes, Native Hawaiian organizations, and Alaska Native corporations may petition federal agencies and federally funded museums for the return of human remains and particular classes of Native American artifacts. In his analysis of the cultural disputes NAGPRA has attempted to resolve as well as those it has exacerbated, Watkins calls attention to the long history of mistrust and broken promises between American Indians and federal authorities, and the striking way that history has been ignored in disputes over Native American human remains. Indeed, Watkins notes that it was not until 1979 that the federal government mandated that archaeologists consult with American Indian tribes prior to conducting excavations on lands those tribes owned or controlled.

To Watkins, the issue at the heart of NAGPRA is not the priority of Native Americans versus European settlers (which he shows is what the debate over the ancient skeleton known as Kennewick Man has degenerated into), but rather that "American Indian groups feel more of a need to exercise their responsibilities to provide those human remains with a quiet and undisturbed 'rest' than to continue to contribute to a science that more and more acts to divest contemporary groups of their collective past." In the case of disputed human remains, archaeologists (and museums) are renegotiating their access to this material, as Native Americans are no longer content to be considered as "subjects" without a voice. This is not because Native Americans fear scientific study, but rather, as Watkins shows, because they do not believe Western science is the only method that offers an understanding of past human cultures.

In the second chapter, "The Trial of Marion True and Changing Policies for Classical Antiquities in American Museums," I explore the repatriation of over one hundred works of classical art by American museums since 2006, sparked by the five-year trial in Rome of the former curator of the J. Paul Getty Museum. While this court case was inconclusive—it was dismissed without a verdict—and devastating because True never got the chance to defend herself, the trial still marks the moment in the history of American museums when ideas about the ownership of antiquities shifted irrevocably. I show how the trial served as the catalyst that persuaded premier American museums to enter into negotiations over contested works of Greek and Roman art, ultimately to return some of them in exchange for long-term loans of similar antiquities with archaeological context (such as the Roman statue shown on the cover of this volume), and to revise their acquisition policies for ancient art to abide by the 1970 UNESCO convention on cultural property.[2] Those acquisition guidelines now stress the importance of serious research into provenience (the original findspot of the ancient work of art) and provenance (its modern history). What is still missing, however, is a change in attitude regarding those antiquities that remain in American collections. I argue that museums must similarly redefine their educational mandate to include information about the archaeological context of the masterpieces they display and about the modern history of those works, and stop focusing exclusively on the moment of creation. The public benefits when museum exhibitions combine curatorial knowledge with archaeological context. As educational institutions devoted to the preservation of the past, our prominent museums owe it to the public and the scholarly community to own, and own up to, the full history of their ancient objects.

In chapter 3, "The Salamanca Papers: A Cultural Property Episode in Post-Franco Spain," Oriol Pi-Sunyer and Susan DiGiacomo recount the long dispute over the return of personal and institutional papers seized from Republican groups and individuals by Franco's forces at the end of the Spanish Civil War (1936–1939). The authors show that this was a targeted confiscation, and they situate the efforts to recover these public and private documents within the atmosphere of amnesty and amnesia—the willful forgetting of atrocities committed in the Spanish Civil War—that followed the transition to democracy at the end of the fascist dictatorship in 1975. The opposition to the restoration of the Salamanca Papers, like the opposition to the identification and exhumation of mass graves, most of which contained the bodies of victims of fascism, bears witness to the still unhealed wounds of that war. Efforts to repatriate this "documentary equivalent of a mass grave" date back to 1978, but it was only with the creation of the Comissió de la Dignitat (Dignity Commission), a citizens' group formed in 2002, that the movement gained political traction. The group's strategy framed ownership not as a matter of mere possession, but as a legal and moral issue. In 2006, most of the documents belonging to the Catalan government were finally returned. The argument in favor of return rested not only on the right to ownership of personal and cultural property, but the right to memory, both individual and collective.

Each chapter in this first section thus brings out forcefully the selectivity of memory in ownership disputes, whether it is the conscious forgetting of the fraught history between American Indians and the U.S. government, the deliberate overlooking of the archaeological context and modern history of classical antiquities by some of our most prominent American museums, or the fight against *desmemoria*, the failure of memory, in post-Franco Spain. Each also highlights a critical milestone in the recovery of memory—of Native American practices, of the provenance and provenience of classical antiquities, and of Catalan and Republican identity.

Part II, Shared Stewardship, focuses on the way different kinds of knowledge, and divergent attitudes toward knowledge, lie at the heart of contending claims. The two chapters in this section address, respectively, Navajo language revitalization efforts and anthropological research on Indigenous oral tradition. Each stresses the need for academics to respect the traditions and knowledge of Indigenous groups and to work within parameters that are controlled by Indigenous actors in those communities. In Chapter 4, "Language Ownership and Language Ideologies,"

Margaret Speas shows that different attitudes toward language lie at the heart of power struggles between linguists and Indigenous communities over language revitalization efforts. To the latter, language is the cornerstone of who they are as a people. Not only is it critical for linguists to respect that, but with this understanding must come the recognition that only the indigenous populations—not the linguists—hold the power to create the next generation of native speakers. This, Speas argues, is the obvious but often overlooked reason for the success of language revitalization projects that are community-based. Speas's experience as the coauthor of a textbook on Navajo revealed to her not only that the Navajo lead author knew her audience better than Speas, the outside linguist, did, but also that the ultimate success of the book was the result of a Navajo approach to the specific content and to language learning as a whole, many aspects of which flew in the face of standard linguistic wisdom. The problem, as Speas makes clear, is that standard linguistic wisdom has not taken into account the perspective of the indigenous community. She concludes that it is critical that linguists listen to what the community says it needs, help the community navigate the dominant culture to get it, and acknowledge that sometimes the most valuable contribution they can make might involve something besides their professional expertise.

While dialogue and respect for alternative visions and traditions are essential components of any negotiation over culture, the authors of chapters 1 and 5 stress that it is not easy or even always possible to reconcile such opposing viewpoints. This is especially true when there is a pattern of one side deprecating the other's kind of knowledge. In chapter 5, "Archaeologists, Indigenous Intellectual Property, and Oral History," H. Martin Wobst explores how the development of archaeology as a scientific discipline led its practitioners to separate themselves from the indigenous societies they studied. Claims of scientific detachment and the pursuit of pan-human ideals ultimately produced "the power scenario of late colonialism and early post-colonialism," in which "archaeologists could violate Indigenous human rights and intellectual properties with little fear of legal consequences." After World War II, however, legal developments in the United States as well as Canada, Australia, New Zealand, and South Africa, together with the rise of new fields such as ethnoarchaeology, eventually forced archaeologists to work more closely with descendant populations. The realization by postmodern archaeologists that artifacts not only reflect human behavior but also shape it was a key breakthrough in shifting the focus of research back to social context. As archaeologists acknowledged different stakeholders, they also began to realize that points of contention required negotiation, and thus long-term social relations with indigenous groups. In the last section of his chapter, Wobst outlines some of the consequences for the Indigenous group that occur when such a complex (and nonlinear) social process as Indigenous oral tradition is collected, transformed, and collapsed by archaeologists into a physical and more linear artifact such as a DVD. These include separating knowledge from the social nexus within which it was embedded, destabilizing the social hierarchy based on the acquisition of such knowledge, and flattening the rich tapestry of voices that previously interacted with one another. The archiving of oral history validates certain voices, truncating and distorting the oral communication on which that history is based. The choice of whether or not to record oral history, as Wobst posits it, presents a serious dilemma: "On the one hand the irreplaceable loss of historic substance, on the other the potential sabotage of social process."

Speas and Wobst thus propose a particular form of collaboration, one that is grounded in shared stewardship of Indigenous cultural properties and in helping Indigenous communities navigate the dominant culture to achieve their goals. Wobst suggests that what is needed is a new form of ethical review that goes far beyond current practice to help ensure that, in the long term, archaeologists and their activities do not harm Indigenous groups or their intellectual property. Both authors stress that shared stewardship requires new models and different ways of thinking.

While several chapters address the benefits of bringing together different disciplinary approaches, the need for and value of collaboration is most closely examined in Part III of the volume, Negotiating the Boundary, which analyzes group ownership and the creation, handling, and interpretation of intellectual property with examples drawn from biology and technology. Chapter 6, "Re-owning the Past: DNA and the Politics of Belonging," by Banu Subramaniam, focuses on the application of genetics, specifically DNA research, to population studies, and the need for new interdisciplinary models that move beyond pure biology to recognize the way DNA is deeply intertwined with the social history of groups. In chapter 7, "Digital Commons: The Rise of New Models of Collaborative Ownership," David Bollier explores the new collaborative

communities fostered by the Internet that challenge traditional definitions of ownership.

Like the chapters by Speas and Wobst, Subramaniam's focuses on community and belonging, but through the lens of genetics rather than language or oral knowledge. She is less concerned with the way our DNA is
being patented and owned, even though she recognizes that this shows up
the limits of what she calls a "liberal individual-rights framework." Rather,
she explores one particular (misguided, but not atypical) application of
DNA research, a 2001 study that purported to show a connection between
race and caste in India. Despite widespread scholarly agreement dismiss-
ing any such connection, the new genetic study was then used politically
to reinforce old positions on race and caste and to bolster old disciplinary debates that pit the humanities and sciences against each other. Like
Watkins, Speas, and Wobst, Subramaniam looks at a political controversy
that affects a minority in a larger state (the Dalits, or "untouchables," in
India), together with issues of origins, the use of new data to retell old
stories, and the dangers of proceeding with (scientific) business as usual.
Subramaniam first notes that DNA is both material object (like the examples covered in Part I of the volume) and intellectual property (akin to the
material examined in Part II). The transmission of DNA is thus firmly
grounded in the history of cultural groups; as she points out, "Who reproduces, how many children they have, who survives, who migrates, who
lives and who dies—these are all deeply social and political questions."
Yet most genetic studies refuse to recognize the close connection between
nature and culture. Subramaniam also criticizes the lack of rigor exhibited
in many genetic studies and the "new regime of biologism" responsible for
them. She singles out for particular attention the uncritical use of social
groupings that are not carefully defined (like caste and race), the tiny
sample sizes involved, which contrast sharply with the sensational claims
made from them, and the many assumptions made, over the many generations such studies involve, that compound the problems of analysis. All of
these practices suggest that what results is a partial history only, one that
calls out for contextualization. Genetic stories such as these, Subramaniam
argues, are as potent as they are controversial, important for the way they
reveal matters of identity and its connection to history and nationhood.
She points to the need for multiple stories, multiple histories, that are the
result of different disciplinary investigations.

In Chapter 7, David Bollier examines the way new collaborative models of ownership (the digital commons, Web 2.0, open source software, and social networks like Facebook and Twitter) are challenging traditional economic wisdom. The Internet, Bollier explains, has demonstrated that private ownership of intellectual property can decrease value by limiting social circulation. Instead, new models allow shared access to creative works, albeit with some protections. Thanks to mechanisms such as the General Public License, a modified form of copyright, a programmer can guarantee that his or her open software code will remain in the public domain and not be appropriated by others for private gain. Through Creative Commons licenses, websites like Flickr similarly allow creators to make their works available to the public without cost or permission, provided certain rules and conditions (such as attribution to the author and an agreement not to use the work commercially) are met. Bollier explores how these new online commons (defined as social communities that enforce certain rules) present functional challenges to traditional capitalism, which sees value as monetized and privately owned: "The standard narrative of 'individual originality' that is the justification for copyright privileges is being subverted by modes of creation that are derivative, collaborative, and context-based." While acknowledging the challenges that remain, Bollier also points to the political potential represented by the myriad commons emerging globally. He sees them forming a new kind of democracy, a digital republic. The studies in this third section thus contrast the need for interdisciplinary collaboration and a wider purview in genetic studies related to populations with the collaborative model of the online commons.

In the volume's afterword, "Ownership and the Boundary," Stephen Clingman (who as ISHA's director facilitated the seminar discussions) explores the transitive nature of culture and the way boundaries construct meaning. Clingman defines interdisciplinarity as "a willingness to learn and speak in one another's languages, to hear and absorb what might at first sound alien." Interdisciplinarity, in these terms, means "working in and across the boundaries of the disciplines, and not in some vacuous or abstract sense simply negating or transcending them." He stresses not only the importance of crossing disciplinary boundaries, but also the way ownership, and therefore meaning, is constructed *through* boundaries, rather than being simply limited by them. He identifies circumstances where boundaries have been violated and must be reestablished as a form of respect. In these cases (such as Native American human remains or looted antiquities), Clingman suggests that a closed boundary is a means of restitution for past injustices. He contrasts this with the new online communities analyzed by Bollier, where value and meaning are created not just by the creator but by the user. While here "maximum circulation creates maximum value," the boundaries are still not completely porous, and safeguards are set in place to protect both the creators and the subsequent users. Recognition of those boundaries, he suggests, adds to the value of the work, and thus "there is no meaning without boundaries." He argues that rather than thinking of the boundary as the limit to meaning, we should consider it as the precondition to meaning. Using linguistic analogy, Clingman shows how meaning comes from transition—significance comes from the space of crossing. He posits that culture is similarly transitive; it too gains from exchange and negotiation.

Negotiating Culture thus proposes a series of new models for thinking about the ownership of culture and cultural property, models predicated on dialogue, negotiation, and collaboration. Such dialogue must involve careful listening to and respect for divergent worldviews, including those of Indigenous groups, as well as conversations across existing boundaries, be they social, disciplinary, historical, or political, in order to understand and sensitively act within the cultural context involved. Negotiating these boundaries requires more than dialogue and exchange, however. Protections and safeguards are sometimes needed to make it clear that all partners are respected and to develop long-term, negotiated solutions. These may require limiting access to certain material, such as Native American remains or unprovenanced antiquities, to make up for past abuses, or they may take the form of more meticulous assessments of, for example, the consequences of the gathering of Indigenous oral history. But even restrictions like these can open the door to new kinds of collaborations. Such engagement—the bringing together of different stakeholders, social groups, and disciplines—builds stronger collaboration and helps not only to safeguard culture, but also to disseminate it more broadly.

NOTES

1. Examples include Routledge's series in heritage studies and archaeology, Duckworth's series Debates in Archaeology, and the Public Life of the Arts series published by Rutgers University Press. Two important law titles are Jane E. Anderson, *Law, Knowledge, Culture: The Production of Indigenous Knowledge in Intellectual Property Law* (Cheltenham, UK: Edward Elgar, 2009), and Patty Gerstenblith, *Art, Cultural Heritage, and the Law,* 2nd ed. (Durham, NC: Carolina Academic Press, 2008).
2. The image shown on the cover is the first-century CE Roman marble statue of Peace, excavated in 1986 at Palombara Sabina in Latium and loaned by Italy to Boston's Museum of Fine Arts in 2006 in exchange for the repatriation of contested antiquities.

I

CONTESTED PHYSICAL CULTURE

I

THE POLITICS OF ARCHAEOLOGY
Heritage, Ownership, and Repatriation

Joe Watkins

IT IS PROBABLY safe to say that everyone has an opinion on the repatriation legislation that came out of Congress in 1989 and 1990, the National Museum of the American Indian Act (NMAIA) and the Native American Graves Protection and Repatriation Act (NAGPRA), which require U.S. government agencies and federally funded museums to return cultural items, including human remains, to Native American tribes, and also established procedures governing the excavation of Native American sites on federal or tribal land. Some anthropologists saw the legislation as an opportunity to further their field of study, noting that "NAGPRA will allow bioarcheology to emerge as a vigorous and possibly more publicly relevant and responsible profession," while others, such as Robson Bonnichsen, saw it as a threat to archaeological anthropology, arguing that "repatriation has taken on a life of its own and is about to put us out of business as a profession."[1] These two federal laws injected even more politics into what has always been a political situation concerning heritage and its control. Prior to the legislation of repatriation, archaeologists were constrained primarily by the terms they could negotiate with the tribal groups or federal land managers; after the establishment of strict legal repatriation guidelines, archaeologists have had to renegotiate access to the heritage of local groups.[2]

As an Indigenous archaeologist (I am a member of the Choctaw Nation of Oklahoma), I have always had difficulty seeing the threat to archaeology that Bonnichsen felt. To me, repatriation has created opportunities for archaeologists to draw from the Indigenous knowledge held by those people whose ancestors created the archaeological record we write about. It has opened up hitherto untapped pools of knowledge that can help inform archaeological understanding of the numerous pasts we encounter by legislating consultation and by suggesting the usefulness of Native American involvement in a shared program of heritage investigation.

Archaeology as a Humanist and Scientific Endeavor

Archaeologists are generally united in the understanding that archaeology is a science that uses the scientific method to tease out information about the cultures that existed in the past. It is, as Jeremy Sabloff, a former president of the Society for American Archaeology, notes, "one of the broadest intellectual endeavors in the scholarly world, as it straddles the physical and natural sciences, the social sciences, and the humanities; in its techniques, methods and theories."[3] But even though its subject is *the past*, archaeologists do not work in the past. The descendants of those cultures that the archaeologist studies exist in the present and are faced with contemporary issues that archaeology often does not address, including the struggle to maintain relationships with their ancestral past.

Elizabeth Brumfiel, a past president of the American Anthropological Association, draws attention to the relationship between contemporary, living cultures and the cultures that archaeologists study. She writes that "identities are frequently grounded in socially constructed understandings of the past, and this is true of those identities ascribed to others by outsiders and those identities embraced by individuals for themselves."[4] In this manner, people in the present develop inclusive or exclusive characteristics that can be applied to differentiate archaeological cultures of the past.

The problem is that archaeological cultures often bear no true relationship with contemporary cultures, even though archaeologists might treat them as if they do. As Kurt Dongoske and his colleagues observe, "It is ironic that today many southwestern archaeologists continue to conceive of archaeological cultures in essentially ethnographic terms, considering them to be tribal groups that are synonymous with ethnically distinct groups of people."[5] In essence, archaeologists create "cultures" out of pieces of stone, bone, and pottery and then act as if those cultures were people, not the *products* of people. This disconnect causes archaeologists to have more difficulty understanding relationships between ancestral populations and today's living groups and makes them less likely to recognize the connections between their artificially created cultures with the living cultures of today's groups.

What is it that anthropologists such as Sabloff, Brumfiel, and thousands of others study? Anthropologists study culture, which can be defined in many different ways. Culture is a shared, learned, symbolic system of values, beliefs, and attitudes, which shapes and influences perception and behavior. It is patterned and mutually constructed. It is arbitrary, in that it is not based on "natural laws" external to humans but is created by humans. It is, as Sir Edward Tylor wrote in 1871, "that complex whole which includes knowledge, belief, art, morals, law, custom, and any other capabilities and habits acquired by man as a member of society."[6]

In this sense, the past that archaeologists study is composed of evidence of cultures left for others to uncover. Archaeological artifacts are only a minor portion of the items created by humans to help them deal with their environments. These artifacts *in and of themselves* offer little information about the people who put them to use—it takes other humans to interpret the information contained therein. These interpretations are invariably influenced by the background and culture of archaeologists and suffer or benefit from the experiences they bring to their work, an issue H. Martin Wobst, in his essay elsewhere in this volume, also ties to the Indigenous knowledge that has been either offered to and declined by archaeologists or was known but ignored by the discipline.

As I noted earlier, archaeologists generally use the scientific method to try to reconstruct information about the past. The techniques vary within archaeology and among its practitioners, but information can be gathered through many different procedures, ranging from pedestrian surveys (to look for and record manifestations of archaeological sites) to complete archaeological excavations (to gather information on a particular archaeological manifestation for in-depth or comparative research). In this manner, archaeologists hope to create additional information about human cultures that existed in a particular place at a particular time.

The scientific method is composed basically of four distinct steps:

observation; formulation of a hypothesis to explain the observation; prediction based on the hypothesis; and experimentation to test the validity of the prediction. It is, as Brian Fagan succinctly defines it, a "disciplined and carefully ordered approach to acquiring knowledge about the real world using deductive reasoning combined with testing and retesting."[7]

Archaeologists are at somewhat of a disadvantage in that they cannot ask the participants in the culture being studied about the culture; they can only make educated guesses (hypotheses) about the culture that resulted in the materials being investigated. These educated guesses can be based on personal experience (technical training or experimentation), historical information (historical description of an area or similar areas), ethnographic examples (ethnographic analogy), or any of several other sources of information about human beings and their cultures.

"Managing" Culture and Heritage

Heritage is many different things and has many different definitions. While heritage can be seen to have ties with the past, it is also often the source of conflict within contemporary cultures, as Margaret Speas (see her essay in this volume) and others have shown.[8] Heritage is the product of societies, is inherited, and is often complex. John Tunbridge and Gregory Ashworth have noted that "not very long ago the word 'heritage' had a simple and generally accepted primary meaning; it was the collective generalization derived from the idea of an individual's inheritance from a deceased ancestor." Others argue, however, that such definitions may serve to oversimplify "heritage" in conjunction with other concepts.[9]

While archaeologists might be comfortable with separating "culture" from "heritage" as I have done above, it might not be quite so easy to other researchers. Tolina Loulanski recognizes that "the main controversy in defining heritage seems to originate in its uneasy duality of being both a cultural and economic subject, possessing both cultural and economic values, and performing both cultural and economic functions." And as Tunbridge and Ashworth observe, it often becomes difficult to recognize that there are "distinctions between the past (what has happened), history (selective attempts to describe this), and heritage (a contemporary product shaped from history)." Similarly, Frans Shouten writes: "Heritage is not the same as history. Heritage is history processed through mythology, ideology, nationalism, local pride, romantic ideas, or just plain marketing, into a commodity."[10]

Because of the definitions we use, "heritage" can be seen as a resource in need of protecting, preserving, or managing. It can have multiple levels of value to multiple groups, and its management may be undertaken by individuals, by groups large and small, and by various branches of local, state, or national government. The reasons for heritage management may vary as well. Peter Larkham writes that when one takes into consideration the "value" of heritage, one should consider *preservation*, "the retention, in largely unchanged form, of sites or objects of major cultural significance"; *conservation*, "the idea that some form of restoration should be undertaken to bring old buildings and sites into suitable modern use"; and *exploitation*, which "recognizes the value of heritage sites, particularly for tourism and recreation, and encompasses the development of existing sites and new sites."[11]

Heritage might be somehow seen as benign, but even the intangible aspects of heritage, such as language revitalization or documentation, can become highly problematic because of power imbalances between researchers and community members (see Margaret Speas's essay in this volume). As a result, Graeme Aplin sees heritage as "both intensely personal and intensely political," and he adds that "in effect, these two elements go hand in hand, as heritage is hotly contested because we each have our own views on what represents heritage, and what is worth conserving." And because of this, issues can arise when it is put to use in particular ways, especially when this is done by larger political bodies. David Harvey calls attention to this aspect: "Heritage should be understood as a process, related to human action and agency, and as an instrument of cultural power."[12]

Nations (or particular subsets of nations) can therefore use heritage as a symbol of group ethos and to increase relationships within a population, or it can also be used to exclude other portions of the population—those economically, politically, philosophically, or socially on the fringes of the dominant culture—purposefully or inadvertently. Oriol Pi-Sunyer and Susan DiGiacomo's example of the deliberate exclusion of Catalan cultural patrimony in Spain elsewhere in this volume calls attention to ways that heritage can be a distinctly political weapon. Again, Aplin writes, "National heritage is sometimes used by a government or dominant group in society as a concept to legitimize the state, to help define it, and to advance individuals' identification with it." Nationalistic constructs of a shared heritage thus serve as a method of developing a structure within which the past can become a political weapon, creating out of many pasts a singular one around which people can rally. "Social solidarity," as Andrew Smith points out, "requires a sense of cultural unity based on a myth of common ethnic descent and shared vernacular codes."[13]

This political aspect of heritage and its management can have a strong impact on local and Indigenous groups within a nation. Lynn Meskell and Lynette S. M. Van Damme have examined the sorts of issues that arise when heritage environments change as a result of social and political upheavals, focusing on "sets of relationships between descendant communities and a familiar arm of the government in the form of national parks" in South Africa.[14] Such issues are not encountered only in the so-called Third World, but also in First World countries such as Australia and the United States.[15]

The Politics of Archaeology as Public Heritage

In the United States, archaeological resources on public land are considered to be a subset of the American heritage. Three aspects of the Antiquities Act of 1906 can be seen as the foundation for public archaeological and historic preservation policies: "(1) archaeological resources are public resources and their uses should be regulated publicly for a public benefit rather than for private commercial or personal gain; (2) the primary values of archaeological resources are educational and commemorative; and (3) archaeological resources should be investigated and interpreted by qualified professionals using the best historical and scientific methods and techniques."[16] Later, the Historic Sites Act of 1935 and the National Historic Preservation Act of 1966 extended these policies to a much wider range of cultural and historic resources as well as to nonpublic lands. In short, the Antiquities Act of 1906 established the policy that archaeological remains and manifestations of archaeological cultures "belong" to the American taxpayer; remains on public land belonged to the nation, regardless of whether any specific subset of that public agreed to share ownership.[17]

I have discussed elsewhere the apparent conflict between various schools of thought concerning the rights to control cultural heritage, and I will not repeat that here.[18] But the point still remains: the right of

Indigenous groups to the ownership and control of their archaeological and cultural heritage is rarely equivalent to that of the nations within which they exist. We, as archaeologists, contribute to that inequality as we set ourselves up as the "experts" on the archaeological and cultural heritage under study. As Sandra Scham notes, "the archaeology of the disenfranchised can be defined as a unique combining of culture with current and past political realities," and she adds that "to the extent that archaeologists in all societies typically place themselves in the role of mediator between the past and the present, . . . it is disingenuous to suggest that popular views do not affect our work."[19]

The history of the relationship between American Indians and archaeologists is one of strife and mistrust and has been recounted by too many authors to list here.[20] But Larry Zimmerman makes an important point about the conflict: "It is difficult to see the historical relationship between archaeologists and Native Americans as anything but scientific colonialism"—a process in which, as Dell Hymes writes, knowledge about a people is acquired and then "exported" out of the "country of origin" to be used for "processing" into intellectual material.[21]

It is within this culture of "scientism" that American Indian concern with the free practice of archaeology came to a head in the 1970s. Perhaps in response to the social and political unrest of the times, American Indians began showing their distrust of archaeology and archaeologists. These protests revolved primarily around what American Indians perceived as a threat to the human remains of their ancestors. In 1971 the American Indian Movement disrupted excavations at Welch, Minnesota, and a group of Indians occupied the Southwest Museum in Los Angeles in an attempt to get American Indian human remains and sensitive material out of public displays.

These political actions created discomfort between archaeologists and American Indians, but they served to create an awareness of archaeology as a political action as well as a science. The anthropologist Bruce Trigger was one of the first to recognize that science does not operate within a vacuum but rather is an integral part of the social and culture milieu within which it is practiced: "Problems social scientists choose to research and (hopefully less often) the conclusions that they reach are influenced in various ways and sometimes to a highly significant degree by the attitudes and opinions that are prevalent in the societies in which they live."[22]

The practice of American archaeology changed slowly from the 1970s onward (especially within the academy), but change was quicker within those areas of archaeology affected or controlled by federal legislation. In 1979, with the passage of the Archaeological Resources Protection Act, archaeologists who conducted work on federal lands were required to consult with American Indian tribes concerning archaeological excavations. So powerful was the anthropological and scientific hold on America's past that this was the first legislated mandate that *required* such consultation prior to conducting excavations of sites on tribally owned or controlled lands. While this was a great step forward, the act itself defined human remains as archaeological resources, something the tribes held as unfathomable.

While the excavation of American Indian archaeological sites has been seen by some as disruptive to contemporary populations, perhaps the most discussed, analyzed, and highly publicized conflict between anthropologists and American Indians has been over the excavation of American Indian human remains. In 1973, the archaeologist Eldon Johnson listed the excavation of burials first among four recurrent themes of protests by American Indians, and ended with the hope that those themes would "be dealt with collectively by responsible members of a professional society and that the issues will not continue to be met *post hoc* by individuals and single institutions as reactions to protests." But his article was not the only reaction to the call for the cessation of archaeological excavations of American Indian graves.[23]

Anthropology has generally been political as it has dealt with American Indians over the last one hundred years in the mistaken belief that the Native cultures would soon disappear. Working from this myopic perspective, anthropologists saw it as necessary to gather—to salvage—as much information as possible about those cultures while practitioners of them were alive. Native cultures did not and have not disappeared, but anthropologists and archaeologists continue to operate as if "salvaging" is still necessary. As Stuart Fiedel has written, "Anthropologists whose livelihoods and passionate interests require unfettered access to prehistoric sites, artifacts, and skeletons are threatened by legislation that awards primary control of these data to Native Americans."[24] But it is not only the control of the "resource" that apparently threatens anthropologists.

NAGPRA and Repatriation

To many American Indians, "the only difference between an illegal ran-sacking of a burial ground and a scientific one is the time element, sun screen, little whisk brooms, and the neatness of the area when finished." While illegal excavators of burial grounds might face legal punishment if they are caught, the products archaeologists produce, as Wesley Ber-nardini points out, "increasingly have legal and ethical implications that affect descendant communities." In this regard, as many authors have indicated, repatriation has had and will continue to have an impact on the practice of archaeology.[25]

As I mentioned at the beginning of this chapter, the repatriation leg-islation of 1989 and 1990 created a mechanism whereby federally recog-nized Indian tribes, Alaska Native corporations, and Native Hawaiian organizations could petition federal agencies, federally administered museums, and other museums that receive federal funds for the return of human remains and particular classes of artifacts. The National Museum of the American Indian Act (NMAIA) of 1989, which deals specifi-cally with the Smithsonian Institution, was the precursor to the Native American Graves Protection and Repatriation Act (NAGPRA) of 1990, which covers all other federal agencies and museums. Following the pas-sage of NAGPRA, amendments to NMAIA brought the two legislative acts more in line with each other.

A great deal has been written about NAGPRA from legal perspectives as well as anthropological ones—too much to warrant discussion here.[26] But American Indians hailed the passage of NAGPRA as "civil rights legislation" aimed at providing protection to American Indian human remains and associated grave furniture equal to that afforded "white" Americans, along with a mechanism for their return and the return of sacred objects and objects of cultural patrimony.[27] Some anthropologists have drawn attention to the fact that "reburial and repatriation have been thorns in the side of archaeology . . . , pitting Native American against archaeologist and archaeologist against archaeologist. This conflict appar-ently revolves around one central issue: whether archaeology's claim on human remains and items of cultural patrimony as scientific data out-weighs Native American ones based on ancestry and cultural affiliation."[28]

At the time of the passage of these two repatriation acts, archaeologists were on both sides of the discussion. On one end of the spectrum was Clement Meighan, who argued that "it is ironic that evil Whites are making every effort to preserve the evidence of Indian history and communicate it to the citizens, while some Indian activists seem to be doing their best to destroy and conceal collections and prohibit any further studies from being conducted (except by politically safe and government-controlled bureaucrats)." Others, such as Andrew Gulliford, saw an appropriate opportunity: "As cultural barriers fall and the hegemony of whites over the curation and interpretation of native objects lessens a new kind of museum may emerge." It is likely that the perspectives of archaeologists and American Indians on archaeology and repatriation fall somewhere between these two extremes. The historian Devon Mihesuah, herself American Indian, wrote that "Indians are curious about their histories, and they do not believe that all scientific and social scientific studies are worthless"; even in the midst of the Kennewick situation (discussed in the following section), Don Sampson, former chairman of the Confederated Tribes of the Umatilla, pointed out, "We do not reject science. In fact, we have anthropologists and other scientists on staff, and we use science every day to help in protecting our people and the land."[29]

Anthropologists have continued to press for concern. Doug Owsley and Richard Jantz believe that "NAGPRA was a compromise to resolve potentially conflicting interests including those of American Indians, museums and scientists, and the public." Shirley Powell, Christina Garza, and Aubrey Hendricks write, "Archaeologists believe so strongly in the importance of knowledge and their responsibility to contribute to that knowledge that not to do so would be unthinkable and unethical." One biological anthropologist also comments that "the reburial of remains detracts from the ability of anthropologists to scientifically study humankind. In fact, the ideology surrounding reburial threatens freedom of scientific inquiry."[30]

American Indian authors believe that "the political goal of reburial opponents is to make Indian ways of knowing 'religious' and to make all religion into the 'religion' that reasonable people will be happy to be rescued from by science." Owsley and Jantz see the political climate differently: "The original intent [of NAGPRA] is being replaced in some quarters by politically expedient decisions that favor some American Indian interests to the detriment of sound scientific inquiry and the public's right to information about the past."[31] The "politically expedient decisions" that concern Owsley and Jantz are part of the changing relationships between "science" and American Indian groups who are no longer politically powerless. Repatriation is by all means a political action, but so too is the *retention* of the items under question, and nowhere was politics more apparent than in the Kennewick Man court case.

The Politics of Repatriation: Kennewick Man as Epitome

There is no need to recount in depth the nearly eight-year-long legal battle over the prehistoric human remains known alternately as "Kennewick Man" and "the Ancient One," which were discovered in 1996 along the banks of the Columbia River in Kennewick, Washington.[32] Because this case presents many rather complex issues, I will focus only on particular aspects of the controversy that relate specifically to the political situation regarding the renegotiation of the past. The case is, as Susan Bruning, an attorney and archaeologist, points out, "a prominent, yet enigmatic, icon of the ongoing struggles over controlling ancient human remains."[33]

First, the failure of the courts to recognize the initial inhabitants of the North American continent as "Native American" under NAGPRA politicized the idea of American Indians as this continent's "Indigenous inhabitants." I have discussed the case itself in more detail elsewhere, especially the ways that the decision carries with it political implications far beyond the rights of scientists to study this particular set of human remains.[34]

Second, when Kennewick Man's skull was mistakenly identified in the newspapers as "of European descent," it set off a series of events that struck at the heart of American Indian sovereignty issues.[35] I focus here on three of these—the first by a right-wing journalist, the second by a nonprofit organization reflective of the scientism I discussed earlier, and the third by several anthropologists.

Lowell Ponte, a reporter for the online conservative journal FrontPage Magazine, wrote that the Kennewick Man case might prove that "some of the first 'Native Americans' had white skin and European ancestry."[36] This, Ponte suggested, would have continuing implications: "If evidence shows that white-skinned Americans were exterminated by invading ancestors of today's Indians, then this genocide could give Caucasian Americans a claim to victim status even stronger than that of Native Americans. Had such genocide not taken place, the argument would go, perhaps most of America's population and territory would have been Caucasian. Columbus might have been greeted by natives with faces whiter than his own."

According to this nonsense, based as it was on a mistaken identification, American Indians would not have been the first settlers but rather second-wave immigrants. That is, if the Indians killed off "white-skinned Americans" and stole their land, then the European actions since 1492 are much more easily justified. American politicians need no longer honor treaties, because the treaties were unnecessary to regain land stolen from white ancestors. Another of Ponte's statements summarizes this scenario succinctly: "The European invasion of the past five centuries, in this potential revisionist history, merely reclaimed land stolen 9,000 years earlier from their murdered kin."

The second political incursion into the Kennewick situation was by a nonprofit organization called Friends of America's Past. Dedicated to "promoting and advancing the rights of scientists and the public to learn about America's past," it was organized in 1998 to "alert the public to the issues and implications of the Kennewick Man lawsuit"; its mission is "to keep the door of scientific inquiry open and to work to maintain the integrity of scientific inquiry in this country."[37] The organization was active in the Kennewick Man case and in the similar Spirit Cave Man case, but has been relatively inactive since 2006, with only minor postings and action. Their "target," according to their website, is "the threat to a factual understanding of what actually happened in the past." In reality, however, the "past" this groups wants to promote is constructed with a Western ideology firmly implanted at its core, one that refuses to acknowledge Indigenous voices or allow them to be heard and fails to recognize that there are alternative ways of knowing (or constructing) the past.

The implication of the Friends of America's Past statement is that only archaeologists can provide a factual understanding of the past, and that researchers have a "right" to investigate anything that intrigues them, including the Indigenous dead.[38] This is not unexpected, given that archaeologists, as Brumfiel notes, "seem prepared to speak out assertively against what they perceive to be the misuse of prehistory, and the material nature of archaeological data seems to give archaeologists a degree of public credibility."[39] It is this credibility as "scientist and expert" that creates much of the power differential between Indigenous groups and researchers, but Indigenous groups are becoming more active in challenging this power by drawing attention to the seemingly "racist" practice of excavating Indigenous human remains for scientific "knowledge."[40]

The third political aspect of the Kennewick Man controversy was the claim by a number of anthropologists that the tribes were afraid that the scientific study of the human remains would "disprove" their religious stories and origin myths. Elizabeth Weiss wrote that the Umatilla wanted to "bury evidence regarding the prehistory of the Americas to prop up myths" about tribal origins; Clement Meighan called for the power of archaeology "to discriminate those tales which are entirely mythical from those which can be confirmed by scientific truth."[41] American Indian authors reacted as could have been anticipated. Responding to a *New York Times* article patently in favor of repatriation of the Kennewick Man skeleton, Jace Weaver noted that the "fear among many Natives about scientific testing is not that it will contradict or disprove sacred accounts concerning tribal origins but that it will further desecrate the remains."[42] More recently, D. S. Pensley put the situation in blunter terms: "Despite media claims to the contrary, Native American demands for the repatriation of human remains and funerary objects are unrelated to fears that scientific study or DNA testing will disprove stories of tribal origins. Put simply, Natives are generally uninterested in findings generated via archaeological curiosity because their own oral traditions adequately explain the past."[43]

Culturally Unidentifiable Human Remains

One aspect of NAGPRA that has also been greatly politicized is the disposition of remains that can't be easily or clearly affiliated with particular cultural groups. The disposition of this class of human remains is addressed in one section of the act, but they are defined as remains that cannot be identified as affiliated with any particular Indian tribe or Native Hawaiian organization. An important point to remember is that "Indian tribe," as defined within this regulation, means "any tribe, band, nation, or other organized Indian group or community of Indians . . .

which is recognized as eligible for the special programs and services provided by the United States to Indians because of their status as Indians."[44]
Thus, if the remains are not from *federally recognized* Indian groups, they
are considered to be "culturally unidentifiable." This is but one of the
issues related to this class of remains that are deeply political.

This circumstance pits "federally recognized tribes" and "non-federally-recognized tribes" against one another. While a lot of tribes agree
that many non-federally-recognized tribes are likely to be (and to have
always been) Indians, they are afraid that repatriating human remains will
give some level of "recognition" to those tribes *outside* of the federal recognition process.[45] Some of these federally recognized tribes believe that
the human remains should be repatriated to a recognized tribe, which can
then return the remains to the non-recognized tribe.

But this sort of disagreement by American Indian groups serves to
enhance the arguments by non-Indians that human remains are being
used merely as pawns in a game of politics. The politics of federal recognition surely have an impact on each and every tribal group—recognized
and non-recognized—in different ways, but the use of the skeletons of
dead ancestors as "bargaining chips" is odious. Whether "recognized" or
not, the dead deserve to be reburied, even if in a cultural pauper's grave.
But this is not the only (or even the most political) issue in relation to
culturally unidentifiable human remains.

The initial writing of the NAGPRA regulations reserved a section
for culturally unidentifiable human remains. The National Park Service
published "draft principles" to address the disposition of these remains on
July 29, 1999; the Park Service's NAGPRA Review Committee provided
these as a "beginning point for consideration of this topic" and as a means
of initiating discussion on the ultimate regulations regarding these items.
On June 8, 2000, the Review Committee published a proposed rule in the
Federal Register.[46] On October 16, 2007, a proposed rule on the regulations
for the disposition of culturally unidentifiable human remains was published. It was also within this proposed rule that the NAGPRA Review
Committee identified three distinct categories of culturally unidentifiable
human remains: (1) those for which cultural affiliation could be determined, but the appropriate Native American group is not federally recognized as an Indian tribe; (2) those that represent an identifiable earlier
group, but for which no present-day Indian tribe has been identified by

the museum or federal agency; and (3) those for which the museum or federal agency believes that evidence is insufficient to identify an earlier group.[47]

The political implications relevant to the first category I have already addressed. Categories 2 and 3, however, further continued the politicization of NAGPRA. One area of particular concern to anthropologists in relation to category 2 was the proposal to expand the rights of tribes to claim human remains that come from a geographical area with which the tribe claims a "cultural affiliation," or allow tribes from the geographical area within which the museum or federal agency is situated to claim the remains if no geographical location for the human remains is known.[48] At issue is whether the mere fact that a museum or federal repository is located within a geographical area (but not necessarily where the human remains in question might have originated) is sufficient to allow the American Indian group to gain control over those remains.

The defining limits of the geographical areas under consideration have been created by actions of the United States government and are not as capricious as it might initially seem. The section of the new rule on the disposition of cultural unidentifiable human remains requires that the lands under which tribes might initiate a claim must have been defined as recognized by a final judgment of the Indian Claims Commission or the United States Court of Claims, or a treaty, act of Congress, or Executive Order. While anthropologists might believe this requirement to be biased toward American Indian interests, it seems consistent with international law, which allows for the repatriation of military dead from the field of battle—a somewhat implicit parallel given the "Indian Wars" waged by the United States against American Indians.

Ryan Seidemann, an attorney and archaeologist, has published an in-depth discussion of the attempts by the National Park Service's NAGPRA Office to create the final rule on the disposition of the culturally unidentifiable human remains still held in museums and federal repositories, including other actions by the Review Committee not discussed here. Seidemann believes his analysis supports a finding that the Department of the Interior, the parent agency of the National Park Service, "lacks the authority to promulgate regulations for culturally unidentifiable human remains" and that "the 2007 Draft Regulations are also inconsistent with the legislative history of NAGPRA."[49] In part, Seidemann believes that, since NAGPRA is silent on the issue of culturally unidentifiable human remains, the Department of the Interior has no authority to create regulations on them—in essence, that such an action would be creating "new" aspects of the law without legal authority to do so.

In spite of this, the National Park Service issued a Final Rule on culturally unidentifiable human remains on March 10, 2010.[50] Would this rule create a mechanism enabling tribes to rebury all the human remains within museums and federal repositories, or would the political aspects of the rule lead anthropological and archaeological associations to return to the courts for a legal decision regarding the right of tribes to obtain the human remains that have resided in archaeological and museum collections?

Indigenous groups would argue that the intent of NAGPRA is to return human remains and associated funerary objects to the cultural groups that can demonstrate affiliation with them. The regulations concerning culturally unidentifiable human remains mirror that intent. As a scientist I can understand the hesitancy to return items that can give information about the "human" past of the western hemisphere, but I can't continue to support the scientific colonialism that has plagued archaeology and anthropology. While the dead have no "rights," living people have obligations toward the dead that are spelled out within contemporary cultural mores.

The new regulations have reignited the fear in archaeologists and anthropologists that museum collections will be wiped clear of human remains. These "resources" are deemed to be irreplaceable specimens from which to gather bits of knowledge to help us understand humanity's rise on this planet. It might be a valid concern, but the historical and political aspects of such a perspective must be considered as well. Science has always weighed the social consequences of data acquisition in relation to human rights; for example. the information gathered from experiments conducted by German scientists during World War II would be beneficial for cold-water (hypothermia) survival studies, but the world has agreed that to use the data would give a blush of respectability to the experiments themselves.

As a member of the Choctaw Nation of Oklahoma and an archaeologist, I believe that American Indians recognize the scientific advances that provide additional information from human populations in the past.

I also believe that those groups, on an objective level, understand why scientists feel the need to gather such data. On a personal and societal level, however, I recognize that American Indian groups feel more of a need to exercise their responsibilities to provide those human remains with a quiet and undisturbed "rest" than to continue to contribute to a science that more and more acts to divest contemporary groups of their collective past.

The ultimate fate of the National Park Service's Final Rule is uncertain. Some notable archaeologists have indicated privately that litigation is imminent and perhaps necessary in order to "protect" the resource from repatriation and reburial; others have indicated that while repatriation is expected and a logical outgrowth of the original legislative intent, they believe the proposed rule will create an undue burden on the museums and federal repositories as well as on the tribal groups involved. Still others see this as a purely political means of trying to legislate archaeology and physical anthropology out of business. Regardless, almost all see this as a political response to an unwieldy problem, one that will require continual negotiation and renegotiation as individual situations dictate. As American Indian groups garner more political power, archaeologists will need to recognize the extent to which negotiation will be in their best interests.

Repatriation legislation has further politicized a volatile situation that threatens to erode any positive relationships between anthropologists and American Indians, and it has also influenced the development of a cadre of professional archaeologists who are working to find ways to expand the collaboration between their work and Indigenous groups of North America. In 2001 Tamara Bray observed: "At the dawn of the new millennium, American archaeology finds itself at the threshold of a new, more humanistic orientation toward the past. . . . [This] somewhat reluctant turn toward a more self-conscious, inclusive and humanistic approach to the construction of knowledge about the past has been accelerated by the passage of repatriation legislation."[51]

In some ways, repatriation is part of the renegotiation of the relationship between American archaeologists and American Indians that is taking place.[52] Bray's linkage of the development of a more humanistic approach to the construction of knowledge about the past to the passage of repatriation legislation is an interesting interpretation of the trajectory of contemporary archaeology. Today's practitioners of archaeology are renegotiating not only their constructions of knowledge about the past but also their very access to that knowledge.[53] Such collaborations are not without pitfalls, however, as both H. Martin Wobst and Margaret Speas note in their essays in this volume.

But even though archaeologists are moving toward sharing the construction of knowledge about the past, not all anthropologists see this as a necessarily good thing. Elizabeth Weiss believes that repatriation legislation grew out of a concerted effort by an anti-science coalition: "Native Americans alone would not have had the political power to create or enforce NAGPRA. In getting it enacted, they received help from some very unlikely allies, including agencies of the government, Christian fundamentalists, and liberal activists." Others see that "the reburial and repatriation conflict did not just pop out of thin air but instead rose from long-held attitudes toward the place of American Indians in the greater society of the United States."[54]

Some archaeologists and anthropologists suggest that it was religious concerns that fueled the passage of NAGPRA, or even the putative fears American Indians have about science, but such suggestions are unfounded, given that more than 130 American Indian tribes actively manage the archaeology on their tribal lands.[55] Meighan writes of NAGPRA that "while much of this legislation is intended to legislate 'respect,' its justification is always given in religious terms and the word 'sacred' is abundantly used to justify confiscation of research collections." Mark Tveskov, perhaps more realistically, identifies conflicts such as the one over Kennewick Man, or more generally over repatriation laws such as NAGPRA, as "fundamentally battles over slippery concepts of social identity, cultural rights, and political power."[56] In my opinion, it is time for archaeologists to realize that the past can no longer be claimed by any one person or group, but that contemporary politics require renegotiation of the social contracts under which we operate.

Wherever repatriation leads archaeology, or wherever the sometimes strained collaboration between archaeologists and American Indians takes us, there will always be an uneasy truce between the scientists who study "the past" and those whose ancestors created it. NAGPRA is here to stay, and it will likely create more issues as the courts continue to review it and as further legislative actions expand (or decrease) its purview. Regardless of whether those complaining about NAGPRA are archaeologists or American Indians, the sociologist Clayton Dumont warns, "These political attacks on NAGPRA can only be successful if they succeed in convincing law-makers and their publics that scientific claims are made in the pursuit of what is 'truthful,' 'objective,' and thus *extrapolitical*, while native arguments are conversely rooted in the 'irrationality' of 'myth,' 'superstition,' and 'religion.'"[57]

Politics abound in all things, even within so-called "objective" science, and to believe otherwise is naive, as H. Martin Wobst demonstrates elsewhere in this volume. Recognition of the political aspects of the issues should, if anything, prepare archaeologists for the need to renegotiate with American Indian groups about access to the material culture of the past. American Indian groups are not totally opposed to the practice of archaeology, but they are more actively seeking to become equal partners in the construction of information about the past. In this regard, the practice of archaeology in the twenty-first century can benefit from listening to voices other than those of its practitioners.

NOTES

1. Jerome C. Rose, Thomas J. Green, and Victoria D. Green, "NAGPRA Is Forever: The Future of Osteology and the Repatriation of Skeletons," *Annual Review of Anthropology* 25 (1996): 82; Bonnichsen quoted in George Johnson, "Indian Tribes' Creationists Thwart Archeologists," *New York Times*, October 22, 1996.

2. As the term is used by anthropologists in the United States, 'archaeology' refers to a subfield of the broader discipline of anthropology, and I will use the two terms more or less interchangeably throughout this chapter.

3. Jeremy Sabloff, *Archaeology Matters: Action Archaeology in the Modern World* (Walnut Creek, CA: Left Coast, 2008), 28.

4. Elizabeth M. Brumfiel, "It's a Material World: History, Artifacts, and Anthropology," *Annual Review of Anthropology* 32 (2003): 207.

5. Kurt Dongoske, Michael Yeatts, Roger Anyon, and T. J. Ferguson, "Archaeological Cultures and Cultural Affiliation: Hopi and Zuni Perspectives in the American Southwest," *American Antiquity* 62 (1997): 602.

6. Edward B. Tylor, *Primitive Culture* (1871; repr., New York: Harper, 1958), 1.

7. Brian Fagan, *Ancient Lives: An Introduction to Archaeology* (Upper Saddle River, NJ: Prentice-Hall, 2000), 403.

8. See Joe Watkins, "Cultural Nationalists, Internationalists, and 'Intra-nationalists': Who's Right and Whose Right?," *International Journal of Cultural Property* 12.1 (2005): 78–94.

9. John E. Tunbridge and Gregory J. Ashworth, *Dissonant Heritage: The Management of the Past as a Resource in Conflict* (London: John Wylie & Sons, 1996), 1; Joe E. Watkins and John Beaver, "What Do We Mean by 'Heritage'? Whose Heritage Do We Manage and What Rights Have We to Do So?," *Heritage Management* 1 (2008): 10–15.

10. Tolina Loulanski, "Revising the Concept for Cultural Heritage: The Argument for a Functional Approach," *International Journal of Cultural Property* 13 (2006): 209; Tunbridge and Ashworth, *Dissonant Heritage,* 20; Frans Shouten, "Heritage as Historical Reality," in *Heritage, Tourism and Society,* ed. David T. Herbert (London: Mansell, 1995), 21.

11. Peter Larkham, "Heritage as Planned and Conserved," in Herbert, *Heritage, Tourism and Society,* 86.

12. Graeme Aplin, *Heritage Identification, Conservation, and Management* (Melbourne: Oxford, 2002), 358; David C. Harvey, "'National' Identities and the Politics of Ancient Heritage: Continuity and Change at Ancient Monuments in Britain and Ireland, c. 1675–1850," *Transactions of the Institute of British Geographers,* n.s., 28 (2003): 475.

13. Aplin, *Heritage Identification,* 16; Anthony Smith, "Culture, Community and Territory: The Politics of Ethnicity and Nationalism," *International Affairs (Royal Institute of International Affairs 1944–)* 72.3 (1996): 458.

14. Lynn Meskell and Lynette Sibongile Masuku Van Damme, "Heritage Ethics and Descendant Communities," in *Collaboration in Archaeological Practice: Engaging Descendant Communities,* ed. Chip Colwell-Chanthaphonh and T. J. Ferguson (Lanham, MD: AltaMira, 2008), 131.

15. Watkins, "Cultural Nationalists," 87–89. H. Martin Wobst's essay in this volume explores this political aspect of heritage management of Indigenous heritage by former colonial nations.

16. Francis P. McManamon, "The Foundation for American Public Archaeology: Section 3 of the Antiquities Act of 1906," in *The Antiquities Act: A Century of American Archaeology, Historic Preservation, and Nature Conservation,* ed. David Harmon, Francis P. McManamon, and Dwight T. Pitcaithley (Tucson: University of Arizona Press, 2006), 153.

17. See Joe Watkins, "The Antiquities Act at 100 Years: A Native American Perspective," in Harmon, McManamon, and Pitcaithley, *The Antiquities Act,* 187–98.

18. Watkins, "Cultural Nationalists."

19. Sandra Arnold Scham, "The Archaeology of the Disenfranchised," *Journal of Archaeological Method and Theory* 8 (2001): 190.

20. See, among many others, Alice Beck Kehoe, *The Land of Prehistory: A Critical History of American Archaeology* (New York: Routledge, 1998); Randall H. McGuire, "Archeology and the First Americans," *American Anthropologist* 94 (1992): 816–36; James Riding In, "Without Ethics and Morality: A Historical Overview of Imperial Archaeology and American Indians," *Arizona State Law Journal* 24 (1992): 11–34; Bruce Trigger, "Archeology and the Image of the American Indian," *American Antiquity* 45 (1980): 662–76; Jack F. Trope and Walter R. Echo-Hawk, "The Native

American Graves Protection and Repatriation Act: Background and Legislative History," *Arizona State Law Journal* 24.1 (Spring 1992): 35–77; and Joe Watkins, *Indigenous Archaeology: American Indian Values and Scientific Practice* (Walnut Creek, CA: AltaMira, 2000).

21. Larry J. Zimmerman, "Usurping Native American Voice," in *The Future of the Past: Archaeologists, Native Americans, and Repatriation,* ed. Tamara Bray (New York: Garland, 2001), 169; Dell Hymes, "The Use of Anthropology," in *Reinventing Anthropology,* ed. Hymes (New York: Vintage, 1974), 49; see also Lawrence A. Kuznar, *Reclaiming a Scientific Anthropology,* 2nd ed. (Lanham, MD: AltaMira, 2008), 89.

22. Trigger, "Archaeology and the Image," 662.

23. Eldon Johnson, "Professional Responsibilities and the American Indian," *American Antiquity* 38 (1973): 129–30; for further reactions see Watkins, *Indigenous Archaeology,* 11–17.

24. Stuart J. Fiedel, "The Kennewick Follies: 'New' Theories about the Peopling of the Americas," *Journal of Anthropological Research* 60 (2004): 77.

25. Devon A. Mihesuah, "American Indians, Anthropologists, Pothunters, and Repatriation: Ethical, Religious, and Political Differences," *American Indian Quarterly* 20 (1996): 233; Wesley Bernardini, "Reconsidering Spatial and Temporal Aspects of Prehistoric Cultural Identity: A Case Study from the American Southwest," *American Antiquity* 70 (2005): 47; T. J. Ferguson, "Native Americans and the Practice of Archaeology," *Annual Review of Anthropology* 25 (1996): 63.

26. For legal perspectives see Renee M. Kosslak, "The Native American Graves Protection and Repatriation Act: The Death Knell for Scientific Study?," *American Indian Law Review* 24 (1999/2000): 129–51; Kieran McEvoy and Heather Conway, "The Dead, the Law, and the Politics of the Past," *Journal of Law and Society* 31 (2004): 539–62; and Peter Welsh, "Repatriation and Cultural Preservation: Potent Objects, Potent Pasts," *University of Michigan Journal of Law Reform* 25 (1992): 837–65. For an overview of anthropological perspectives, see Susan B. Bruning, "Complex Legal Legacies: The Native American Graves Protection and Repatriation Act, Scientific Study, and Kennewick Man," *American Antiquity* 71 (2006): 501–21.

27. Sherry Hutt, "Illegal Trafficking in Native American Human Remains and Cultural Items: A New Protection Tool," *Arizona State Law Journal* 24 (1992): 135–50; Sherry Hutt, Elwood W. Jones, and Martin E. McAllister, *Archeological Resource Protection* (Washington, DC: Preservation Press, 1992).

28. Shirley Powell, Christina Elnora Garza, and Aubrey Hendricks, "Ethics and Ownership of the Past: The Reburial and Repatriation Controversy," *Archaeological Method and Theory* 5 (1993): 2.

29. Clement W. Meighan, "Another View on Repatriation: Lost to the Public, Lost to History," *Public Historian* 14 (1992): 43; Andrew Gulliford, "Curation and Repatriation of Sacred and Tribal Objects," *Public Historian* 14 (1992): 31–32; Mihesuah, "American Indians, Anthropologists, Pothunters, and Repatriation," 231; Don Sampson, "(Former) Tribal Chair Questions Scientists Motives and Credibility" (1997; www .umatilla.nsn.us/kman2.html), quoted in Watkins, *Indigenous Archaeology,* 149–50.

30. Douglas W. Owsley and Richard L. Jantz, "Archaeological Politics and Public Interest in Paleoamerican Studies: Lessons from Gordon Creek Woman and Kennewick Man," *American Antiquity* 66 (2001): 571. Powell, Garza, and Hendricks, "Ethics and Ownership," 3–4; Elizabeth Weiss, "Kennewick Man's Funeral: The Burying of Scientific Evidence," *Politics and the Life Sciences* 20 (2001): 16.

31. Clayton W. Dumont Jr., "The Politics of Scientific Objections to Repatriation," *Wicazo Sa Review* 18 (2003): 109; Owsley and Jantz, "Archaeological Politics," 571.

32. Many articles and books have been written about this situation; a good (if minimal) review of the basic facts is available through a National Endowment for the Humanities website that uses the situation as part of a lesson plan for grades 9–12: "Kennewick Man: Science and Sacred Rights," http://edsitement.neh.gov/lesson-plan/kennewick-man-science-and-sacred-rights. For an overview of the case see "Kennewick Man Virtual Interpretative Center," *Tri-City Herald* (Kennewick, WA), available at www.tri-cityherald.com/kman/.

33. Bruning, "Complex Legal Legacies," 519.

34. Joe Watkins, "Becoming American or Becoming Indian? NAGPRA, Kennewick, and Cultural Affiliation," *Journal of Social Archaeology* 4 (2004): 60–80.

35. The misidentification was reported in Dave Schafer, "Skull Likely Early White Settler," *Tri-City Herald* (Kennewick, WA), July 30, 1996.

36. Quotations in this and the following paragraph are from Lowell Ponte, "Politically Incorrect Genocide, Part 2," *FrontPage Magazine* October 5, 1999, http://archive.frontpagemag.com/readArticle.aspx?ARTID=22976.

37. Quotations in this paragraph are from the website of Friends of America's Past, www.friendsofpast.org.

38. McEvoy and Conway, "The Dead, the Law, and the Politics," 546.

39. Brumfiel, "It's a Material World," 213.

40. The Ipperwash Inquiry (2004–2006; led by Justice Sidney B. Linden) noted the importance of burial sites to Aboriginal peoples of Ontario (www.ipperwashinquiry.ca/); Paul Turnbull and Michael Pickering's *The Long Way Home: The Meaning and Values of Repatriation* (Oxford: Berghahn, 2010) offers discussion of the value of human remains and the process of repatriation to Australian Aboriginal groups; Brian Hole's "Playthings for the Foe: The Repatriation of Human Remains in New Zealand," *Public Archaeology* 6 (2007): 5–27, offers New Zealand Maori perspectives on such issues.

41. Weiss, "Kennewick Man's Funeral," 17; Meighan, "Another View," 41.

42. Jace Weaver, "Indian Presence with No Indians Present: NAGPRA and Its Discontents," *Wicazo Sa Review* 12 (1997): 21. The original article was George Johnson, "Indian Tribes' Creationists Thwart Archaeologists," *New York Times,* October 22, 1996.

43. D. S. Pensley, "The Native American Graves Protection and Repatriation Act (1990): Where the Native Voice Is Missing," *Wicazo Sa Review* 20 (2005): 52.

44. Native American Graves Protection and Repatriation Act Regulations, 43 CFR Part 10.2(e)(2) and Part 10.2(b)(2).

45. See Joe Watkins and Tom Parry, "Archeology's First Steps in Moccasins," *Common Ground* 2 (1997): 46–49.

46. Notice of Draft Principles of Agreement Regarding the Disposition of Culturally Unidentifiable Human Remains—Extended Date for Comments," *Federal Register* 64:145 (July 29, 1999): 41135–36, quotation on 41135; "Recommendations Regarding the Disposition of Culturally Unidentifiable Native American Human Remains," Notice, *Federal Register* 65:111 (June 8, 2000): 36462–64.

47. "Native American Graves Protection and Repatriation Act Regulations—Disposition of Culturally Unidentifiable Human Remains. Proposed Rule," *Federal Register* 72:199 (October 16, 2007): 58582–90, paraphrased material on 58584.

48. "AAA Comment Letter re: Proposed NAGPRA CUHR Regulations," American Anthropological Association, www.aaanet.org/issues/policy-advocacy/upload/Draft-AAA-Comment-Letter-re-NAGPRA-CUHR-Regulations-Final-121907.pdf.

49. Ryan M. Seidemann, "Altered Meanings: The Department of the Interior's Rewriting of the Native American Graves Protection and Repatriation Act to Regulate Culturally Unidentifiable Human Remains," *Temple Journal of Science, Technology & Environmental Law* 28 (2009): 1–45, quotation on 24.

50. "Native American Graves Protection and Repatriation Act Regulations—Disposition of Culturally Unidentifiable Human Remains; Final Rule," *Federal Register* 75:49 (March 15, 2010): 12378–405.

51. Tamara Bray, "American Archaeologists and Native Americans: A Relationship under Construction," in *The Future of the Past: Archaeologists, Native Americans, and Repatriation,* ed. Bray (New York: Garland, 2001), 1.

52. See Chip Colwell-Chanthaphonh and T. J. Ferguson, eds., *Collaboration in Archaeological Practice: Engaging Descendant Communities* (Lanham, MD: AltaMira, 2008), as well as Jonathan Kerber, ed., *Cross-cultural Collaboration: Native Peoples and Archaeology in the Northeastern United States* (Lincoln: University of Nebraska Press, 2006).

53. See, for example, Colwell-Chanthaphonh and Ferguson, *Collaboration in Archaeological Practice;* Kerber, *Cross-cultural Collaboration;* Stephen W. Silliman, ed., *Collaborating at the Trowel's Edge: Teaching and Learning in Indigenous Archaeology* (Tucson: University of Arizona Press, 2008); and Swidler, Dongoske, Anyon, and Downer, *Native Americans and Archaeologists.*

54. Weiss, "Kennewick Man's Funeral," 17; Powell, Garza, and Hendricks, "Ethics and Ownership," 17.

55. National Association of Tribal Historic Preservation Officers website at www.nathpo.org/map.html.

56. Meighan, "Another View," 40; Mark A. Tveskov, "Social Identity and Culture Change on the Southern Northwest Coast," *American Anthropologist* 109 (2007): 431.

57. Dumont, "Politics of Scientific Objections," 122.

2

THE TRIAL OF MARION TRUE AND CHANGING POLICIES FOR CLASSICAL ANTIQUITIES IN AMERICAN MUSEUMS

———∞∞∞———

Laetitia La Follette

THE INDICTMENT OF Marion True, curator of classical art at the J. Paul Getty Museum, by a Roman court in 2005 on charges of conspiring to traffic in illicit antiquities marked a dramatic shift in the history of ownership claims over contested works of ancient art. This chapter shows how the indictment changed the way premier museums in the United States acquire classical Greek and Roman art and resulted in the repatriation of over a hundred such cultural artifacts to Italy and Greece so far. In its impact on art museum policy, True's trial, together with the negotiations that led up to and followed it, thus ranks in importance with the Native American Graves Protection and Repatriation Act of 1990 (see Joe Watkins's essay elsewhere in this volume) and the task force established in 1997 to investigate art looted by the Nazis during World War II.[1] The trial also demonstrated some of the flaws implicit in the policy advocating the free flow of cultural materials across national borders, known as cultural property internationalism.[2] By negotiating directly with premier museums in the United States—and when that failed, indicting one of their curators—the Italian authorities succeeded in altering museological attitudes and long-standing practices in the United States that had condoned the purchase of stolen antiquities.

True's trial and its fallout redefined the ownership of ancient cultural artifacts in two important ways. With the restitution of some looted antiquities and the revision of guidelines for future purchases, our leading museums now acknowledge restrictions on their ability to collect and own ancient art. In particular, they agree to exercise better due diligence to ascertain that any antiquity they seek to acquire left its country of origin before November 17, 1970, the date of UNESCO's Convention on the Means of Prohibiting and Preventing the Illicit Import, Export, and Transfer of Ownership of Cultural Property.[3] The new museum guidelines thus address some of the more egregious past mistakes and lay out reforms, but they still ignore those antiquities acquired since 1970 that remain in American collections. In this chapter I argue that the status of these more recent acquisitions must be addressed, and that the way museums present ancient art must also change, replacing a valuation based predominantly on aesthetics with one that reflects the importance of an object's context and its multiple histories.

Some have questioned the need for the dramatic changes ushered in by True's trial, asking "Who owns antiquity?" or "Who owns the past?"[4] Staking a claim to the past does not, however, justify purchasing purloined artifacts. Since there is still some confusion about why the changes in museum ownership policy were necessary, I offer first a review of the evidence for past purchases of looted antiquities, the museums' rationale for doing so, and the way such purchases have shortchanged our understanding of the ancient Greek and Roman worlds. In the next two sections I trace the way museum policy for the acquisition of antiquities began to change in the late 1990s and examine the central figure associated with the changes, Marion True, and lessons learned from her trial and ancillary investigations. Finally, I return to the educational mission of the museum, showing how the gaps in the history of unprovenanced antiquities—works whose modern ownership history is unknown or murky—have undermined that mission. I conclude that True's trial, the revised acquisition policies, and the restitutions, together with new long-term loans, have contributed to a new model of international collaboration over cultural property, one based on shared stewardship instead of ownership.

Museums and Looted Antiquities

Marion True's indictment in April 2005 prompted prominent museums that feared similar suits to reach accommodations to avoid litigation. Within months, New York's Metropolitan Museum of Art and the Museum of Fine Arts in Boston rushed to negotiate deals in which they transferred title of disputed objects to Italy in exchange for long-term loans of comparable material from that country. Three years after the opening of True's lengthy trial, her former employer, the J. Paul Getty Museum in southern California, as well as the Princeton Art Museum and the Cleveland Museum of Art, had done the same.[5] By 2010 over a hundred works of Greek and Roman art had been returned to Italy and Greece from these institutions and others (see the appendix to this chapter), and more are likely. Despite the careful wording of the settlements, the objects were clearly repatriated because they were recognized as stolen goods, looted from Italian or Greek soil. These returns demonstrate that even after the United States ratified the 1970 UNESCO convention in 1983, many American museums not only continued but even increased their purchases of problematic antiquities.[6]

Some have questioned the need for the returns, in part because the agreements that led to the repatriated items are rarely published.[7] Unfortunate though this is—more transparency could have put such objections to rest—it is hardly surprising that museums did not wish to call even more attention to past errors. The tracing of the provenance (the transmission history) and/or the provenience (the archaeological findspot) of many of the objects suggests the returns were in fact justified.[8] A few key examples also show how scholarship and our understanding of the past were stymied as the museums in question resisted research that might have proven the origins of undocumented or poorly documented items. For example, a Hellenistic silver set of fifteen pieces returned by the Metropolitan Museum had been purchased in two batches in 1981 and 1982 from an American dealer, Robert Hecht Jr., for $3 million.[9] It was subsequently determined that the silver had been removed illegally from an ancient house in Morgantina, Sicily. The Metropolitan stalled both the Italian authorities and American archaeologist Malcolm Bell's investigations into the origins of this silver set for over a decade, and this delayed the scholarly publication more than twenty years.[10] The same museum purchased a Lydian hoard smuggled out of Turkey in the 1960s, keeping it out of sight in its storerooms until 1984. It was only after the items were returned to Turkey as the result of a court case that the scholarly study finally appeared, in 1996.[11] Another example is the so-called Aphrodite of Morgantina, an overlifesize acrolithic (that is, made of mixed materials, in this case marble and limestone) statue returned by the Getty Museum to Italy in late 2010. It was acquired in 1988; the first full study took place nearly twenty years later, in 2007.[12]

Two British archaeologists, David Gill and Christopher Chippendale, have reconstructed the background history of many of the objects returned from the Museum of Fine Arts in Boston and the Getty Museum in Malibu. They traced the objects back to dealers such as Hecht, Giacomo Medici, Gianfranco Becchina, and others known to have trafficked in looted objects. Gill and Chippendale also identified the assigning of fictitious pedigrees to the artifacts (often to old collections that would have been hard to corroborate), the myriad alliances and partnerships among international dealerships, galleries, and auction houses involved in the illicit trade, and the sheer volume of material that passed through Hecht's hands.[13]

A pair of journalists, Peter Watson and Cecilia Todeschini, have also helped clarify the role played by Medici, whose storerooms in Geneva were raided by Italian police in 1995, yielding a cache of thousands of Polaroid photographs of works of art in varying states of preservation, from dirt-encrusted and broken to fully restored. Medici sold these works to international museums through a variety of fronts.[14] For example, an overlifesize marble portrait statue of the Roman empress Sabina was acquired by Boston's Museum of Fine Arts in 1979 from Fritz Bürki, a Swiss restorer who fronted for Hecht. It was said then to have come from an "aristocratic family collection in Bavaria," but since it appeared in Medici's Polaroid archive, that provenance was obviously made up. The Italians believe that the statue and a Roman candelabrum relief also returned from Boston had been removed illicitly from the imperial villa at Tivoli built for Sabina's husband, the emperor Hadrian.[15]

The journalist Sharon Waxman has illuminated the role investigative reporters in Turkey and Greece have played in uncovering the illicit trade, and two reporters, Jason Felch and Ralph Frammolino, have exposed the star-crossed history of the Getty Museum and the Getty Trust, which oversees it. Well before October 2010, when True's trial was finally dismissed without verdict under Italy's five-year statute of limitations, an elaborate tapestry of obfuscations concerning the buying and selling of classical art had begun to unravel.[16]

The Rationale for "Don't Ask, Don't Tell"

There is more evidence for the reconstruction of acquisition policies at the Getty Museum than for any other museum, and this evidence goes back before Marion True was made chief curator at the museum in 1986. In a series of confidential memos to Getty Museum director John Walsh in 1983, Arthur Houghton III, interim curator of antiquities, explained the way museums had for generations justified their participation in the market in looted antiquities. Houghton acknowledged the direct link between the demand for new objects by museums and looting in places like Italy and Greece. He rationalized continuing to purchase undocumented antiquities, claiming the laws in the source countries were vague and unenforceable and that the international market would likely continue to exist even if museums stopped purchasing from it. He pointed out that the Getty's policy was already more stringent than that of many other American museums, because it required notifying foreign governments of objects the museum intended to purchase.[17]

Houghton argued that the educational mission of the museum—its obligation to make available to the general public and scholars the objects it purchased, through study and publication—helped preserve the past, even when the objects in question were looted. In further conversations with the Getty's outside counsel about the legal repercussions of this stance, Houghton stated: "The reality is that 95% of the antiquities on the market have been found in the last three years. The only way one obtains them is if you do not ask the specific question that would elicit the specific answer about provenance that would make the material unbuyable." Houghton recommended that the museum limit potential legal problems by what he called "optical due diligence," creating the impression that the objects acquired had been carefully screened but avoiding certain knowledge of where they actually came from.[18]

An analysis of purchases of antiquities going back to the 1970s shows that this policy of plausible deniability was followed not just by the Getty but also by other major museums, including the Metropolitan Museum, the Museum of Fine Arts in Boston, the Cleveland Museum of Art, and the Princeton Art Museum, up until True's indictment in 2005. That policy required ignoring the 1970 UNESCO convention on cultural property, ratified by the United States in 1983.[19] But this, and "breaking the export laws of a neglectful foreign country, especially when the goal was to educate and enlighten Americans . . . , neither he [Houghton] nor most American curators saw . . . as a major concern."[20] In contrast, the Archaeological Institute of America (AIA) and museums like the University of Pennsylvania Museum of Archaeology and Anthropology in Philadelphia argued for the importance of following the UNESCO guidelines either soon after the 1970 convention was finalized (in the case of the AIA) or even before (the Penn Museum).[21]

The Euphronios krater demonstrates the effect of museum purchases of looted antiquities. This large Attic krater (a two-handled vase used for mixing wine and water), decorated in the red-figure style with a scene from the *Iliad* and another of Athenian youth arming for battle, dates to the late sixth century BCE and is signed by the renowned vase-painter Euphronios. In his 1993 memoir, Thomas Hoving, former director of the Metropolitan Museum, bragged about how he and Dietrich von Bothmer, the museum's curator of Greek art, managed the acquisition of the krater in 1972, slipping it in "under the wire"—that is, after the UNESCO convention on the protection of cultural property was pro-mulgated in 1970, but before its 1983 ratification by the United States. Both Hoving and von Bothmer knew by the end of 1973 that the vase had been looted from an Etruscan tomb near San Antonio di Cerveteri in central Italy, even though they continued to deny it. Their rationale was that many more people would see it in New York City than would in an Italian museum, a view echoed by some journalists since its return to Italy in 2006.[22] But this attitude raises the question of what is learned from such looted objects.

How did this Greek vase created in Athens twenty-five centuries ago find its way into an Etruscan tomb near Rome? Who were its Etruscan purchasers? Did they intend from the beginning to use it as a funerary offering, or was that only its final function, after the krater served them as a punchbowl for wine, as vessels of this type were used in Greece? Based on the iconography, modern scholars assume that the vase must have been used for a male burial, but is this a reasonable hypothesis? We cannot answer these questions because the vase was illegally removed from its archaeological context and not scientifically excavated. The looting destroyed evidence about the gender and age of the tomb's occupants, its date, contents, and context, and the use to which the vase had been put there, together with any information about its earlier function or functions.[23] This, sadly, is the norm with looted objects, but in the case of this vase it gets worse. The extraordinarily high price paid by the Metropolitan Museum for the Euphronios krater made headlines; it also prompted a new merchandizing ploy on the part of Italian tomb robbers. Eager to cash in on the desire for vases by well-known Greek artists, they scavenged tombs for such pieces and then smashed them in order to sell the fragments, for tens of thousands of dollars, to museums like the Getty and collectors like the Metropolitan's own curator, von Bothmer.[24] Scores if not hundreds of Greek vases were damaged as a result. And because they were also looted and not properly excavated, knowledge about the Etruscans who purchased them, and the use to which the vases were put by that culture, was lost for all of them, as it was for the Euphronios krater. This did not concern Hoving or von Bothmer, though; all that mattered to them was the vase's first history—that of its original manufacture in ancient Athens—and not its travel from Athens to Etruria and its use there (provenience, or second history) nor its journey from its discovery to the museum (provenance, or third history).

They could ignore the vase's later history because the tendency in art museums is to focus first and foremost on the aesthetics of a work of ancient art. Antiquities are thus valued primarily as beautiful and exotic treasures from a distant time and place.[25] This helps to explain why some of our most prominent museums were willing to dispense with so much historical information about ancient objects they acquired. They ignored unpalatable evidence about the antiquities' third, modern history and the journey these objects took to reach them, but they also ignored information about their second history, namely a work's function, its reception, and its meaning over time, which could have been recovered through scientific excavation and examination of the work's archaeological context. The result presents the public with a surprisingly narrow view of what is worth knowing about antiquity: the object becomes little more than eye candy. The idea that beauty alone is enough, and that cultural context, archaeological provenience, and modern provenance are not important—or worse, are dispensable elements of the history of a work of art—represents a dumbed-down view of the stories ancient art has to tell us. Such an ahistorical approach also reflects a serious misunderstanding about the way antiquities differ from other types of fine art, such as Old Master paintings. No art historian today would support the idea that only the aesthetics of a work of art matter. My art-history colleagues scour archives in search of material that will help them reconstruct not only the historical circumstances under which a work of art was created, but also the context within which it operated, since both shaped its meaning. For antiquities, however, such archival material does not exist. Most of what can be reconstructed of the history, function, and meaning of an ancient work of art comes from the scientific study of its findspot and the objects that surrounded it when it was buried. This archaeological context, properly excavated, is thus the equivalent of the regional archive for a scholar of Old Masters, indispensable because it tells the story of the work of art. But the critical importance of archaeological context seems to be a surprisingly hard concept for some to grasp. Instead of recognizing unexcavated sites as worthy of the same protection as standing monuments, some curators claim that archaeologists "only care about the dirt"—that is, they focus only on the dirt the object is buried in and not on the work itself.[26]

In the case of the Euphronios vase, and the silver hoard also returned by the Metropolitan, the findspots were eventually determined. Since the objects were found in Italy and under Italian law belonged to that country, they would have required export licenses to leave it legally, which they lacked. The museum agreed to return them in exchange for long-term loans of comparable material from Italy. While it is too early to say whether such loans will catch on as a viable substitute for new acquisitions, the restitutions, and the recognition of Italian patrimony law they reflect, represent a major change in museum policy regarding ownership. This can be seen from the position adopted by professional museum organizations a decade before in a case known as *United States v. An Antique Platter of Gold.*

This court case of the late 1990s involved an ancient Greek libation bowl, or phiale, from Sicily that was purchased in December 1991 by a collector, Michael Steinhardt, for some $1.2 million through the agency of Robert Haber, a New York art dealer.[27] American customs agents seized the gold phiale from Steinhardt's apartment on a warrant issued by a federal magistrate in New York City after the Republic of Italy, in February 1995, requested the assistance of American authorities in tracking down the illegal export of the work from Italy and its importation into the United States. The U.S. government then initiated a civil forfeiture action in federal district court. An initial decision in favor of forfeiture was appealed. Four professional museum associations—the American Association of Museums, the Association of Art Museum Directors, the Association of Science Museum Directors, and the American Association for State and Local History—filed an amicus curiae brief against forfeiture and in support of Steinhardt's ownership. On the other side, supporting forfeiture, was the American archaeological community: the Archaeological Institute of America, the American Anthropological Association, the Society for American Archaeology, and the Society for Historical Archaeology, joined by the American Philological Association as well as the U.S. National Committee of the International Council on Monuments and Sites. The opposing perspectives, principles, and positions of the two sides have been carefully analyzed by Claire Lyons and need not be reiterated here. Particularly important for this discussion, however, is the way the professional museum organizations supported the collector's ownership rights over Italy's, downplaying the importance of the Sicilian provenience of the phiale, what was known of its provenance, and Italian patrimony laws in their argument against repatriation.[28] The decision went against them and the collector. In February 2000 the bowl was returned to Italy, a forfeiture based on the materially false customs declaration prepared by Haber's agent, which listed the origin as Switzerland (through which the bowl had passed from Italy), and its value as $250,000, less than a quarter of the purchase price.

A Changing Policy for the Acquisition of Antiquities

As the final verdict in the Steinhardt case was looming, the Republic of Italy requested a Memorandum of Understanding with the United States. Such bilateral agreements fall under the provisions of the Cultural Property Implementation Act of 1983, the American legislation that implemented the 1970 UNESCO convention on the protection of cultural property. They allow the United States to place import restrictions on certain types of cultural property from a country in return for certain actions by that country, such as promoting cultural exchanges and taking steps to curb looting. On October 12, 1999, the State Department's Cultural Property Advisory Committee held a public hearing on the Italian request. The measure was supported by archaeologists such as Malcolm Bell, and opposed by dealers, including Frederick Schultz, president of the National Association of Dealers in Ancient, Oriental and Primitive Art. Given their position in the Steinhardt case, it is not surprising that most from the museum world opposed it as well; the exception was Marion True from the Getty Museum.[29] Italy's request was approved, and in January 2001, when the bilateral agreement was signed by representatives from both countries, restrictions on the importation of antiquities into the United States from Italy were imposed for the next five years. This agreement has been renewed twice, in 2006 and 2011.[30] The United States thus committed itself to international collaboration over the problem of looted antiquities from the Mediterranean, as it had earlier for Mali and for Central and South American countries such as El Salvador, Guatemala, Nicaragua, and Peru.

In February 2002, Schultz, one of the dealers opposed to the Memorandum of Understanding with Italy, was convicted under the National Stolen Property Act for conspiring to traffic in illicit Egyptian artifacts. The case was critical, not only because Schultz was a recent president of the leading international association of antiquities dealers, but also because the U.S. court recognized the validity of Egyptian patrimony laws.[31] Schultz was fined $50,000 and sentenced to thirty-three months in jail. By excluding the "conscious avoidance" defense, the judge in this case spelled the end of the "Don't ask, don't tell" approach. Legal restrictions were thus placed on the free flow of cultural property; its origins and the way it was acquired now mattered.

In April 2003 the looting of the Iraq Museum during the invasion of Baghdad by U.S. and allied forces brought the issue of the illicit market for antiquities to public attention. Shortly thereafter, the Association of Art Museum Directors (AAMD) agreed to revisit its policy on the acquisition of ancient art. New guidelines initially published in June 2004 were revised in 2006 and again in 2008 in the wake of True's indictment and the repatriation of objects to Italy and Greece. The 2008 guidelines urge curators to ensure that new acquisitions (as of 2008) can be documented to have left their probable country of modern discovery before November 17, 1970, the date of the UNESCO convention on the protection of cultural property, or if exported after that date, that they have documentation to attest to the legality of export from that country and import into the United States.

Some experts in cultural heritage law have expressed skepticism that these revised policies will alter the status quo. They point out that the guidelines are voluntary, that they provide loopholes for the acquisition of some objects whose movements and history cannot be documented, and that most antiquities available on the market lack both provenance and provenience.[32] But the official adoption of even stricter guidelines by the Getty Museum in 2006 constitutes a significant step, one that brings American museum policy closer to that of their European counterparts.[33]

The AAMD has also set up an online object registry where member museums are urged to post information and photographs of archaeological material and works of ancient art they acquire that lack complete provenance information going back to 1970. This marks a useful beginning, but the registry includes only ancient art acquired since June 4, 2008, the date of the new guidelines. By the end of 2012 the database included 579 objects from 16 institutions.[34] It is nowhere near as comprehensive as the Nazi-Era Provenance Internet Portal established by the American Association of Museums to facilitate the investigation of works of art in their collections that have gaps in their provenance history between 1933 and 1945 and that may have been looted by the Nazis before and during World War II, which as of December 2012 included 28,848 objects from 173 participating museums.[35] The AAMD registry is far less ambitious; it does not includes works from non-AAMD institutions, nor does it address works of ancient art in American collections acquired between the 1970 UNESCO convention and the revised guidelines of 2008, even though the repatriations that followed True's indictment indicate that a substantial number of antiquities in American museums came from sites looted after 1970. The bronze Apollo acquired by the Cleveland Museum of Art in 2004 from Phoenix Ancient Art, a prominent gallery with offices in New York and Geneva, is one controversial item with little documentation of its provenance and provenience. Another controversy is brewing over the same firm's sale of an Egyptian mummy mask to the St. Louis Art Museum in 1998.[36] Clearly, the provenance of antiquities acquired by

American museums between 1970 and 2008 needs to be addressed, that is, first researched and then made available to the public. This can be best done if each institution creates its own registry and posts this information on its website, as indeed a few museums are starting to do.[37] At present, though, more museums seem to be adopting a "wait and see" approach, not engaging in provenance research on items they acquired since 1970 until prompted by a claim.[38] This seems short-sighted, given the high cost Marion True paid for avoiding the issue of provenance.

The Case against the Getty Museum and Marion True

True's trial, which was conducted intermittently for almost five years, from November 2005 to October 2010, focused much attention on the J. Paul Getty Museum and Trust and on the former curator—True had by then resigned her position—personally.[39] Many questions remain. Why did the Italian suit wind up focusing more on True herself than on her institution, which clearly approved every acquisition? Why did the Italians go after True at all, given her attempts at reform? After all, it was True who first suggested (in 1991) the idea of long-term loans from Italian storerooms; she was also the only museum curator to support Italy's request for a Memorandum of Understanding at the State Department hearing in 1999.[40] It is evident that True was walking a fine line, pushing reform while still wielding the monetary power of the wealthiest museum in the United States. Did she begin to decide to do so only after she had finished building most of the Getty's ancient collection? Or was she the scapegoat for an American museum policy in transition, as some have argued?[41] A closer look at the reforms True tried to put in place suggests not only that they were unsuccessful in tackling the problem of looted antiquities, but also that True herself may have been ambivalent about them.

In November 1995 the Getty Museum announced a new policy, touted as a step to eliminate the purchase of unprovenanced antiquities. As True put it, "Now we would only consider buying from an established collection that is known to the world, so that we do not have the issue of *undocumented provenance*."[42] True was breaking ranks with the prevailing "Don't ask, don't tell" policy. Even this small, initial step antagonized museum directors and curators at similar big museums, many of whom at the time were supporting Steinhardt's retention of the unprovenanced Sicilian gold libation bowl.

Within months True wound up undermining the new policy by urging the Getty to accept the combination gift and purchase of the Barbara and Lawrence Fleischman collection of some three hundred antiquities in 1996. Most of the Fleischman collection had little information about provenance. Like the collections of antiquities amassed by other private collectors (such as Maurice Tempelsman, Shelby White, and Leon Levy), it had been put together after the UNESCO convention of 1970.[43] The exhibition of Fleischman material that the Getty had put on with the Cleveland Museum of Art in 1994, a year and a half earlier, also aroused suspicion; it seemed a convenient way to provide a published pedigree for the collection without supplying new information about the modern history or origin of the works. Ninety-two percent of the works in the catalog produced for the 1994 exhibition lacked known findspots.[44] True's decision to acquire the Fleischman collection thus showed that, at best, she was adopting a strictly literal interpretation of the new policy—splitting hairs, since the only documentation for the collection came from the catalog she had produced for the 1994 exhibition. Interviews with her assistant at the time suggest that she anguished over the decision, but once she made up her mind, her concern was for the collectors over the museum's own interests.[45] When push came to shove, True and the Getty demonstrated through this 1996 acquisition that pleasing collectors and amassing more objects was more important than serious reform.

Then there were the voluntary returns of objects by the Getty to Italy in the late 1990s, heralded by True as part of a new transparency. On September 13, 1995, Italian *carabinieri* raided Medici's warehouse in Geneva. The smoking gun that broke the Medici ring was a handwritten organizational chart of the chain of command in the illicit antiquities trade. This sheet of paper listed at the top (as buyers) Hecht and international museums and collectors, and below them (as suppliers) Medici and a series of European dealers and various criminal elements. Although the Getty was not listed by name on the chart itself, it turned up in Medici's extensive records, which included, in addition to the thousands of Polaroid snapshots I described earlier, letters between True and Medici about some of the objects in the photographs.[46]

A few weeks after that September 1995 raid, an assistant U.S. attorney came to the Getty to depose True about the subject of two of those letters, a bronze tripod initially borrowed for study in 1987 and acquired in 1990. Stolen in Rome from the Guglielmi collection (a distinguished private collection now housed at the Vatican), the tripod and a companion candelabrum had been purchased from Medici through Fritz Bürki & Sons in Zurich.[47] The tripod was published and put on display, which led to its recognition by the Italian authorities with whom it had been registered. The federal prosecutor came to the Getty at the Italians' request to question True, the curator; her sworn testimony at that time (October 4, 1995), was that she had first seen the tripod in Zurich in Bürki's restoration shop, although this conflicts with her later testimony on March 15, 2005, when she indicated she has seen it in Medici's Geneva warehouse in 1987, an account corroborated by other evidence. The tripod was returned on November 21, 1996, by True herself on a trip to meet with senior Vatican and Italian cultural officials.[48] Oddly, the companion piece, the candelabrum stolen from the same collection, was not returned until 2005. Why was the candelabrum not researched more carefully after the return of the tripod in 1996, or when the decision was later made to include it in a handbook to the Getty's antiquities published in 2002?[49] Was the Getty waiting for an official request for it? Was this another example of the literal interpretation of transparency: waiting until the item had to be returned? In the event, the museum sent it back without an official request, as a goodwill gesture on the eve of True's trial in 2005.[50] How long had the Getty known it was purloined? If provenance was key, as stated in the new policy, why didn't that involve following up on suspicious facts like these?

In the case of the next three returns, which were far more publicized, the research was done by scholars outside the Getty Museum, although it is to True's credit that she followed up on it. Two of them were, like the Guglielmi tripod and candelabrum, stolen from existing collections. A graduate student identified the first, a sculpted torso of the god Mithras, purchased in 1982 by True's predecessor, Jiri Frel. It had been published in 1958 as part of a private eighteenth-century collection. A German scholar similarly notified the museum that the second sculpture, a Roman copy after the Greek sculptor Polykleitos acquired as part of the Fleischman collection, came from an excavation storeroom in Venosa in southern Italy. The third item, a large Greek kylix, or drinking cup, painted by

Onesimos and potted by Euphronios, was looted from an archaeological site. In contrast to the other two objects, there was no prior documentation for this kylix, because it had been taken out of the ground illegally and had never been part of a collection. The lack of documentation makes it difficult to prove such objects have been stolen. But an Italian archaeologist put together the forensic evidence and confronted True about it publicly at a conference in Italy in October 1997, demanding its return.[51] The Greek vase had been looted from Cerveteri, just like the Euphronios krater purchased by the Metropolitan, and had clearly been broken up for sale and then acquired in fragments over several years in the 1980s from a variety of different sources, including Medici, Hecht, and von Bothmer, the curator at the Metropolitan.[52] This was the first looted object returned to Italy by the Getty. But neither this nor the other stolen examples prompted the vetting of the dealers from whom the museum was buying, such as Hecht and Medici, or any further research into the provenance of other works purchased from them.

Nor did True always pursue the leads. In 1996 she put off Renzo Canavesi—the man from whom the London dealer Robin Symes purportedly purchased the now infamous acrolithic statue mentioned earlier—when Canavesi contacted the Getty with information about the provenance of the statue. Even later, in 2002, when it was clear that True was the focus of an Italian investigation, she drafted a proposal to the museum's board that the Getty acquire a bronze statue of Poseidon she had seen and placed on reserve at the winter antiquities show in New York City. The statue had surfaced first in the collection of Robin Symes, the London dealer from whom True had acquired many objects for the Getty, including the acrolithic Aphrodite. Apparently True did not include Symes's name in the draft proposal, which went back only as far as the period of the late 1970s when the Poseidon statue belonged to the British Rail Pension. This was an odd omission, since the point of provenance history is to go back as far as possible. True's history already went back well past 1995, the date of the museum's new policy, and even past 1983, the date of the ratification of the UNESCO convention by the United States. In any case, the omission did not keep Symes's name out of the picture, since he provided a file on the bronze, claiming the statue had come out of Alexandria in Egypt in the 1930s, was transferred to Switzerland in the 1950s, and finally purchased by him in 1973. Since by 2002 Symes had become the target of litigation in Britain, the Getty lawyers insisted on scrutinizing the documents and soon found significant holes. Some of the affidavits looked fishy, and there was an Italian investigation that claimed the statue had been found in the Bay of Naples in the late 1970s and smuggled out of Italy.[53] It was clear to all but True and Deborah Gribbon, then the director of the Getty Museum, that the Poseidon was suspicious. The ethics were changing, as True had been advocating in public for seven years. But now she appeared to be on the other side.

In all three cases—the Fleischman collection, the pre-trial returns of the 1990s, and the Poseidon—what True didn't do (or have done by her staff) was to take the task of establishing provenance seriously, which is what her new policy called for: doing serious research and fact-checking, not just accepting a dealer's story. Instead, True split hairs over the definition of provenance for the first, turned a blind eye to the facts the fragments of the Onesimos-Euphronios kylix indicated in the second, and refused to vet her sources or the information they provided on the acrolithic statue or the Poseidon sculpture. The result was disastrous, not just for her, but for the Getty and the public it serves.

The Educational Mission of Museums

As Thomas Hoving knew in 1972, and Arthur Houghton reiterated in 1983 and John Walsh again in 1986, unprovenanced antiquities are looted.[54] True's trial has shown that in the search for ancient masterpieces, curators and directors at some of our most prominent museums acted more like treasure hunters than professionals. They condoned buying from fences and others who looted and damaged antiquities to meet demand, and they spent millions on objects with huge gaps in their histories. And they justified doing so in the name of education.

Yet both the public and the scholarly community are poorly served when museums purchase undocumented objects. First, these masterpieces, selected primarily for their beauty, fuel the tendency to stress the aesthetic appeal of the works and to promote their visual allure over other historical information. Second, when a historical context is provided for the work of art, it is invariably a truncated one focused only on the artist, school, or location that had produced the object initially, and not on the subsequent history of the work after its creation. The viewer is told nothing about its function(s), reception, and meaning over time. This is because looted objects lack provenience: their original findspot is rarely indicated by the criminal elements who scavenge for them and then destroy the context in which an object was found to cover their tracks.

The importance of provenience and the way it illuminates the meaning of a work of art may be shown by the case of a tenth-century BCE terracotta centaur whose head and body were found in two graves at Lefkandi on the Greek island of Euboea.[55] The careful separation of the centaur for burial in two distinct graves, likely belonging to the same family, makes it clear that this, the earliest known representation of a mythological being in Greek art, was no toy. The grieving family must have identified the mythical man-horse as Chiron, the only wise centaur, who embraced death as a release from endless suffering. Without the knowledge of its provenience, we might have identified the figure as one of the rowdy, drunken, and uncontrollable centaurs of Greek myth, rather than as a metaphor for the welcoming of death. Likewise, knowing where the magnificent Sicilian silver set was buried—under the floor of the house of Eupolemos, whose name is carved on it—brings to life the circumstances of the ancient town of Morgantina in 211 BCE, as inhabitants rushed to hide their valuables and escape before the Romans sacked it. Eupolemos clearly did not survive to retrieve his treasure, which lay buried until tomb-looters dug it up and spirited it away two thousand years later. In both examples, it is the second history of the works, not the details of their creation and first history, that provides the more gripping story. Yet this is precisely what our premier museums have been ignoring.[56] In contrast, the Moregine Treasure, a silver set from the region of Pompeii, one of the long-term loans from Italy to the Metropolitan Museum, provides a counterexample of the critical importance of provenience. Although the hoard was buried during the eruption of Vesuvius in 79 CE, two of the drinking cups were clearly made in Egypt around 40 BCE, over a century before the eruption, and thus were surely prized as heirlooms by the Pompeian family that owned them.[57]

True's trial, the returns that followed her indictment, and the subsequent revision of museum policies for the acquisition of ancient art have also shown the importance of the object's third, modern, history, or provenance—its journey from discovery until it was purchased by the museum. The educational and scholarly repercussions of not paying attention to provenance may be illustrated by the nude statue of a Greek youth, or kouros, initially borrowed by the Getty Museum in 1983 and finally purchased in 1985 for $9.5 million.[58] The museum only later did the necessary research to determine that the documentation about its provenance had been forged. This again underscores how little value they attributed to such historical information. Although the museum under True invested even more time and money in determining whether the statue was authentic or a modern forgery, even flying the statue to a conference in Greece in 1992 for analysis by experts, the jury—at least officially—is still out.[59]

Indeed, this example may best demonstrate the drawbacks of buying from shady dealers. Felch and Frammolino sketch True's unsuccessful attempts to get to the bottom of the kouros's provenance by pressing the dealer, Gianfranco Becchina, for information, first after payments had begun and again later after the surfacing of a similar but manifestly fake torso in 1990. They cite further work by Jeffrey Spier, a scholar and antiquities dealer, who claims both statues were made by the same Roman copyist from a block of Sicilian marble, and that both were commissioned by Becchina's rival, Medici. The authors' conclusion, that the kouros was an elaborate ruse by Medici to discredit Becchina, is speculative, but it gives a good impression of the sorts of people from whom the Getty was buying. Even more important is True's alleged comment to Spier that the torso—purchased by the Getty for another $1 million for the light it shed on the kouros—proved the kouros almost certainly a fake.[60] If this report is accurate, what does it say about the museum's educational mandate that the statue is still labeled "late 6th c. BCE or modern forgery"? There is no mention of any of this modern history, nor the names of the dealers involved, nor a hint that the 1992 colloquium with its attribution of the marble to the Greek island of Thasos might not be the final word.

Toward a More Complete History of Antiquities

The revision of museum guidelines for the acquisition of ancient art suggested that as of 2008, new purchases of antiquities would be more carefully vetted. There will likely be fewer of them as a result, but that should give museums more time to focus on their collections, specifically on antiquities acquired between 1970 and 2008. Provenance research is needed on items that were not subject to proper due diligence, for at least two reasons. First, it would help museums anticipate claims for forfeiture. The restitutions to Italy and Greece are likely to stimulate similar requests from other countries on the same grounds, and museums need to be prepared for them. The second reason has to do with the educational mission of our great museums. For too long some of them have been satisfied with a mere fraction of the history of the works of art they present to the public. It is time to address the critical gaps that have stymied our understanding of these ancient artifacts. A tall order, perhaps, but not an impossible one. This research need not be done solely by the museums themselves, but should be done in collaboration with them, so that the full history of the ancient work of art—as fully as it can be reconstructed—can be made public, for example by posting on museum websites. This should go beyond what some are already doing in posting provenance information to address issues of provenience as well.

Although much information about provenience has been lost, some of it irretrievably, there is still much that can be learned. In the case of Attic pottery, for example, the work of the prolific art historian and vase-painting expert J. D. Beazley (1885–1970) allows for the tracing of the output of artists whose hands he identified. Thousands of their vases were shipped in antiquity from Athens to Etruria and other parts of Italy.[61] Their current locations, as well as the dealers and museums through which these vases have passed, are known, thanks to Beazley's and other scholars' compilation of that data. Statistical analysis of this network of information about a given artist and the shapes he favored that were exported together can suggest likely proveniences or findspots, as has been recently demonstrated.[62] More information on the individual journeys these vases have taken—their second and third lives—together with greater emphasis on their role as commodities in an extensive and widespread ancient market would help enliven their appeal to a modern viewer, beyond the usual museum categorization by shape and iconography that addresses only their first life.

The restitutions and revised museum policies acknowledge the international right of countries to stolen elements of their standing monuments, as well as to antiquities looted from unexcavated sites, as specified in the UNESCO convention of 1970. This is not the result of excessive nationalism, as some have charged.[63] Rather, what has developed is a different form of cultural property internationalism, one that focuses less on the right to possess than on the importance of shared stewardship. As Francesco Rutelli, Italy's former minister of culture, put it, "Ours is not a nationalist discourse. On the contrary: it is a universal one, because each national patrimony belongs to the world, and circulation cannot be left to illegal organizations."[64]

True's trial showed that the international market in undocumented antiquities, fed by criminal elements, was concerned only with increasing the monetary value of the illegally acquired works. In contrast, Italy's willingness to implement a program of long-term loans of properly excavated antiquities represents an important new model, since those cultural artifacts cross national borders to educate the public and increase scientific knowledge. This stress on shared stewardship, over possession or ownership, is an essential part of a collaborative series of international agreements that are being forged around the world to protect priceless cultural works for the future.[65]

NOTES

Earlier versions of this essay have benefited from the suggestions from several groups and individuals. These include students in my Greek art classes at the University of Massachusetts Amherst, with whom I first began to explore issues of cultural ownership, colleagues in the initial Interdisciplinary Seminar in the Humanities and Fine Arts seminar on that topic, members of an audience at the Springfield (MA) Museums, and colleagues in the Beyond Reproduction writing group at the University of Massachusetts Amherst. I also thank Patty Gerstenblith and George Ryan for their comments on an early draft, as well as Patricia Warner, who saw the essay take shape and offered constructive criticism throughout.

1. See "Report of the AAMD Task Force on the Spoliation of Art during the Nazi/World War II Era (1933–1945)," www.aamd.org/papers/guideln.php.

2. Cultural property internationalism was first advocated by John H. Merryman in "Two Ways of Thinking about Cultural Property," *American Journal of International Law* 80.4 (1986): 831–53, and reiterated in his article "Cultural Property Internationalism," *International Journal of Cultural Property* 12 (2005): 11–39. For criticism, see Nora Niedzielski-Eichner, "Art Historians and Cultural Property Internationalism," *International Journal of Cultural Property* 12 (2005): 183–200; and Lyndel V. Prott, "The International Movement of Cultural Objects," *International Journal of Cultural Property* 12 (2005): 225–48.

3. See Association of Art Museum Directors, "New Report on Acquisition of Archaeological Materials and Ancient Art" (June 3, 2008), available at www.aamd.org. The AAMD

issued a further revision of their guidelines on the acquisition of archaeological material and ancient art on January 29, 2013, as this volume was going to press. The major contribution of the revised document is the careful listing of all the reasons that can now be used to justify acquisition of a questionable object. Hardly a step forward.

4. See, for example, Kate Fitz Gibbon, ed., *Who Owns the Past? Cultural Policy, Cultural Property and the Law* (New Brunswick, NJ: Rutgers University Press, 2005); James Cuno, *Who Owns Antiquity? Museums and the Battle over Our Ancient Heritage* (Princeton: Princeton University Press, 2008); and Cuno, "Art Museums, Archaeology, and Antiquities in an Age of Sectarian Violence and Nationalist Politics," in *The Acquisition and Exhibition of Classical Antiquities*, ed. Robin F. Rhodes (Notre Dame: University of Notre Dame Press, 2007), 9–26.

5. On the Metropolitan see "The Metropolitan Museum of Art–Republic of Italy Agreement of February 21, 2006," *International Journal of Cultural Property* 13 (2006): 427–34; on the Museum of Fine Arts see David Gill and Christopher Chippendale, "From Boston to Rome: Reflections on Returning Antiquities," *International Journal of Cultural Property* 13 (2006): 311–31; on the Getty see Jason Felch and Ralph Frammolino, *Chasing Aphrodite: The Hunt for Looted Antiquities at the World's Richest Museum* (Boston: Houghton Mifflin, 2011), 304, and David Gill and Christopher Chippendale, "From Malibu to Rome: Further Developments on the Return of Antiquities," *International Journal of Cultural Property* 14 (2007): 205–40; on Princeton see "Princeton to Return Disputed Art to Italy," *New York Times*, October 27, 2007; and on the Cleveland Museum of Art see "Pact Will Relocate Artifacts to Italy from Cleveland," *New York Times*, November 19, 2008.

6. The high-profile museums in question, which have large budgets and ample private funding, are not representative of the museological community as a whole. Most museums focus more on preserving their collections than on new acquisitions; see Robert Hallman, "Museums and Cultural Property: A Retreat from the Internationalist Approach," *International Journal of Cultural Property* 12 (2005): 201–23, esp. 203. University and college art museums that occasionally acquire new objects have long had rigorous policies of due diligence about the purchase of antiquities on the art market.

7. The agreement between Italy and the Metropolitan is the exception, but even then the grounds were not made clear, and at least one observer questioned whether the Getty's repatriations were really necessary; see Hugh Eakin, "What Went Wrong at the Getty," *New York Review of Books*, June 23, 2011.

8. The word 'provenance' refers specifically to the ownership or transmission history of a work of art; 'provenience' refers to the tracing of an archaeological object's history back to its the spot where it was discovered. Both are critical for determining valid title and authenticity. See Patty Gerstenblith, *Art, Cultural Heritage, and the Law: Cases and Materials*, 2nd ed. (Durham, NC: Carolina Academic Press, 2008), 298. In common parlance, however, 'unprovenanced' is used to describe antiquities lacking information about both provenance and provenience, that is, works that did not come out of an official excavation or a long-established private collection.

9. See Peter Watson and Cecilia Todeschini, *The Medici Conspiracy: The Illicit Journey*

of Looted Antiquities from Italy's Tomb Raiders to the World's Greatest Museums (New York: Public Affairs, 2006), 103–6; Gill and Chippendale, "From Boston to Rome," 312–13.

10. The silver was briefly presented in 1984 (Dietrich von Bothmer, "A Greek and Roman Treasury," *Bulletin of the Metropolitan Museum of Art* 42.1 [1984]: 54–60), but it was not analyzed until 2003; see Pietro G. Guzzo, "A Group of Hellenistic Silver Objects in the Metropolitan Museum," *Metropolitan Museum Journal* 38 (2003): 45–94. (I thank Carla Antonaccio for this reference.) For a summary of the detective story and the Metropolitan's obfuscation, see Maura Singleton, "Plunder: The Theft of the Morgantina Silver," *University of Virginia Magazine*, Spring 2006, available at http://archives.uvamagazine.org. The fifteen pieces were returned to Sicily in 2010 (see the appendix to this chapter).

11. See Sharon Waxman, *Loot: The Battle over the Stolen Treasures of the Ancient World* (New York: Times Books, 2008), 135–74, which also covers the subsequent theft of some of the works from the regional museum in Turkey. For a summary of the case, *Republic of Turkey v. Metropolitan Museum of Art*, 762 F. Supp. 44 (S.D.N.Y. 1990), by the International Foundation for Art Research (IFAR), see www.ifar.org/case_summary.php?docid=1184689520. The final publication was Ilknur Özgen and Jean Öztürk, *Heritage Recovered: The Lydian Treasure* (Istanbul: Okman, 1996).

12. *Cult Statue of a Goddess: Proceedings of a Workshop Held at the Getty Villa, May 9, 2007*, published online at www.getty.edu. For what is known of the statue's modern history, see Felch and Frammolino, *Chasing Aphrodite*, 84–110, 203, 286–88.

13. On the mythical attributions to old collections see Gill and Chippendale, "From Boston to Rome," 313–14; on the dealerships (including the Medici–Bürki–Hecht–Atlantis Antiquities nexus, Palladion–Antike Kunst, Sotheby's, Royal Athena Galleries, and Jerome Eisenberg in New York), see Gill and Chippendale, "From Boston to Rome," 314–21, and also Gill and Chippendale, "From Malibu to Rome," 217–20. On the one thousand objects in Boston's Museum of Fine Arts reportedly handled by Hecht, see Gill and Chippendale, "From Boston to Rome," 323. Hecht supplied many other museums as well, so this figure reflects a fraction of his total and explains why the Italian court also indicted him.

14. Watson and Todeschini, *The Medici Conspiracy*, 20–23, 66–79.

15. On Bürki as a front for Hecht, see Felch and Frammolino, *Chasing Aphrodite*, 153, and Gill and Chippendale, "From Boston to Rome," 315 with n. 30; on the manufactured provenance, Gill and Chippendale, "From Boston to Rome," 314; and on the Tivoli provenance, Benedetta Adembri and Rosa M. Nicolai, *Vibia Sabina: Da Augusta a diva* (Milan: Electa, 2007).

16. Waxman, *Loot*, 135–74. On the dismissal of the case against True see Felch and Frammolino, *Chasing Aphrodite*, 312.

17. Felch and Frammolino, *Chasing Aphrodite*, 59–62. True later conceded that such notification was a fig-leaf, because countries cannot track objects they do not know have been stolen; ibid., 185.

18. Houghton quoted ibid., 61.

19. The UNESCO convention is available at http://eca.state.gov/files/bureau/unesco01 .pdf; for the 1983 Cultural Property Implementation Act see http://eca.state.gov/files /bureau/97-446.pdf.

20. Felch and Frammolino, *Chasing Aphrodite*, 62.

21. The AIA adopted a first resolution to urge museums and institutions in the U.S. to follow the UNESCO convention's guidelines in December 1970 (www.archaeological. org/news/advocacy/108), and another in 1973 specifically focused on the acquisition of antiquities by museums (www.archaeological.org/news/advocacy/101). The statement of the University of Pennsylvania Museum of Archaeology and Anthropology ("the Pennsylvania Declaration," dated April 1, 1970) was the first of its kind; see www.penn .museum/about-our-collections.html.

22. Thomas Hoving, *Making the Mummies Dance: Inside the Metropolitan Museum of Art* (New York: Simon & Schuster, 1993), 318, 334. Hoving cites confidential carabinieri reports that confirmed the theft after the vase was purchased. True testified in her 2001 sworn deposition that von Bothmer showed her the exact location of the tomb from which it came, Felch and Frammolino, *Chasing Aphrodite*, 209. For journalists' reactions see Eakin, "What Went Wrong at the Getty"; and Michael Kimmelman, "Stolen Beauty: A Greek Urn's Underworld," *New York Times*, July 8, 2009.

23. I use the terms "looted" and "looting" here to refer to the illegal removal of objects from their archaeological context, and "stolen" for items taken illegally from an existing, documented collection. While both are legally considered stolen, the lack of documentation for looted objects makes tracing that type of theft much harder.

24. Watson and Todeschini, *The Medici Conspiracy*, 222–29; confirmed by Gill and Chippendale, "From Malibu to Rome," 226–27.

25. This ahistorical bent is true not just of museum displays, but of some museum publications as well, as in the case of the Morgantina silver set. It affects media coverage of the works, too. For example, Christian Sahner's essay on the Euphronios vase in the *Wall Street Journal* ("Through Death, Glory," August 11, 2007) devotes one sentence to the Etruscan context of the work.

26. Carlos Picón (curator in charge of ancient Greek and Roman art at the Metropolitan Museum), quoted in Rebecca Mead, "Den of Antiquity," *New Yorker*, April 9, 2005, 61. In contrast, Claire Lyons argues that archaeological sites "are essentially monuments—monuments that go down into the earth rather than rise up from it." Lyons, "Objects and Identities: Claiming and Reclaiming the Past," in *Claiming the Stones, Naming the Bones*, ed. Elazar Barkan and Ronald Bush (Los Angeles: Getty Center, 2002), 116–37, quotation on 131.

27. See the case summary on the IFAR website, www.ifar.org/case_summary.php?docid =1184703034.

28. Lyons, "Objects and Identities." On the lack of inquiry about provenience or export restrictions, she writes, "Both questions could have been readily addressed in a few minutes' research, since the phiale was published in a major scholarly journal" (121).

29. For an account of the public hearing see Felch and Frammolino, *Chasing Aphrodite*, 183–86.

30. The text of the document is available at http://exchanges.state.gov/heritage/culprop /itfact.html.

31. See the case summary on the IFAR website, www.ifar.org/case_summary.php?docid =1192024714. Schultz had remained president of the National Association of Dealers in Ancient, Oriental and Primitive Art until shortly before his indictment. For more on the way this case affirmed the precedent established in the 1970s with *United States v. McClain*, which convicted dealers of conspiring to deal in antiquities stolen from Mexico, see Patty Gerstenblith, "The McClain/Schultz Doctrine: Another Step against Trade in Stolen Antiquities," *Culture without Context* 13 (2003), www.mcdonald .cam.ac.uk/projects/iarc/culturewithoutcontext/issue 13/gerstenblith.htm.

32. Erin Thompson, "What Effect Will the AAMD Guidelines Have on the Antiquities Markets?," *Art and Cultural Heritage Law Newsletter* 1.3 (Summer 2008): 1, 19, available at www.law.depaul.edu/centers_institutes/art_museum/pdf/VolumeI_IssueIII .pdf. For similar reaction to the January 29, 2013 revisions, see Lee Rosenbaum's post "AAMD's "Strengthened" Antiquities-Collecting Guidelines Boost the Loopholes" (January 31, 2013), at www.artsjournal.com/culturegrrl.

33. The Getty policy, announced in October 2006, went further than any of the AAMD guidelines; see www.getty.edu/news/press/center/revised_acquisition_policy_release _102606.html.

34. The registry is maintained on the AAMD website at http://aamdobjectregistry.org. As of December 2012 the institutions included the Asia Society Museum in New York City (2 items), the Asian Art Museum in San Francisco (4), the Dallas Museum of Art (14), the Denver Art Museum (9), the Detroit Institute of Arts (2), the Iris and B. Gerald Cantor Center for the Visual Arts at Stanford (66), the Memorial Art Gallery in Rochester, NY (21), the Museum of Fine Arts in Boston (17), the Philadelphia Museum of Art (1), the Portland (Oregon) Art Museum (1), the Seattle Art Museum (25), the Art Institute of Chicago (11), the Cleveland Museum of Art (2), the Metropolitan Museum of Art (15), the Walters Art Museum in Baltimore (358), and the Virginia Museum of Fine Arts (31). It should be noted that the 2008 guidelines made institutions responsible for uploading information about their material, but they were not required to fill out all fields, such as that providing the rartionale for a controverial acquisition. The 2013 guidelines now make this mandatory.

35. The Nazi-Era Provenance Internet Portal is at www.nepip.org/.

36. On the Cleveland Apollo see www.stanford.edu/group/chr/drupal/ref/cleveland-apollo -sauroktonos; on the Egyptian mummy mask see the June 30, 2012, summary of the case by Ricardo St. Hilaire at http://culturalheritagelawyer.blogspot.com/2012/06 /notice-of-appeal-filed-by-us-attorney.html. Phoenix Ancient Art, which is owned by Hicham and Ali Aboutaam, returned 251 objects to Italy in 2009; see http://loot ingmatters.blogspot.com/2009/06/operation-phoenix-ali-aboutaam-urges.html.

37. The online database of the Metropolitan Museum's Department of Greek and Roman Art, www.metmuseum.org/Collections/search-the-collections, includes provenance information, in some cases via a clickable tag. The Department of the Ancient World at Boston's Museum of Fine Arts has made determined efforts to post provenance

information; it can be accessed through the collection tours or through the collection page, www.mfa.org/collections. In August 2011, the Getty Museum launched its Getty Search Gateway, http://search.getty.edu/gateway/landing, which provides online access to its collection database. By December 2012, research on provenance information on the antiquities collection was being added to the database, beginning with the objects currently on display at the Getty Villa in Malibu. I am grateful to Claire Lyons, acting senior curator of antiquities at the Getty, for information about this project.

38. This is the case for the Harvard University Art Museums, according to Jennifer Allen, the university's director of collections management, who participated in a roundtable discussion, "Challenges and Rewards of Collections Management," at the University of Massachusetts Amherst on April 12, 2011.

39. On the indictment and trial see "Indictment Targets Getty's Acquisitions," *Los Angeles Times*, May 20, 2005, available at www.elginism.com/20050520/102/; Hugh Eakin, "Treasure Hunt: The Downfall of the Getty Curator Marion True," *New Yorker*, December 12, 2007; and Eakin's *New Yorker* blog post, "Marion True on Her Trial and Ordeal," October 14, 2010, www.newyorker.com; Watson and Todeschini, *The Medici Conspiracy*, and Eakin's review of the book, "Notes from the Underground," *New York Review of Books*, May 25, 2008; Felch and Frammolino, *Chasing Aphrodite*; and Eakin, "What Went Wrong at the Getty."

40. On True's suggesting long-term loans see Felch and Frammolino, *Chasing Aphrodite*, 118.

41. See for example Eakin, "Notes from the Underground"; also Malcolm Bell, "The Beautiful and the True," *Wall Street Journal*, July 2, 2011.

42. *Art Newspaper*, December 1995, 1, 16, emphasis added. See commentary by Mark Rose, "The Getty's Mea Culpa," especially the sections "Staying Clear of Costly Court Cases" and "The Lure of Priceless Collections," and that of Jason Kaufman, "Getty Sticks with Antiquities," *Art Newspaper*, July–August 1996, 1, 17.

43. The Fleischmans did most of their antiquities buying after 1982; see Felch and Frammolino, *Chasing Aphrodite*, 126, 204. On the history of the three objects purchased by the Getty from Tempelsman through Robin Symes in 1985 (see Appendix), see Gill and Chippendale, "From Malibu to Rome," 210–12; also Felch and Frammolino, *Chasing Aphrodite*, 64–65. For the Levy-White collection see Shelby White, "Building American Museums: The Role of the Private Collector," in Fitz Gibbon, *Who Owns the Past?*, 170–71, and the appendix to this chapter for returned items.

44. Gill and Chippendale, "From Malibu to Rome," 213. The exhibition catalog is *A Passion for Antiquities: Ancient Art from the Collection of Barbara and Lawrence Fleischman* (Malibu, CA: J. Paul Getty Museum in Association with the Cleveland Museum of Art, 1994).

45. Felch and Frammolino, *Chasing Aphrodite*, 144, 205.

46. Watson and Todeschini, *The Medici Conspiracy*, 16–18, 20, 54, 265, 290, 336; see also Felch and Frammolino, *Chasing Aphrodite*, 173–74.

47. In the letters True acknowledged Medici as the supplier, even though Bürki was invoiced; see Watson and Todeschini, *The Medici Conspiracy*, 85; Felch and Frammolino, *Chasing Aphrodite*, 153, 343.

48. Watson and Todeschini, *The Medici Conspiracy*, 86; Felch and Frammolino, *Chasing Aphrodite*, 154.

49. J. Paul Getty Museum, *Handbook of the Antiquities Collection* (Malibu, CA: Getty Trust, 2002), 134–35, 90.AC.17. See also Eakin, "Notes from the Underground," for an earlier publication (1991) with photograph.

50. Watson and Todeschini, *The Medici Conspiracy*, 87; Felch and Frammolino, *Chasing Aphrodite*, 267.

51. Felch and Frammolino, *Chasing Aphrodite*, 177, 156–57.

52. On the history of the Onesimos kylix fragments, see Watson and Todeschini, *The Medici Conspiracy*, 209–10.

53. Felch and Frammolino, *Chasing Aphrodite*, 155–65, 219–20.

54. See ibid., 89, on the 1986 conversation between John Walsh and Harold Williams about the acrolithic statue ("We are saying we won't look into provenance. We know it's stolen . . . we know Symes is a fence.")

55. See Jane Sweeney, Tam Curry, and Yannis Tzedakis, *The Human Figure in Early Greek Art* (Athens and Washington, DC: Greek Ministry of Culture and National Gallery of Art, 1988), 59–60.

56. See also Jenifer Neils's review of Joan Mertens, *How to Read Greek Vases* (New York: Metropolitan Museum of Art and Yale University Press, 2010), noting the lack of discussion of provenience in this museum publication (*Bryn Mawr Classical Review*, July 23, 2011, http://bmcr.brynmawr.edu/2011/2011-07-23.html).

57. On the Moregine silver set, see "Important Antiquities Lent by Republic of Italy on View at Metropolitan Museum," www.artdaily.com/index.asp?int_sec=2&int_new=36381.

58. Felch and Frammolino, *Chasing Aphrodite*, 57–58, 64, 80–82.

59. See Nicholas P. Goulandris Foundation Museum of Cycladic Art and the J. Paul Getty Museum, *The Getty Kouros Colloquium* (Athens: Kapon Editions, 1993).

60. Felch and Frammolino, *Chasing Aphrodite*, 333–34.

61. See, for example, the discussions by Nigel Spivey and Alan Johnston on Greek vases found in Etruria and other parts of Italy in *Looking at Greek Vases*, ed. Tom Rasmussen and Nigel Spivey (Cambridge: Cambridge University Press, 1991), 131–50 and 214.

62. Isabella Donadio, "Three Attic Vases at the Mead Art Museum (Amherst College): Researching Provenance and Provenience" (BA honors thesis, art history, University of Massachusetts Amherst, 2011).

63. See for example Cuno, *Who Owns Antiquity?*, and Fitz Gibbon, *Who Owns the Past?*

64. Quoted in Felch and Frammolino, *Chasing Aphrodite*, 308.

65. As of December 2012, the United States, through the Department of State's Bureau of Educational and Cultural Affairs, is currently engaged in bilateral Memoranda of Understanding with thirteen countries; see http://eca.state.gov /cultural-heritage-center/cultural-property-protection/bilateral-agreements/.

APPENDIX
Art Repatriated to Italy and Greece through 2010

Returns to Italy
FROM THE METROPOLITAN MUSEUM OF ART,
FEBRUARY 2006, 20 OBJECTS

SOURCES: "The Metropolitan Museum of Art–Republic of Italy Agreement of February 21, 2006," *International Journal of Cultural Property* 13 (2006): 427–34; "Statement by the Metropolitan Museum of Art in Its Agreement with Italian Ministry of Culture," available at www.metmuseum.org.

Greek Attic red-figure krater by Euphronios, ca. 515 BCE (1972.11.10); purchased from Robert Hecht Jr. for $1 million in 1972

Greek Apulian red-figure dinos, attributed to the Darius Painter, 340–320 BCE (1984.11.7); David Gill and Christopher Chippendale, "From Boston to Rome: Reflections on Returning Antiquities," *International Journal of Cultural Property* 13 (2006): 313n19

Greek Attic red-figure amphora by the Berlin Painter, ca. 490 BCE (1985.11.5); ibid., 313n18

Greek red-figure psykter decorated with horsemen, attributed to Smikros, ca. 520 BCE (1996.250); ibid., 313n17

Greek Laconian kylix, 6th c. BCE (1999.527)

Hellenistic silver set of fifteen pieces, 3rd c. BCE, acquired through
Robert Hecht Jr. for $3 million in 1981 and 1982:

Kyathos (1981.11.15)

Hemispheric cup (1981.11.16)

Skyphos, ovoid cup with raised handles (1981.11.17)

Vessel in the shape of a truncated cone, with convex base provided with three forged metal supports with theatrical masks (1981.11.18)

Deep conical cup (1981.11.19)

Two deep concave cups (1981.11.20 and 1981.11.21)

Circular set, composed of a plate with embossed decoration soldered to a plate having a flared shape, with upper profiling (1981.11.22)

Pair of corrugated horns with pointed extremities (1982.11.7–8)

Cylindrical small altar on quadrangular base formed by four pieces (1982.11.9a–d)

Phiale mesomphalos (1982.11.10)

Pyxis with figured medallion on the cover, currently consisting of three pieces (1982.11.11a–c, 1982.11.9e)

Vessel in the shape of a truncated cone with convex base provided with three forged metal supports with theatrical masks (1982.11.12)

Ovoid body olpe (1982.11.13)

FROM THE MUSEUM OF FINE ARTS, BOSTON, JULY 2006, 13 OBJECTS
SOURCE: Gill and Chippendale, "From Boston to Rome."

Lucanian nestoris (1971.49)

Greek Attic red-figure lekythos (1977.713)

Greek Attic red-figure hydria, attributed to the Berlin Painter (1978.45)

Greek Attic red-figure pelike (1979.40)

Roman portrait statue of Empress Sabina, 2nd c. CE (1979.556)

Greek Attic black-figure hydria (1979.614)

Apulian loutrophoros (1988.431)

Apulian bell-krater, dated to 380–370 BCE (1988.532); illustrated in Gill and
    Chippendale, "From Boston to Rome," 322 fig. 5

Greek Attic black-figure lekythos (1989.317)

Apulian amphora (1991.437); sold by Fritz Bürki & Son, Switzerland, and pur-
    chased jointly by the MFA together with Shelby White and Leon Levy

Roman candelabrum shaft (1992.310)

Lucanian nestoris, late 5th c. BCE (1998.588); illustrated ibid., 322 fig. 4

Greek Attic red-figure bell-krater (1999.735)

FROM THE J. PAUL GETTY MUSEUM, LOS ANGELES AND MALIBU,
AUGUST 2007, 40 OBJECTS

SOURCE: Getty Museum press release, www.getty.edu/news/press/center/italy_getty_
joint_statement_080107.html; David Gill and Christopher Chippendale, "From Malibu to Rome: Further Developments on the Return of Antiquities," *International Journal of Cultural Property* 14 (2007): 205–40; and Elisabetta Povoledo, "Getty Agrees to
Return 40 Antiquities to Italy," *New York Times*, August 2, 2007

Roman fresco fragments (71.AG.111); purchased from the Royal Athena
    Galleries, New York

Group of Greek red-figure calyx fragments (Berlin Painter, Kleophrades Painter):
    (77.AE.5), gift of Herbert Lucas: (a) Berlin painter (attributed by Frel): gift of
    Herbert Lucas (77.AE.5); gift of Vasek Polak (82.AE.124); gift of Dietrich von
    Bothmer (84.AE.972); purchased from Galerie Nefer (84.AE.68); purchased
    from Frederick H. Schultz, Jr. (87.AE.51); (b) Kleophrades painter (attributed
    by Robertson): gift of Herbert Lucas (77.AE.5.5, 77.AE.5.8)

Apulian red-figure volute krater, attributed to the White Saccos Painter (77.
    AE.13); gift of Gordon McLendon

Apulian red-figure volute krater (77.AE.14); gift of Gordon McLendon

Greek Attic red-figure amphora with lid (79.AE.139)

Greek Attic red-figure bell krater (81.AE.149); gift of Max Gerchik

Fragmentary Corinthian olpe (81.AE.197); gift of Werner Nussberger. (This
    may be one of the olpai referred to in a letter from True to Medici in
    January 1992: "I was also very grateful to have the information on the prov-
    enance of our three fragmentary proto-Corinthian olpai. To know that they
    came from Cerveteri and the area of Monte Abatone is very helpful for
    the research of one of our staff members." A Getty press release lists it as a

"group of three fragmentary Corinthian Olpai": www.getty.edu/news/press
/center/italy_getty_joint_statement_080107.html.)

Douris phiale fragments: (81.AE.213), gift of Werner Nussberger; (85.AE.18,
85.AE.185, 88.AE.30), purchased from Galerie Nefer; (L.92.AE.88.2–3),
anonymous loan; Polaroids seized in Geneva

Greek Attic red-figure calyx krater ("Birds") (82.AE.83)

Etruscan red-figure plastic duck askos (83.AE.203); said to be from S. Schweitzer
collection (1940), gift of Vasek Polak (Canada); known from Polaroid in Geneva

Greek Attic Janiform kantharos (83.AE.218)

Greek Attic red-figure kylix (83.AE.287)

Greek Attic red-figure neck amphora (84.AE.63)

Greek Attic red-figure kylix (cup, type B), signed "Douris egraphsen" (84.
AE.569); purchased from Robin Symes; Polaroids seized in Geneva

Apulian red-figure loutrophoros, attributed to the Metope Group (84.AE.996);
purchased from Atlantis Antiquities, New York

South Italian polychromed marble sculpture of two griffins attacking a fallen
doe (85.AA.106); purchased from Maurice Tempelsman, New York

South Italian lekanis, marble, polychrome (85.AA.107); purchased from
Maurice Tempelsman

South Italian marble statue of Apollo (85.AA.108); purchased from Maurice
Tempelsman

Marble bust of a man (85.AA.265)

Apulian red-figure volute krater, attributed to the Sisyphus Painter (85.AE.102);
purchased from Fritz Bürki & Son, Switzerland

Greek Attic red-figure mask kantharos, attributed to the Foundry Painter
(Robert Guy), Euphronios as potter (85.AE.263); purchased from Fritz
Bürki & Son for $200,000

Greek Attic red-figure kalpis (hydria), attributed to the Kleophrades Painter
(85.AE.316); purchased from Robin Symes; known in fragments from
Polaroids seized in Geneva

Apulian pelike with arms of Achilles, attributed to Near the Group of Ruvo
423 (86.AE.611); purchased from Fritz Bürki & Son

Greek Attic black-figure zone cup, manner of the Lysippides Painter (attributed by Robert Guy) (87.AE.22); purchased from Fritz Bürki & Son

Apulian red-figure pelike, attributed to the Darius Painter (87.AE.23); purchased from Fritz Bürki & Son

Greek acrolithic cult statue of a goddess, possibly Aphrodite, late 5th c. BCE
(88.AA.76)

Greek Attic red-figure calyx krater, attributed to the Copenhagen/Aegisthus
Painters (88.AE.66); purchased from Christoph Leon

Askos in the shape of a siren, bronze (92.AC.5); purchased from Lawrence
Fleischman, New York

Greek Attic red-figure calyx-krater, Syriskos (signature) (92.AE.6 and
96.AE.335); known from Polaroids seized in Geneva

Hellenistic marble statuette of Tyche (Malibu 96.AA.49); first purchased from Robin Symes by Barbara and Lawrence Fleischman, then purchased from the Fleischmans for $2 million

Marble Greek statuette of Dionysos with an animal (96.AA.211); gift of Barbara and Lawrence Fleischman

Bronze mirror with relief-decorated cover (96.AC.132)

Etruscan antefix in the form of a maenad and Silenos dancing (96.AD.33); "said to come from Cerveteri," and purchased from Lawrence Fleischman; known from Polaroid in Geneva

Apulian red-figure bell-krater, "reconstructed from fragments," attributed to the Choregos Painter (A. D. Trendall) (Malibu 96.AE.29); purchased from Fritz Bürki

Greek Attic black-figure amphora showing Herakles attacking Geryon, "reconstructed from fragments," attributed to the Painter of Berlin 1686 (Dietrich von Bothmer) (Malibu 96.AE.92); reassembled by Fritz Bürki in 1988 and purchased from Atlantis Antiquities in 1988

Greek Attic black-figure amphora, attributed to the Three-Line Group (Dietrich von Bothmer) (Malibu 96.AE.93); purchased from Fritz Bürki in 1989 (said to have been found with two other pots in the possession of Robert Hecht and Robin Symes)

Greek Attic red-figure cup, "reconstructed from a few large fragments," attributed to the Nikosthenes Painter (Robert Guy), potter Pamphaios (Robert Guy) (Malibu 96.AE.97)

Paestan squat lekythos, attributed to Asteas (96.AE.119); gift of Barbara and Lawrence Fleischman

Pontic amphora, attributed to the Tityos Painter (96.AE.139); sold by Fritz Bürki to Barbara and Lawrence Fleischman in 1988; gift of the Fleischmans; known from a Polaroid seized in Geneva

Roman fresco fragment, lunette with mask of Herakles (Malibu 96.AG.171); purchased from Fritz Bürki & Son; associated with a fragment in the Shelby White collection

FROM THE PRINCETON UNIVERSITY ART MUSEUM, OCTOBER 2007, 8 OBJECTS

SOURCE: Elisabetta Povoledo, "Princeton to Return Disputed Art to Italy," *New York Times,* October 27, 2007; Peter Monaghan, "Princeton Agrees to Return 8 Art Objects to Italy but Will Keep 7 Others," *Chronicle of Higher Education,* October 29, 2007, http://chronicle.com.

Apulian red-figure loutrophoros, attributed to the Darius Painter (y1989-29)

Apulian red-figure volute-krater, attributed to the Iliupersis Painter (y1989-40)

Carian round-mouthed oinochoe, attributed to the Ivy Leaf Group (originally listed as Etruscan) (y1989-53)

Greek Attic red-figure psykter, attributed to the Kleophrades Painter (y1989-69)

Etruscan head of a winged lion (y1994-58)

Etruscan black-figure skyphos fragment with a sprinting youth (1995-64); gift of Brian T. Aitken

Etruscan terracotta plaque with relief centaur (presumably 1995.129); gift of Ali and Hicham Aboutaam (dealers and owners of Phoenix Ancient Art)

Etruscan oinochoe (presumably 1995.149)

FROM JEROME EISENBERG (NEW YORK CITY DEALER), NOVEMBER 2007, 8 OBJECTS

SOURCE: David Gill, "Jerome Eisenberg Returns Antiquities: Further Details," November 7, 2007, http://lootingmatters.blogspot.com/2007/11/jerome-eisenberg-returns-antiquities_07.html

Greek Attic black-figure neck-amphora showing Hephaistos, attributed to the Leagros Group, said to be from Etruria

Greek Attic red-figure column-krater showing Dionysos, Geras Painter, said to be from south-central Italy

Greek Attic red-figure hydria showing women, said to be from south-central Italy

Etruscan bronze athlete with strigil; stolen from Museo Archeologico Nazionale "Spina" di Ferrara on August 3, 1970

Etruscan bronze figure; stolen from Museo Nazionale Etrusco di Chiusi on April 28, 1971

Etruscan bronze Nike; stolen from la Soprintendenza archeologica di Ercolano (Napoli) on July 23–24, 1975

Pontic oinochoe showing warriors, Tityos Painter, said to be from Etruria

Roman marble nymph from fountain, said to be from central Italy

FROM THE PRIVATE COLLECTION OF SHELBY WHITE, JANUARY 2008, 9 OBJECTS

SOURCES: Lee Rosenbaum, "Italy Posts the Shelby White List of Relinquished Objects," April 1, 2008, www.artsjournal.com/culturegrrl/2008/04/italy_posts_the_shelby_white_l.html; David Gill, "Homecomings: 'Glories' with Lost Contexts," March 31, 2008, http://lootingmatters.blogspot.com/2008/03/homecomings-glories-with-lost-contexts.html (Gill's list differs slightly)

Amphora from Chalkidiki with young riders, ca. 550–540 BCE

Fragment of a wall fresco decoration: a lying Maenad, Pompeiian style, ca. 50–79 CE

Fragment of a wall fresco decoration: architectural perspective and theater mask, Pompeiian style, ca. 50–30 BCE

Greek Attic black-figure amphora with Dionysos and Ariadne banqueting, attributed to the Painter of the Medea Group, ca. 520 BCE

Greek Attic black-figure panathenaic amphora with runners, attributed to the Painter of the Louvre F6, ca. 540 BCE

Greek red-figure calyx krater with Zeus and Ganymede, attributed to the
    Eucharides Painter, ca. 490–480 BCE

Greek small bronze statue of kouros, ca. 480–470 BCE

Hydria from Cerveteri with the flight of Ulysses from Polyphemus' cavern,
    attributed to the workshop of the Aquila Painter and associates, ca. 530–500
    BCE

Hydria from Cerveteri with panther and lioness attacking a mule, attributed to
    the Busiride Painter, ca. 530–500 BCE

FROM THE CLEVELAND MUSEUM OF ART, NOVEMBER 2008, 13 ANCIENT OBJECTS PLUS RENAISSANCE CROSS

SOURCE: David Gill, "Cleveland: The List," November 19, 2008, http://lootingmatters.blogspot.com/2008/11/cleveland-list.html

Etruscan red-figure duck askos, Italy, probably Chiusi (ancient Clusium), ca.
    350 BCE (1975.23)

Sicilian plastic vase in the form of a pig, Sicily, provincial Greece, ca. 425 BCE
    (1975.91)

Greek donkey-head rhyton, ca. 475 BCE (1977.92)

Apulian or Campanian red-figure lid with bowl, South Italy, Apulia, 4th c.
    BCE (1986.200); gift of Jonathan P. Rosen

Apulian Gnathia flat-bodied epichysis, Italy, Middle Gnathia, ca. 340–320 BCE
    (1986.201); gift of Jonathan P. Rosen

Apulian Gnathia round-bellied epichysis, Italy, Middle Gnathia, ca. 340–320
    BCE (1986.202); gift of Jonathan P. Rosen

Apulian Gnathia lekythos, Italy, Middle Gnathia, ca. 340–330 BCE (1986.203);
    gift of Jonathan P. Rosen

Campanian red-figure acorn lekythos, South Italy, Campania, ca. 350–320 BCE
    (1986.204); gift of Jonathan P. Rosen

Campanian bird askos, South Italy, northern Campania, ca. 310–280 BCE
    (1987.209); gift of Mr. and Mrs. Lawrence A. Fleischman

Apulian volute-krater, Darius Painter, ca. 330 BCE (1988.41)

Sardinian warrior, ca. 900–700 BCE (1990.1)

Greek column krater, Greece, Late Early Corinthian–Early Middle Corinthian,
    ca. 600–590 BCE (1990.81)

Two Etruscan bracelets, Italy, 6th c. BCE (1996.16 and 1996.17); gift of Edoardo
    Almagia and Courtney Keep in honor of Arielle P. Kozloff

Renaissance processional cross, Tuscany, Siena, ca. 1350 CE (1977.75)

FROM THE J. PAUL GETTY MUSEUM, MAY 2009, 1 OBJECT

SOURCE: Getty Museum press release, April 7, 2009, www.getty.edu/news/press/center/fresco_return.html

Roman fresco fragment depicting part of a landscape scene, 3rd quarter of the 1st century BCE (96.AG.170); acquired by the museum in 1996

FROM THE PRIVATE COLLECTION OF SHELBY WHITE, 2010, 1 OBJECT
SOURCE: Gill, "Homecomings"; see also Peter Watson and Cecilia Todeschini, *The Medici Conspiracy: The Illicit Journey of Looted Antiquities from Italy's Tomb Raiders to the World's Greatest Museums* (New York: Public Affairs, 2006), 128–32; and John Boardman, *The History of Greek Vases* (London: Thames & Hudson, 2001), fig. 120

Greek Attic red-figure calyx-krater by Euphronios, showing Herakles slaying Kyknos; according to Watson and Todeschini, this vase, included in Medici's Polaroid collection, was sold by Medici to Hecht as part of Hecht's partnership in the Summa Gallery in Los Angeles, whence it was acquired by the Hunt brothers, and later sold as part of their collection at Sotheby's (New York) in June 1990, when Robin Symes purchased it for $1.76 million for Leon Levy and Shelby White (Watson and Todeschini, *The Medici Conspiracy*, 131)

Returns to Greece
FROM THE J. PAUL GETTY MUSEUM, FEBRUARY 2007, 4 OBJECTS
SOURCE: Hugh Eakin, "Getty Museum Agrees to Return Two Antiquities to Greece," *New York Times*, July 1, 2006; and Malcolm Brabant, "Getty Returns Ancient Wreath to Greece," BBC News, March 29, 2007, available at www.elginism.com/20070330/696/.

Greek votive relief, marble, depicting two female figures approaching the shrine of a goddess, early 5th c. BCE, acquired by J. P. Getty himself in 1955; stolen from French excavation storeroom in Thasos, where it had been dug up in 1911 (see Eakin, "Getty Museum Agrees to Return Two Antiquities")
Greek kore of Parian marble, late 6th c. BCE (93.AA.24); purchased from dealer Robin Symes, London; shown in Polaroids from Medici's storeroom in Geneva
Greek grave stele of Athanias, Boiotian limestone, ca. 400 BCE (93.AA.47); purchased from Safani Gallery, New York
Macedonian gold funerary wreath, late 4th c. BCE (93.AM.30); purchased from dealer Christoph Leon, Basel

FROM THE PRIVATE COLLECTION OF SHELBY WHITE, AUGUST 2008, 2 OBJECTS
SOURCE: David Gill, "Shelby White and Greece: Antiquities in Athens," August 27, 2008, http://lootingmatters.blogspot.com/2008/08/shelby-white-and-greece-antiquities-in.html; dates are from Maria Petrakis, "Collector Shelby White to Return Two Antiquities to Greece," Bloomberg News, July 11, 2008, www.bloomberg.com/apps/news?pid=newsarchive&sid=aIACdZ7p1E6k

Bronze calyx-krater, said to be from Pieria, with a silver wreath on the walls
  and maenads under the handles, ca. 340 BCE

Fragmentary funerary stele from eastern Attica, bearing the personal names of
  Menon and Kleobolos, 4th c. BCE

3
THE SALAMANCA PAPERS
A Cultural Property Episode in Post-Franco Spain

———— ⌘ ————

Oriol Pi-Sunyer
Susan M. DiGiacomo

THE DEVASTATING CIVIL war of 1936–1939 has long been seen, not the least by foreign historians, as the defining moment of modern Spanish history. In its time, the heroic struggle of the Republic aroused the admiration of anti-fascist Western intellectuals to an unprecedented degree and helped turn the conflict into an international cause. Regarding this generation, the Irish poet Louis MacNeice wrote, "our spirit / Would find its frontier on the Spanish front, / Its body in a rag-tag army." Although the war and its aftermath now seem remote in time and strangely archaic in form, it is again generating a good deal of interest in Spain and beyond. Historians of the conflict have been shifting their focus from what the historians Chris Ealham and Michael Richards term "grand narratives" to a "revitalized social and cultural approach to history" with an "emphasis on everyday life and the social and cultural significance of repression."[1]

This attention to culture, coupled with recognition of the challenge posed by a highly complex series of events, brings historiography much closer to ethnography. One of the factors that have drawn historians and others to a reassessment of the conflict is the pivotal role played by violence, particularly the degree to which "terror had a political purpose and

72

violence a social function."[2] Violence as policy, as distinct from violence as a consequence of chaos, fear, and the disruption of public order, rapidly became the trademark of an emergent fascist regime. The institutionalization of violence is evident in the instructions issued three weeks before the July 1936 coup by one of the rebel generals to a co-conspirator concerning the need to use speed and extreme violence to compel loyalty to the rebellion. The first executions took place in Morocco, and the victims were officers who hesitated to join the rebel generals or challenged their authority. It was there, too, that the rebels began arresting, raping, torturing, and murdering women: the wives and daughters of officers loyal to the Republic. These same atrocities were then used to subjugate and terrorize the civilian population as the insurrection advanced across southern Spain. As the historian Antony Beevor observes, in order to destroy the democratic expectations engendered by the Republic, "repression became planned and methodically directed, encouraged by the military and civil authorities and blessed by the Catholic Church," with a clear and sinister goal: the "cleansing" or "purifying" of Spain through a "national crusade" to eliminate the regime's internal enemies. In many instances, execution was accompanied by deliberate acts of cultural or political vandalism. We have, therefore, an early instance of something that became common in midcentury: a culture of destruction that Alan Kramer describes as fascinated by the purifying possibilities of violence.[3]

The "turn" in historical studies we have outlined coincides with a growing anthropological interest in what Hugh Gusterson calls "the phenomenology of war and violence" and how this leads to cultural practices that permit people to live—generally at great psychological cost—in societies wracked by state-sponsored terror.[4] Much in this body of research is relevant to our essay: the role of atrocity memories in creating a sense of "unfinished business" that may endure for generations and reemerge as powerful moral claims; the presence of a public culture of silence regarding atrocities and other "public secrets"; the use of bodies—tortured, killed, or "disappeared"—as semiotic messages intended to terrorize and silence; the social dismemberment of communities and families by military occupation, forced labor, internment, and other practices of totalitarian rule; and finally, in some situations, the emulation by victims of a militarized ethos, whether through resort to counter-violence, the glorification of "fighters," or a general coarsening and hollowing out of everyday life.[5]

Our chapter is informed by these theoretical positions and thematic concerns, and in particular by how they highlight the importance of situated meanings. We begin, however, by positioning ourselves as a particular category of observers. Almost seventy years ago, Clyde Kluckhohn insisted that anthropologists were "morally obligated to look at the world," claiming that this stance represented the essence of democracy.[6] In the first section of this chapter, "Positioned Observers, Situated Knowledge, and Politically Engaged Research," we define engagement as a form of knowledge grounded in the lived experience of social participation, past and present. In the next section, "Of Time and Place," we discuss the key ideological differences that framed the Spanish Civil War, and in "Culture as Symbol and Ideology" we draw attention to the way in which a concept of culture as artistic production came to define the Republican moral order. For many, "the good fight" is still best remembered through the work of artists and writers.

The section "Trauma, Fascism, and Non-remembrance" is devoted to an examination of the human costs of this repression during Europe's longest-lived fascist regime. We argue that episodes of extreme violence are best understood as sophisticated instruments of terror, and that it can take generations for suppressed memories to resurface. A consideration of the recovery of what in Spain is now termed "historical memory" or "democratic memory" brings us to the next section, "The Salamanca Papers," a discussion of the campaign in Catalonia to recover documents and other cultural property, collectively known as the Salamanca Papers, looted following the fall of Barcelona in 1939. We end with an assessment of the campaign's success and the lessons this project offers.

Positioned Observers, Situated Knowledge, and Politically Engaged Research

As Renato Rosaldo noted several years ago, ethnographic writing in the classic mode features a "detached observer [who] epitomizes neutrality and impartiality," having carefully erased all traces of his or her own subjectivity from the text. Rosaldo is one of the first anthropologists to begin systematically questioning some of the most taken-for-granted conventions of his discipline, developing, in what is one of the most deeply affecting essays in the entire anthropological corpus, the concept of the anthropologist as "positioned (and repositioned) subject" whose life experiences "both enable and inhibit particular kinds of insight." This is where the "remaking of social analysis" begins: with the refiguring of the social analyst and the recognition that all knowledge is situated. As Rosaldo himself was well aware, "by invoking personal experience as an analytical category one risks easy dismissal." While that risk is still present, it has begun to lose force. The literature this kind of reflexivity has generated is now too extensive, too rich in insights, and too productive of new approaches to be so easily dismissed.[7]

If the person of the fieldworker has been subjected to significant rethinking, so has the concept of "the field." At an earlier time—that of the ethnographer as detached observer—"the field" was conceived as a place, often remote, where cultural difference was found and ethnographic data gathered. "Home," by contrast, was where the data collected in the field were subjected to anthropological analysis and fashioned into articles and monographs. This dichotomy of "home" versus "the field" supported the self-versus-other dichotomy that differentiated anthropologist from informant, anthropological knowledge from cultural knowledge.

These dichotomies have been destabilized as more and more anthropologists have undertaken collaborative and action-oriented forms of research. For example, Davydd Greenwood and Morton Levin studied communities of which they themselves were a part; others have written autoethnographies, or returned to their native societies to do ethnographic research.[8] In all these cases, the distinction between home and the field, self and other, is significantly blurred, and the anthropologist's own subjectivity becomes an important element in the analysis. This is not a matter of what we might call "full disclosure," but of epistemology. In short, engagement is a form of knowledge.

Both of us have long histories of field research in Catalonia focusing on political issues. Our forms of engagement reflect our different connections to Catalonia, but in both cases, "home" and "the field" interpenetrate significantly. One of us (Pi-Sunyer) was born in Barcelona six years before the Spanish Civil War began, and retains memories of both wartime Barcelona and rural Catalonia, and of the Spanish Republican diaspora that followed. His father, Carles Pi i Sunyer, was a prominent Republican political leader, at different times the mayor of Barcelona and a minister in both the Generalitat (the Catalan autonomous government) and the Spanish government, and later a member of the Catalan government in exile. The "borrowed exile," as discussed in his sister's memoir, involved the forced loss of Spanish nationality, the constant search for security, and an environment that helped forge a powerful bond with Republican exiles throughout the diaspora.[9] The closely linked issues of historical memory and cultural property are not abstractions for them, but are part and parcel of personal memory and experience.

The second author (DiGiacomo) has a different kind of connection to Catalonia, one forged in a period less violent than the Spanish Civil War but no less formative: the transition to democracy following the death of General Franco and his regime in 1975. Someone whose political awareness was shaped in the United States by a sequence of political assassinations, the Vietnam War, and the Watergate scandal, a period when violence, the demonization of dissent, support for right-wing dictatorships, and political dishonesty were all justified by an appeal to patriotism, was not especially well positioned to see nationalism as a personally and collectively liberating force. Witnessing a key phase of the Spanish transition to democracy from the vantage point of Catalonia, and beginning to understand what it meant for Catalans, entailed significant repositioning of a novice ethnographer as anthropological subject. More than three decades later, that novice ethnographer is an anthropologist who lives and works in Barcelona, teaches in Catalan at a Catalan university, and is a member of the Comissió de la Dignitat (Dignity Commission), a citizens' organization led by a politically engaged historian and lawyer, Josep Cruanyes, and an equally engaged journalist, Antoni Strubell i Trueta. Legal and international pressure brought to bear on the Spanish government by this group resulted in the initiation of the return of the Salamanca Papers in early 2006, a process that is still ongoing at this writing.[10]

For us, where does "home" end and "the field" begin? The boundaries, in both cases, are hopelessly blurred, and it seems more productive, as James Clifford has suggested, "to think of the 'field' as a habitus rather than as a place, a cluster of *embodied* dispositions and practices." Central to those dispositions and practices is an emphasis on ethnography as a form of witness, an approach that politically engaged anthropology shares with politically engaged journalism and historiography. This approach to fieldwork as a shifting of conceptual locations in one's own life makes it possible to use autobiographical materials as ethnographic materials, and personal experience as an analytic category. Because of how history has positioned us, and how we have chosen to position ourselves, there is something important at stake for us in the outcome of the memory work and cultural property struggle described here: joining anthropological knowledge to other forms of knowledge, and thereby, as Akhil Gupta and James Ferguson expressed it, "tracing . . . lines of possible alliance and common purpose between them."[11]

Of Time and Place

The core of our essay situates cultural property claims and disputes in post-Franco and post-transition Spain. A generalized interest in "historical memory" (and with it issues of cultural patrimony) is not much older than a decade. Interestingly, it has emerged as a significant movement just as the last living witnesses of the Civil War depart the scene.[12] If the movement is recent, however, the issues are not, for they have to do with the unfinished business of the war and the subsequent decades of repression. Reconnecting with such a past takes many forms and involves tasks of imagining, demarcating, and exploring the "ghosts" of the Civil War. The specifics vary, but in situations of this sort enormously powerful emotions inevitably become attached to locations, material objects, physical space, and specific events.[13]

Current concern with the Franco dictatorship owes much to the fact that 1939 did not so much mark the end of a war as the inauguration of a victorious regime. In formal political terms, this condition was to endure until the late 1970s; psychologically, it lasted much longer and often entailed multiple forms of personal loss: home, livelihood, family and social ties, a sense of security and integrity, and at times language and country.

Later on, Spain's much-heralded transition to democracy was based on an implicit pact of silence: political amnesty in exchange for political amnesia. Among the many issues that were left unattended was the fate (and remembrance) of the thousands of Spanish Republicans in Nazi camps, who had faced "brutality, overwork, executions, the gas chamber, suicide, hunger and disease."[14] Evidence of Nazi atrocities recorded by Spanish prisoners was used at the Nuremberg trials; because of the Cold War, however, not a single Spanish official was held to account for the pro-Axis Franco regime's complicity in these crimes, and there are still powerful forces in Spain that prevent examination of the past. In October 2008 a Spanish judge, Baltasar Garzón, declared the acts of repression and reprisal committed by the Franco regime to be crimes against humanity. His attempt to open an investigation was frustrated on jurisdictional grounds, and in January 2010 the Spanish Supreme Court agreed to hear a case against Garzón brought by the Spanish fascist party (Falange Española de las JONS), which is still in existence. It is as if the Nazi Party were still considered a legitimate political organization in contemporary Germany. Garzón was suspended, and went to work as a consultant at the International Criminal Court, The Hague. In February 2012 the Spanish Supreme Court absolved Garzón of charges related to the investigation of crimes against humanity, but convicted him on an unrelated charge concerning the use of wiretaps in the investigation of a corruption scandal. The court barred him from serving as a judge for eleven years, effectively ending his judicial career. In their verdict, however, the justices paid very little attention to the corruption scandal and devoted a great deal of space to arguing that the amnesty law passed in 1977 closes off any possibility of holding the fascists legally accountable.

Culture as Symbol and Ideology

It might be helpful at this juncture to say something about "culture" in Iberia, not so much in the anthropological or sociological sense as in terms of literary and artistic production. In early 1936, on the eve of the Civil War, Spain was in many respects an exceedingly poor country, still largely agricultural and characterized by huge social inequalities.[15] It was saddled with a bloated bureaucracy, politically powerful church and military establishments, and an unfortunate tradition of centralism. From the second half of the nineteenth century, however, Spain can also be described as a society in rapid socioeconomic transformation. Modern working- and middle-class sectors had expanded significantly, particularly in the Basque Country and Catalonia. Spain was experiencing the tensions between periodic liberal attempts to modernize the country and extend rights to marginalized social sectors, and privileged groups alarmed at what these reforms might entail.[16]

This clash of ideals and sociopolitical projects framed Civil War discourses, and the war and the dictatorship that followed have helped structure a perception of the society as marginal to Europe and the West. It is easy to forget that in the 1930s Spain was something of an artistic and intellectual powerhouse. It had produced three of the greatest contemporary painters—Pablo Picasso, Joan Miró, and Salvador Dalí, each of whom spent formative years in Barcelona—and in the words of the Spanish diplomat and historian Salvador de Madariaga, thanks to Isaac Albéniz, Enric Granados, and Manuel de Falla, music was "better cultivated than ever since the days of the great masters of old."[17] One should also note such renowned instrumentalists as Pau Casals and Andrés Segovia. In literature, leading figures of the "Generation of '98," including José Ortega y Gasset and Miguel de Unamuno, remained influential, while a cohort of younger writers and poets, the best known being Federico García Lorca, was busy making a name for itself.[18] This dazzling creativity in literature and the arts occurred in a world also plagued by unemployment and social unrest, since Spain could escape neither the economic dislocations of the Great Depression nor the rise of totalitarian systems and ideologies.[19]

What this short summary cannot convey is the special role and influence of culture and art in Spain and in Catalonia. In some respects it was something distinctive of Iberia, but in others a phenomenon with clear parallels in several European countries. The distinctiveness is related to a set of historical events, particularly the loss of Spain's overseas empire in the Spanish-American War of 1898.[20] The dispatch of tens of thousands of conscripts to Cuba, Puerto Rico, and the Philippines had enormous social and political consequences. "The Disaster," as it came to be called, gave "old protests new impetus, as the ragged and disease-ridden defeated army returned to Spain."[21] What ensued was both a fervent debate on Spain's future and a reaffirmation by progressive elements of the need for reform and social regeneration that had much in common with the intellectual discourses of pre–World War I central Europe so vividly described by Stefan Zweig in his autobiography: an expectation that the application of reason and science would surely overcome backwardness, disharmony, and violence. Faith in "progress," as Zweig stresses, "had the force of religion."[22]

This modernizing agenda, which was also an attempt to ground liberal democracy, faced many challenges.[23] It also manifested itself in highly specific ways. The historian Thomas Glick has drawn attention to the number of Republican leaders who were doctors, scientists, or engineers, and to the remarkable fact that over four hundred members of the 1931 Constituent Cortes—the parliament charged with drawing up a new constitution following the abdication of Alfonso XIII—had been trained in some branch of science.[24] Many of its members saw themselves as engaged in a process of renewal designed to situate Spain in the community of European democracies.

While Spain was a large state geographically (with more than twice the area of the United Kingdom), its population in 1930 stood at less than 24 million. This made it a "small nation" in the sense used by Milan Kundera: "The small nations form 'another Europe,' whose evolution runs in counterpoint with that of the large nations. An observer can be fascinated by the often astonishing intensity of their cultural life."[25] Both Catalonia and Spain as a whole met this description, producing brilliant artists and intellectuals, but from a relatively small potential pool. A rough measure is the number of university students enrolled in Spanish universities—in 1930, just over 37,000, or 153 university students per 100,000 inhabitants. This helps explain other features of intellectual life in a small country: a high level of intimacy—what Kundera calls "family ties," characterized by dense social networks and powerful attachments (and at times, strong antipathies)—and a tendency, common in countries that are not powerful by the standard measures, to value writers and artists highly as representatives of the nation to the outside world.

The vast majority of Spanish writers, artists, and intellectuals firmly supported the Republic. This stance further reinforced Franco's abiding suspicion of all things related to the intellect. As a result, "culture," to the extent that it survived the dictatorship, went underground, and many people believe that it has never fully recovered. According to J. M. Cohen, editor of *The Penguin Book of Spanish Verse*, "By the end of that war all Spain's principal poets were dead or silenced, in prison or in exile."[26] But the war itself and the long dictatorship also made a concern for cultural issues a key element of progressive and contestatorial ideologies.

The defining moment of this culture clash came early in the war. It took place at the University of Salamanca on October 16, 1936, in celebration of the Día de la Raza (celebrated in the United States as Columbus Day). Salamanca was Franco territory, and most of the speeches were predictable. Miguel de Unamuno, who presided as the rector of the university, stood up and complained of all the talk of war and death, and of what he termed an *un*civil war. At this, General José Millán Astray, founder of the Spanish Foreign Legion, rose to his feet and shouted *"Viva la muerte!"*—Long live death!—to which his supporters cried out "Death to intelligence!" Unamuno's response is lapidary: "This is the temple of intelligence. And I am its high priest. You are profaning this sacred precinct. . . . You may win, but you will not convince."[27]

A significant feature of this cultural environment was the degree to which writers, poets, musicians, and painters were seen as the moral conscience of the Republic, and how this quality differentiated them from the enemy. In October 1938, when the war was already going badly for the Republic, Carles Pi i Sunyer opened an art exhibit in Barcelona with these words: "In times to come, when the history of these years is calmly recalled, . . . one of the most remarkable and admirable aspects will be the intense cultural work undertaken in Catalonia, as throughout Republican Spain."[28] For him, as for many others, culture was not an abstraction but a weapon wielded to protect the Republic. The cultural role of art and artists in progressive Spain attempted to meld the political realities of a society defending itself against global fascism with the liberties characteristic of an advanced democracy.

It was also chiefly through art and literature that an embattled society worked to influence the outside world, in particular foreign intellectuals.[29] Picasso's *Guernica*, originally commissioned for the 1937 Paris International Exhibition, has lost none of its power. Nor was art in its sundry forms simply the face that Loyalist Spain showed to the outside world. The Spanish government produced newsreels and documentaries; it supported theater companies and the production of a great deal of poster art, all primarily for internal consumption. This was equally true of Catalonia. At the height of a horrendous war, the Catalan government spent major human and economic resources protecting material cultural property, supporting art and literature, publishing magazines, and sending mobile "bibliobuses" to the front. Part of what explains this remarkable effort and expenditure is that literature and art were not only thought valuable for sustaining the troops' morale, but also marked a moral and ethical divide between "us" and "them."

Trauma, Fascism, and Non-remembrance

Culture still matters, perhaps particularly in Catalonia, a non-state nation with an old and rich literary and artistic tradition. Cultural and artistic concerns, including language, were both the substance of and the vehicle for political demands during the transition to democracy that began after Franco's death in late 1975 and continued into the early 1980s, a situation with parallels to events in central and eastern Europe in the terminal phases of state socialism. What needs explanation is why, in the context of these changes, so much remained hidden and unspoken, and for this we need to examine not only competing meanings and claims to ownership of history and memory, but the role of a violent regime in defining and censoring past and present.

Spanish has a term, *desmemoria*, that may be rendered as "a failure of memory": not simple forgetting, but erasure. To understand the social and political uses of this word, one should first bear in mind the cost of the Civil War itself. The country was shattered and impoverished by almost three years of fighting; casualties, civilian and military, were enormous. Close to half a million people were forced into exile, and about the same number were imprisoned; of these, many—the commonly accepted figure is 50,000—were executed, and others turned into forced labor, incarcerated in what Antony Beevor terms "the Franquist gulag."[30] Certainly this is trauma enough, but there are other costs, including the loss of links to Western culture, an involuntary complicity with the regime, and the oppression and contempt with which "regional" cultures were treated during the dictatorship.

Postwar forms of social dislocation included massive internal and external migration, the uprooting of rural communities, and industrialization at all costs. All of this changed the social landscape to a degree never seen or imagined, and at a heavy price in human suffering. The postwar period shares with the Civil War some of the same qualities of an unremembered past, what Antonio Barr, an early observer of the phenomenon, termed a "collective memory block." In a review of the English translation of Javier Cercas's prize-winning novel *Soldados de Salamina* (2001), Colm Tóibin first explains the strangeness of the Spanish transition, grounded as it was in an informal but clearly understood agreement that neither victors nor vanquished would bring up the past. But in the post-Franco world of democracy, "the silence exerted its sinister power and influence in the private realm . . . and there, in families and villages, it did a great deal of harm." What he is noting are modalities of a self-censorship that have yet to be fully abandoned. Tóibin argues that forgetting has made its way into the core of Spanish political life, and he attributes the enormous success of Cercas's novel to the fact that it manages to further the process of reconciliation for which Spain has been striving, "while reminding readers . . . that the shadow of the Civil War is a shadow they live with, and that what creates this shadow . . . continues, whether they like it or not."[31]

Things have changed, quite fast—but not without clamor and dispute. The recovery of what in Spain is termed "historical memory" or "democratic memory" is best understood as a number of distinct social movements sharing similar aims and functioning as political actors. Many of these groups have joined together as the Asociación para la Recuperación de la Memoria Histórica, or ARMH.[32] Those who personally experienced the Civil War and the initial dictatorship have either died or are now of very advanced age. The baton has been passed not so much to the second generation, the children of the Civil War, as to the third, the grandchildren.[33] This generation carries fewer burdens of fear and anguish; it is also a generation fully at home with the Internet, social media, and other aspects of information technology, which helps to explain the rapid spread and growth of the movement.

In his article "The Return of Civil War Ghosts," the Spanish anthropologist Francisco Ferrándiz discusses the most dramatic feature of the historical memory movement. Unmarked mass graves are found throughout Spain; most of those interred in them were victims of fascism. Quite correctly, we believe, he regards these episodes of extreme violence as "a sophisticated instrument of terror . . . intended to bury the social memory of violence and thus to strengthen the fear-based regimes of the perpetrators, which can survive for decades." He goes on to point out that exhuming those who died by violence is inevitably controversial, and that "state institutions often become involved in the exhumations in one way or another"—sometimes in order to prevent them.[34] At the symbolic level, episodes of extreme violence are crucial evidence of the wounds of history, and a key to understanding the dynamics of terror. The social or ethnographic analysis of mass graves, skeletons, war monuments, and suppressed memories, Ferrándiz argues, makes for a productive convergence of anthropological interests: issues of violence, victimhood, human rights, memory, ritual, and mass media and art. And, one might add, social movements and political mobilization.

The Salamanca Papers

It is within this framework that we would position the movement for the return of documents and other war booty taken from Catalonia in 1938–39. In April 1938, Ramón Serrano Suñer, Franco's minister of the interior and a great admirer of the Nazis, created the Delegación del Estado para la Recuparación de Documentos (State Office for the Recovery of Documents), an agency designed to confiscate materials from organizations and individuals deemed dangerous to the state—in short, a police archive. The primary goal was the collection of evidence to be used in courts-martial and other political trials. These "enemies" came in various forms, some difficult to imagine. To the expected "reds," "separatists," trade unionists, and other people who had supported the Republic, we can add a strange mélange of Freemasons, nudists, pacifists, theosophists, and members of the Rotary Club. In the reigning demonology, this collection of undesirables constituted a "Judeo-Masonic concubinage" (it makes no more sense in Spanish: *contubernio judeo-masónico*). In keeping with the fascist model, much of the seized material was ritually burned, and a lot more turned into pulp—altogether, some 80 percent of the total.

Since the seizures were massive and random, however, substantial quantities were carted away. These included the archives of the Generalitat (the Catalan autonomous government) and all its dependencies, material from the Catalan parliament and the offices of political parties and trade unions, property from the homes and offices of political and intellectual figures, books and documents from the community center and temple of the Jewish community of Barcelona, and, according to the records, "seven sacks of Protestant bibles" categorized as "Masonic documents."[35] Until 2006, the bulk of this material seized from so many locations was housed in an institution known as the Salamanca Civil War Archive (Archivo Histórico Nacional Sección Guerra Civil), the same facility used by the "political brigade" of the state police when its function was strictly repressive. It is the documentary equivalent of a mass grave.

The Salamanca archive contains material from all over Spain, and this raises the moral issue of ownership rights over cultural and institutional property seized by force, which brings us back to an earlier section of this essay. It was in Salamanca that Miguel de Unamuno (hardly a man of the left) made his historic appeal for reason over hate in 1936. Salamanca was then the capital of Francoist Spain, and as such it also became the headquarters of the political police and its files. None of this was the fault or responsibility of the citizens of Salamanca. Possession, however, sometimes gives rise to a sense of entitlement, and this was certainly true of the authorities in Salamanca, and not just during the Franco era. On March 30, 1995, when the Spanish government, under the leadership of the Socialist party (Partido Socialista Obrero Español, or PSOE), had decided in principle to turn over the papers, the municipal authorities of Salamanca, also socialists, organized the city's largest demonstration in living memory to oppose it. From the balcony of the Salamanca city hall, the novelist Gonzalo Torrente Ballester shouted to the crowds below, "[The archive] is yours by right of conquest!" Ten days later, a motion presented in the Spanish senate defending the "unity" of the archive based on laws dictated by Franco during the Civil War brought the incipient process of return to a halt. This right of conquest was invoked again ten years later, in the spring of 2005, by a Salamanca city government of the far right, as another socialist Spanish government prepared to revisit the question of restitution.

The demand that these Catalan documents and other items be returned is not new; what is new is the language in which this demand is now framed. Josep Benet, a Catalan historian and senator in the first democratically elected Spanish parliament after the dictatorship, made the initial demand for protection of the Salamanca Papers in 1978—almost thirty years before the first phase of the return. His fear was that they would be burned or otherwise destroyed in order to protect those who had seized them. This appeal was followed up by a formal request by the Catalan minister of culture in 1980, which was also rejected. In 1989 the Catalan parliament passed a motion demanding the return of all Catalan cultural property. The case is stated clearly: "The point of our motion is this: to recover for the people of Catalonia archival material that belongs to them, by virtue of its institutional and private heirs, material that is essential for the understanding and the analysis of the history of our country."[36]

All most proper and professional, if not exactly a stirring call to action.

The spokesman for the government responded in the Congress of Deputies (Congreso de los Diputados, the lower house of Spain's legislature), "Gentlemen, I believe that, since in Salamanca we have managed to house one of the best archives in the world relating to the Civil War . . . it would be a mistake to destroy its unity in order to satisfy the perhaps legitimate wish to hand them over to the Catalan government."[37] This is neither the first nor the last time the concept of "integrity" was invoked in a discussion of property seized at gunpoint, and what is fascinating about this exchange (and others that followed) is the implicit sense that these "archives" are better housed and curated by some outside body, rather than by their rightful owners. At this juncture the PSOE enjoyed an overwhelming majority in parliament. If the Spanish left was unwilling to negotiate a return, what hope remained?

There were other demands and other rejections (by governments of the left and the right). In 2002 the Dignity Commission (Comissió de la Dignitat) was formed. Its goal was simple: the return of all looted material. The discourse was no longer framed in terms of "science" or "scholarship," but something much more visceral and attuned to the power of popular opinion and global exposure. These materials were described as "blood papers," "papers of remembrance," "looted papers," "papers of memory," "papers that cry out for justice." This discourse was accompanied by a very different strategy—mass mobilization at home and support from abroad—and claims based both on morality and on such treaties as the Hague Convention for the Protection of Cultural Property in the Event of Armed Conflict (1954). The very name of the commission was based on the term "dignity," and taken from a phrase that had recently been used by the Portuguese writer and Nobel laureate José Saramago, who had "defined a 'nation' as 'a community of people who have not yet lost their capacity for indignation,'" thus framing the issue in terms of Catalan national identity and its political expression.[38] The Dignity Commission rapidly became a household word in Catalonia, and it began to collect a roster of highly visible international supporters that would eventually include Noam Chomsky, Rigoberta Menchú, Danielle Mitterand, and the Argentinian human rights association Madres de la Plaza de Mayo. At the University of Massachusetts Amherst, where both authors of this chapter have taught, the Department of Anthropology held a small but inspiring demonstration in front of the Student Union building. A photo of this event was published in the two leading Barcelona periodicals. Coverage in the media of national and international support was extensive.

It worked . . . in part, and not without protest. On June 11, 2005, the Salamanca city government, with the support of the right-wing Partido Popular, organized a demonstration against the return of the papers and in favor of maintaining "our history, our dignity," and "the unity of the General Archive of the Civil War." The demonstration featured general insults directed at Catalonia, condemnation of the Spanish prime minister, José Luis Rodríguez Zapatero, as a "traitor" for permitting the return, and explicit death threats against Josep-Lluís Carod-Rovira, the president of Esquerra Republicana, a Catalan party that had pressed consistently for the return of the papers.

Repatriation required the passage of a special law explicitly mandating the return of not only the Generalitat's papers, but also those belonging to public and private entities and private persons all over the Spanish state. After several attempts to block its approval, this law was finally passed on September 15, 2005, by the Congress of Deputies in Madrid and later ratified by the legislature's upper house, the Senate (Senado). A spokesman for the Salamanca city government issued a statement in which he said that the new law "placed the cultural patrimony of Castilla-León and of all Spaniards in the hands of those who feel more affinity with ETA terrorists than with their fellow Spaniards."[39] The municipal government of Salamanca and the autonomous government of Castilla-León immediately announced that they would explore the possibility of blocking application of the law by appealing it on the grounds that it was unconstitutional, and the Constitutional Court agreed to take up the case. This tactic, however, was not expected to delay the return of the papers, which was anticipated by the end of 2005 or the beginning of 2006.

Unexpectedly, an eleventh-hour decision by another of Spain's high courts, the Audiencia Nacional, to suspend the return prevented the papers from leaving Salamanca as planned on January 19, 2006. The Audiencia Nacional is another fascist institution that underwent a change of name in the course of the transition to democracy. It is the lineal descendant of the Tribunal de Orden Público (Tribunal of Public Order), the fascist judicial body created in 1963 to assume the functions of the Tribunal Especial para la Represión de la Masonería y el Comunismo (Special Tribunal for the Repression of Freemasonry and Communism) formed in 1940; that is, the prosecution of anything deemed a political crime.[40] In the Basque country in recent years, it has closed down newspapers, outlawed political parties, and ordered the arrest of journalists and Basque political leaders favoring Basque political sovereignty. In Catalonia, in 2004, it chose to prosecute as a terrorist a fourteen-year-old boy who sent an e-mail message to a Spanish company asking them to label their products in Catalan and, inspired by the Harry Potter books, signed it in the name of the "Army of the Phoenix."[41]

The Audiencia took its time, but finally, on the symbolic date of January 26, 2006, the sixty-seventh anniversary of the entry of the victorious fascist troops into Barcelona, it reached a unanimous decision to let the return of the papers proceed. On January 31, the long-awaited papers arrived in Sant Cugat, the comfortable upper-middle-class suburb of Barcelona where the National Archives of Catalonia are located. Their return was, as the February 1 editorial in the Catalan newspaper *AVUI* noted, carried out with "excessive discretion." The file boxes (which were first transferred from Salamanca to Madrid to make the point that the Spanish ministry of culture, and not the Generalitat, was in charge of the operation) were quietly loaded into unmarked white vans by night and driven under cover of darkness to Sant Cugat, where they arrived in the winter predawn on a weekday morning. The Catalan minister of culture was notified of their arrival only a few hours beforehand. As the Catalan journalist Ignasi Aragay noted angrily in an *AVUI* article on February 1, when the Spanish state legislates in Catalonia's favor it resorts to stealth, as if ashamed to be seen doing so. The Spanish ministry of culture, he pointed out, bent over backwards to avoid giving offense to the far right, but wasted no tact on the Generalitat and all the organizations and private persons whose property was looted, people who deserved to receive the papers in public, in broad daylight, with reporters waiting to take down their words. In this he perceived a pattern. He was not alone, and he spoke for many when he wrote, "Nothing can take away the bittersweet aftertaste of this ending. It is as if we were supposed to apologize for celebrating the fact that justice has, at last, been done." This was not, however, the end of the story. Of the 507 numbered file boxes scheduled for return in this first phase, seven were inexplicably missing, and it required two more years, legal threats by the Dignity Commission, and pressure from both the Catalan government and civil society to repatriate them.

In the summer of 2011 the return entered a second phase. Like the first, it was a tortuous process marked by broken promises, delays, legal maneuvering, and protests on both sides. On July 20 of that year, 365 file boxes of documents belonging to organizations—primarily political parties and trade unions—and to private persons were delivered to the National Archive of Catalonia. The organizations and groups affected include the Jewish community of Barcelona and the Barcelona Masonic Lodge, mythic enemies of the Franco regime, and political parties and trade unions across the ideological spectrum—republicans, federalists, Christian democrats, socialists, communists, anarchists, anarchosyndicalists—but also the Barcelona Society of Jesus (Jesuits), the Gran Teatre del Liceu (the Barcelona opera house), the Catalan Association of Handicapped Persons, the Barcelona Music-Hall Association, the Catalan Federation of Amateur Theater Groups, and the Vegetarian Society of Catalonia.[42]

The list makes clear the breadth of the fascist assault on the entire fabric of Catalan society. Documents belonging to governments, political parties, and trade unions are as much "cultural property" as the contents of intellectuals' libraries and artists' studios. Catalan society of the late nineteenth and early twentieth centuries is distinctive for the variety and density of voluntary associations to which it gave rise, including but by no means limited to political parties and labor unions. The fascists correctly recognized this as an obstacle to totalitarian rule, and in fact associations of this type later constituted the ground from which clandestine (and later open) opposition to the dictatorship emerged. Politics and culture converged in multiple ways. Amateur theater groups and choral societies mobilized the Catalan working and middle classes in the defense of their class interests even as they served as mechanisms for cultural production and reproduction. The music-hall world of the Avinguda del Paral·lel, one of early twentieth-century bohemian Barcelona's most famous streets, was where the Catalan working class went for entertainment and the Catalan middle classes went slumming, and its appeal to the appetites of the flesh (and its ability to create female stars) flew in the face of fascist national-Catholic sexual morality and conceptions of gender. Even the Barcelona opera house, that temple of high culture and bastion of conservative social values, was targeted because it represented a particularly dense Catalan social network of eminent families connected in multiple ways to social, economic, and political power.[43] The archives of all these groups form part of the national narrative; they are the stuff of which personal, family, and collective memory is made. There is much we do not know and will never be able to reconstruct about Catalan society under the Second Republic (and this is true for the rest of Spain as well) because even if all the surviving stolen documents were returned, they represent only a tiny fraction of what was seized. Most of it was destroyed.

Some six hundred boxes, roughly a quarter of the total, still remained in Salamanca, and a third phase of repatriation was scheduled for the end of 2011. In the general elections held in November 2011, however, the right-wing Partido Popular—which has always opposed the return of the papers—won an absolute majority in the Cortes Generales, the Spanish legislature. A month later, in one of the final moves of the demoralized outgoing socialist government in Madrid, the minister of culture, acting on orders from the prime minister, halted the process and announced that in the circumstances it would be "inappropriate" to proceed with the return, and that she would be leaving it in the hands of the incoming government. This announcement came not twelve hours after the Catalan minister of culture had received official confirmation that the documents would arrive in Catalonia before December 31. As both the Catalan government and the Dignity Commission pointed out, this was not a simple matter of the Spanish minister of culture breaking her word; it was the government breaking its own 2005 law, which mandated specific time frames for the return of the papers. The Dignity Commission threatened to bring the matter to the attention of the United Nations Commission on Human Rights, the International Council on Archives, and the Council of Europe. Finally, in April 2012, a meeting was scheduled with the new Spanish minister of culture, and an agreement was reached to return the papers before June 30, 2012. The municipal government of Salamanca immediately issued a statement questioning the legality of returning any papers at all, and demanding that no further documents be returned pending a review of the 2005 law by the Constitutional Court. As of this writing (December 2012), there has been no more movement.

Unfinished Business

In late February 2012 a ceremony was held at the National Archive of Catalonia. The guests of honor were representatives of political parties, unions, other organizations (the Catalan Federation of Amateur Theater Groups among them), and the few surviving individual owners of the looted documents returned in July 2011. Teresa Rovira, 93, the daughter of the journalist and political philosopher Antoni Rovira i Virgili, was able to recover a portion of the forty-seven sacks of books looted from her father's library, including the first books she learned to read as a small child. Mercè Romeva, 92, the daughter of Pau Romeva i Ferrer, an educator, translator, and Christian democratic leader, was able to hold in her hands again her father's translation of a book by G. K. Chesterton. Jaume Bosch, a member of the Catalan Parliament, was the person delegated to receive the papers belonging to the Partit Socialista Unificat de Catalunya (PSUC), the ancestor of the left-wing green party he represents. In a brief essay published in the newspaper *ARA* on February 21, 2012, he wrote about mixed and powerful emotions, the weight of history, and how frustratingly little progress has been made toward real democracy:

> If we explained to someone in France, Germany, or Italy that only now, thirty-five years after democracy was reestablished, have the papers seized by the Francoists been returned, they wouldn't believe it. And it is hard to believe that it has required the constant effort of the Dignity Commission to get them back. And that a quarter of the documents belonging to Catalonia . . . are still in Salamanca. Perhaps if we told them that there are people who believe they are entitled to keep them "by right of conquest," they would find it easier to understand what is happening today in the Spanish state.

This story is unfinished, an open-ended process in which issues of cultural property, memory, identity, and political legitimacy are intertwined. The willed obliteration of historical memory is one of the strategies through which the state is rendered not only normal but normative, Spanish nationalism is rendered unproblematic and unmarked, and Catalan nationalism is not only marked as problematic but demonized as a threat to Spanish "national" unity, and sometimes even as a form of terrorism. If many Catalans are today unable to see themselves as also

Spanish, it is in part because of the refusal of the Spanish state, whether governed by the right or by the left, to face the past squarely and openly and return the war booty of seventy years ago. Failure to do so continues to define some people, and some peoples, as citizens of a lesser category.

As the Spanish Civil War historian Paul Preston has pointed out on many occasions, and as the ceremony described above shows, the seizure of these materials is one of the few crimes perpetrated by the Franco regime that can still be put right because there are still living victims to whom the documents can be returned. There is some urgency about this, however, as the youngest of those directly affected are now in their seventies. There have been too many cases like that of the artist Carles Fontserè, who created some of the Republic's most memorable war posters. His entire studio was looted and removed to Salamanca. He died in 2007, at the age of 91, without having recovered so much as a single sketch. A member of the extended Pi-Sunyer family, Rosa Maria Carrasco, the youngest child of Manel Carrasco i Formiguera, a Christian democrat and Catalan nationalist captured by the fascists early in the war and shot in 1938, has long tried, without success, to recover from Salamanca the letter her father wrote to her mother on the eve of his execution. At that time she was just months old, and at this writing she is in her mid-seventies. She cannot wait much longer.

Paradoxically, the erasure of the past makes its presence all the more vivid and tangible, and intensifies the work of memory. Our conclusions are mixed. As this account shows, civil society can be more powerful than governments in the struggle against *desmemoria*, and that is a cause for optimism. But we also argue that *desmemoria*, in the name of peace and unity, creates conflict and division, and in so doing it continues the dirty work of the Franco regime into the present. The refusal to return the Salamanca papers—like the obstacles placed in the way of people trying to recover the remains of family members murdered by the fascists, or the Spanish courts' repeated rejection of appeals for the annulment of convictions imposed by fascist military courts, starting with the "conviction" of the Catalan president, Lluís Companys, shot in 1940 after a simulacrum of a court-martial—is the perpetuation of civil war by other means, decades past the fascist victory in 1939 and the transition from dictatorship to democracy. This requires us to question the conventional view of the Spanish transition to democracy as an unmitigated success and a model for other countries emerging from totalitarian rule. Truth and reconciliation (as we know from the case of South Africa) are not by themselves sufficient, but they are a necessary first step to healing the wounds of the past. The Spanish Civil War is, on some level, still going on.

NOTES

1. Louis MacNeice, *Collected Poems*, ed. E. R. Dodds (New York: Oxford University Press, 1967), 112; Chris Ealham and Michael Richards, eds., *The Splintering of Spain: Cultural History and the Spanish Civil War* (Cambridge: Cambridge University Press, 2005), 11.

2. Mary Vincent, "'The Keys of the Kingdom': Religious Violence in the Spanish Civil War, July–August 1936," in Ealham and Richards, *The Splintering of Spain*, 68–69.

3. Paul Preston, *L'Holocaust espanyol: Odi i extermini durant la Guerra Civil i després* (Barcelona: Editorial Base, 2011), 233; Antony Beevor, *The Battle for Spain* (New York: Penguin, 2006), 88; Alan Kramer, *Culture and Mass Killing in the First World War* (Oxford: Oxford University Press, 2007). After this chapter was completed, the English-language edition of Preston's book was published as *The Spanish Holocaust: Inquisition and Extermination in Twentieth-Century Spain* (New York: Norton, 2012).

4. The quotation is from Hugh Gusterson, "Anthropology and Militarism," *Annual Review of Anthropology* 36 (2007): 161.

5. There is a growing literature on this subject. We were guided by the following studies: Begoña Aretxaga, *Shattering Silence: Women, Nationalism, and Political Subjectivity in Northern Ireland* (Princeton: Princeton University Press, 1997); Victoria Sanford, *Buried Secrets: Truth and Human Rights in Guatemala* (New York: Palgrave Macmillan, 2004); Liisa Malkki, *Purity and Exile: Violence, Memory, and the National Cosmology among Hutu Refugees in Tanzania* (Chicago: University of Chicago Press, 1995); Linda Green, *Fear as a Way of Life: Mayan Widows in Rural Guatemala* (New York: Columbia University Press, 1999); Monique Skidmore, "Darker Than Midnight: Fear, Vulnerability, and Terror Making in Urban Burma (Myanmar)," *American Ethnologist* 30.2 (2003): 5–21; and Michael Taussig, *Walter Benjamin's Grave* (Chicago: University of Chicago Press, 2006).

6. Clyde Kluckhohn, *Mirror for Man: The Relation of Anthropology to Modern Life* (1944; Greenwich, CT: Premier Books, 1965), 226.

7. Renato Rosaldo, "Subjectivity in Social Analysis," in *Culture and Truth: The Making of Social Analysis* (Boston: Beacon, 1989), 168–95, quotation on 168; Rosaldo, "Introduction: Grief and a Headhunter's Rage," in *Culture and Truth*, 1–21, quotations on 7, 19, 11. See also Ruth Behar, "Anthropology That Breaks Your Heart," in *The Vulnerable Observer: Anthropology That Breaks Your Heart* (Boston: Beacon, 1996), 161–77; and Akhil Gupta and James Ferguson, "Discipline and Practice: 'The Field'

as Site, Method, and Location in Anthropology," in *Anthropological Locations: Boundaries and Grounds of a Field Science*, ed. Gupta and Ferguson (Chicago: University of Chicago Press, 1997), 1–46.

8. Davydd J. Greenwood et al., *Industrial Democracy as Process: Participatory Action Research in the Fagor Cooperative Group of Mondragón* (Assen-Maastricht, Netherlands: Van Gorcum, 1992); Davydd J. Greenwood and Morton Levin, *Introduction to Action Research: Social Research for Social Change* (Thousand Oaks, CA: Sage, 1998); Susan Greenhalgh, *Under the Medical Gaze: Facts and Fictions of Chronic Pain* (Berkeley: University of California Press, 2001); Joseba Zulaika, *Basque Violence: Metaphor and Sacrament* (Reno: University of Nevada Press, 1988).

9. Oriol Pi-Sunyer, "Els exilis de 1939: Passar fronteres, reconstruir vides," in *Les ruptures de l'any 1939*, ed. Manel Risques, Francesc Vilanova, and Ricard Vinyes (Barcelona: Fundació Carles Pi i Sunyer and Publicacions de l'Abadia de Montserrat, 2000), 9–33; Oriol Pi-Sunyer, "Pròleg," in *Carles Pi i Sunyer: Londres en guerra, 1939–1942*, ed. Francesc Vilanova (Barcelona: Fundació Carles Pi i Sunyer, 2006), 9–33; Núria Pi-Sunyer, *L'exili manllevat* (Barcelona: Proa, 2006).

10. See Susan M. DiGiacomo, "The Politics of Identity: Nationalism in Catalonia" (PhD diss., University of Massachusetts Amherst, 1985); DiGiacomo, "Images of Class and Ethnicity in Catalan Politics, 1977–1980," in *Conflict in Catalonia: Images of an Urban Society*, ed. Gary W. McDonogh (Gainesville: University of Florida Press, 1986), 72–92; DiGiacomo, "Autobiografia crítica i teoria antropològica: Reflexions a l'entorn de la identitat cultural i professional," *Revista d'etnologia de Catalunya* 25 (2004): 124–34; Josep Cruanyes i Tor, *Els papers de Salamanca: L'espoliació del patrimoni documental de Catalunya* (1938–1939) (Barcelona: Edicions 62, 2003); and Josep Bargalló, "Prologue," in *The Archives Franco Stole from Catalonia: The Campaign for Their Return*, by the Dignity Commission (Lleida: Editorial Milenio, 2004).

11. James Clifford, "Spatial Practices: Fieldwork, Travel, and the Disciplining of Anthropology," in Gupta and Ferguson, *Anthropological Locations*, 185–223, quotation on 199; Liisa Malkki, "News and Culture: Transitory Phenomena and the Fieldwork Tradition," in Gupta and Ferguson, *Anthropological Locations*, 86–101; Susan DiGiacomo, "Noticias, cultura y etnografía: el 11-M desde una perspectiva antropológica," *Revista de Antropología Iberoamericana* 3 (2004): 38–42; Gupta and Ferguson, *Anthropological Locations*, 37.

12. For studies of traumatic historical memory and its repression in Spain and elsewhere, see Paloma Aguilar, *Memoria y olvido de la Guerra Civil española* (Madrid: Alianza, 1996); Alexandra Barahona De Brito and Paloma Aguilar, eds., *Las políticas hacia el pasado: juicios, depuraciones, perdón y olvidio en las nuevas democracias* (Madrid: Istmo, 2002); and María Inés Mudrovcic, *Historia, narración y memoria* (Madrid: Akal, 2005).

13. For comparative views of memory work in different European contexts during the twentieth century, see Francisco Ferrándiz, "The Return of Civil War Ghosts," *Anthropology Today* 22.3 (2006): 7–12; Ferrándiz, "Cries and Whispers: Exhuming and Narrating Defeat in Spain," *Journal of Spanish Cultural Studies* 9.2 (2008):

177–92; Mike Elkin, "Opening Franco's Graves," *Archaeology,* September–October 2006, 38–43; Brian Conway, "Moving through Time and Space: Performing Bodies in Derry, Northern Ireland," *Journal of Historical Sociology* 20.1–2 (2007): 102–25; and Jay Winter, *Sites of Memory, Sites of Mourning: The Great War in European Cultural History* (New York: Cambridge University Press, 1995).

14. Giles Tremlett, *Ghosts of Spain: Travels through a Country's Hidden Past* (New York: Walker, 2006), 82. See also Montserrat Roig, *Els catalans als camps nazis* (1977; Barcelona: Edicions 62, 2001).

15. In 1950, about half of the population made their living from the land, and farm workers and peasants were twice as numerous as industrial workers. As recently as 1962 there were but 14 private motor cars per 1,000 inhabitants, a statistic indicative of relative underdevelopment.

16. This is a simplification of a highly complex environment. For the social and political background to the Spanish Civil War, see Gerald Brenan, *The Spanish Labyrinth: An Account of the Social and Political Background of the Spanish Civil War* (1943; repr., Cambridge: Cambridge University Press, 1962); and Edward E. Malefakis, *Agrarian Reform and Peasant Revolution in Spain* (New Haven: Yale University Press, 1970).

17. Salvador de Madariaga, *Spain* (New York: Creative Age Press, 1943), 282.

18. The Generation of '98 can best be described as rooted cosmopolitans: enormously concerned with the Spanish condition, they were very much at home in European culture, particularly that of France.

19. The Spanish Republic shared several characteristics with the Weimar Republic, another ill-fated experiment in liberal democracy. See Eric D. Weitz, *Weimar Germany: Promise and Tragedy* (Princeton: Princeton University Press, 2007).

20. On this period see Sebastian Balfour, *The End of the Spanish Empire, 1898–1923* (Oxford: Clarendon Press, 1997).

21. Raymond Carr, *Spain: A History* (Oxford: Oxford University Press, 2000), 285.

22. Stefan Zweig, *The World of Yesterday* (1943; Lincoln: University of Nebraska Press, 1964), 3.

23. The challenge to the democratic order came primarily from the traditional right and its historic identification of state and nation with church and monarchy. It is also true that free-thinking liberalism was no protection against factionalism.

24. Thomas F. Glick, "Ciencia, política y discurso civil en la España de Alfonso XIII," in *Nación y estado en la España liberal,* ed. Guillermo Gortázar (Madrid: Noesis, 1994), 225–26.

25. Milan Kundera, *Testaments Betrayed: An Essay in Nine Parts,* trans. Linda Asher (New York: Harper Collins, 1995), 192.

26. J. M. Cohen, ed., *The Penguin Book of Spanish Verse,* rev. ed. (Harmondsworth: Penguin, 1960), xxxvii.

27. We term it *the* defining moment because Unamuno was one of the great philosophers and men of letters of his time, a living symbol of the intelligence he was defending. In Spanish—he was a remarkable wordsmith—the last phrase is *Venceréis, pero no convenceréis.*

28. Quoted in Maria Campillo, *Carles Pi i Sunyer, Conseller de Cultura en temps de guerra* (Barcelona: Fundació Carles Pi i Sunyer, 2007), 46. Unless otherwise noted, all translations from Spanish and Catalan in this essay are by the authors.

29. See, for example, Valentine Cunningham, ed., *Spanish Front: Writers on the Civil War* (Oxford: Oxford University Press, 1986); and John Miller, ed., *Voices against Tyranny: Writings of the Spanish Civil War* (New York: Scribner's, 1986).

30. Beevor, *The Battle for Spain*, 404.

31. Antonio Barr, "A Culture in Transition," in *Culture and Society in Contemporary Europe*, ed. Stanley Hoffman and Paschalis Kitromilides (London: Allen & Unwin, 1981), 164; Javier Cercas, *Soldados de Salamina* (Barcelona: Tusquets, 2001); Colm Tóibín, "Return to Catalonia," *New York Review of Books*, October 7, 2004, 36–37. Cercas's novel was published in English as *Soldiers of Salamis*, trans. Anne McLean (London: Bloomsbury, 2003).

32. See the ARMH website at www.memoriahistorica.org/. The portal of this site reflects the anger and sense of abandonment experienced by descendants of the victims of terror. Next to a photograph of several of the political leaders on both the left and the right who shaped the transition to democracy, all smiling with what now looks like unjustified complacency, is a painful question: "Why did the fathers of the Constitution leave my grandfather lying in a ditch?" (Por qué los padres de la constitución dejaron a mi abuelo en una cuneta?)

33. For example, a key organizer of the Salamanca Papers campaign is Antoni Strubell, whom we might describe as an Anglo-Catalan. His maternal grandparents were exiled in England and his father was English.

34. Ferrándiz, "The Return of Civil War Ghosts," 7–12, quotations on 7.

35. Cruanyes i Tor, *Els papers de Salamanca*, quotations on 233–34; Dignity Commission, *The Archives Franco Stole from Catalonia*.

36. Dignity Commission, *The Archives Franco Stole from Catalonia*, 34.

37. Ibid., 35.

38. Ibid., 48.

39. Quoted in the newspaper *AVUI*, September 16, 2005, 38. ETA (Euskadi Ta Askatasuna, or Basque Homeland and Freedom), founded in 1959, is an organization that until very recently espoused armed struggle as the pathway to Basque independence. It killed its first victim in 1968 and was ultimately responsible for the deaths of 829 people. After the transition to democracy, the victims were increasingly people who were not political targets, which eventually caused ETA to lose an important part of its social support in the Basque country. Under pressure for several years by the Basque nationalist left, it abandoned violence and embraced peaceful and democratic means of political change in October 2011. In the statement quoted in the text, Catalonia's legitimate demand for the return of stolen cultural property is being demonized as not only equivalent to terrorism but also as anti-Spanish in the same way that ETA is treated as radically Other by the Spanish right.

40. See Cruanyes i Tor, *Els papers de Salamanca*, 293–96.

41. For a complete first-person account of this bizarre episode see Èric Bertran, *Èric i l'Exèrcit del Fènix: Acusat de voler viure en català* (Barcelona: Proa, 2006).
42. A complete list of the documents returned as of December 2011 and their owners can be downloaded from the website of the Generalitat's Department of Culture, www20.gencat.cat/portal/site/CulturaDepartament/.
43. One of the best introductions to the elite of Barcelona and the privileges they enjoyed is Gary Wray McDonogh, *Good Families of Barcelona: A Social History of Power in the Industrial Era* (Princeton: Princeton University Press, 1986).

II

SHARED STEWARDSHIP

———⊗⊗⊗———

4
LANGUAGE OWNERSHIP
AND LANGUAGE IDEOLOGIES

———⚬✕✕⚬———

Margaret Speas

IN 2005, FOUR representatives of the Mapuche people of Chile wrote to
Microsoft chairman Bill Gates to express "profound concerns regarding the scope of the agreement between Microsoft and the government of
Chile which aims at creating a Windows operating system in our ancestral language, the Mapudungun." They asserted that "only the Mapuche
People must and can safeguard, maintain, manage, develop and recreate
its cultural heritage."[1] The following year the Mapuche launched a lawsuit to block the Microsoft Mapudungun project, charging intellectual
piracy. This reaction came as a shock to those who believed they were
building a tool that would help the Mapuche people to maintain their
language in the modern world.

Linguists who study indigenous languages of the Americas are aware
that "the loss of Native American languages is directly connected to laws,
policies and practices of European Americans," and many are eager to do
what they can to counter the legacy of these practices.[2] Most linguists agree
that it is important to respect indigenous perspectives and enthusiastically
support measures such as the American Declaration on the Rights of
Indigenous People drafted by the Organization of American States in 1997,
which affirms that states must recognize and respect indigenous languages.
Since most linguists are not themselves speakers of indigenous languages,
however, questions often arise about how (or whether) "outsider" linguists

can contribute to language maintenance or revitalization efforts in a way that respects the ownership rights of the language community.

The fact that language is not a tangible object that can be located or relocated makes issues of cultural ownership more subtle but also more urgent than for concrete pieces of art or other cultural objects. More subtle because a language can in principle be spoken by many people in different places, so it would seem that using a language in, say, Redmond, Washington, would not impinge on rights of speakers in Chile. More urgent, however, because a dominant culture can affect a language even across large distances, and a community that has lost its language cannot simply petition to get it back.

In this chapter I discuss issues of ownership and community empowerment that arise when academic linguists work with communities whose languages are in danger of dying out. I begin by talking about the importance of these issues to language revitalization efforts and the power imbalances that can arise when linguists try to lend their expertise. Then I describe my own experience as coauthor of a textbook of Navajo, which taught me lessons about the limits of my expertise. Finally, I touch on the topic of language attitudes and ideologies, suggesting that the relevant divide is not so much between Western and non-Western ideologies as between the recent discoveries of linguistics and the language experience of nonlinguists.

Language Ownership and Community Empowerment

Issues of language ownership and community empowerment are important to an increasing number of linguists who are concerned about the erosion and disappearance many of the world's languages.[3] In 1992 one linguist, Michael Krauss, estimated that if current conditions continued, over half of the world's languages could be extinct by 2092. Believing that "the world stands to lose an important part of the sum of human knowledge whenever a language stops being used," the community of academic linguists has established several organizations devoted to endangered languages, including a major funding initiative through the National Science Foundation. UNESCO conferences in 2003 and 2009 have affirmed that "there is an imperative need for language documentation, new policy initiatives, and new materials to enhance the vitality of these languages." The 2003 UNESCO working group adds, "There is a pressing need to build support for language communities in their efforts to establish meaningful new roles for their endangered languages." Some linguists argue that documentation of endangered languages should take priority over all other research. Others continue theoretical research but are eager to give back to the communities in which they do their work by creating materials that will be useful for documentation or pedagogy. The linguistic anthropologist Jane Hill, however, has eloquently argued that a great deal of the recent academic literature on endangered languages is at odds with community views on language ownership.[4]

Most linguists who work on indigenous languages of the Americas (and other endangered languages worldwide) would now agree that when working in a speech community, "priority must be given to a community-based approach and to long-term capacity building and support at the most local level."[5] The public archive for Australian aboriginal material explains that "many speakers of endangered languages consider that their language is their intellectual property, passed down to them from their ancestors," adding, "If it is made freely available to others, then their rights in that language can be diminished. Usually they do not want strangers to use words and sentences of their languages in an inappropriate way, and want to be consulted prior to public use." This view of language would seem to contrast with the view expressed by the linguist Geoff Pullum: "A language is not something that could be or should be controlled by a people or its political leadership, and making software available in a certain writing system or language is not a threat to, or a theft of, cultural patrimony."[6]

At the heart of this contrast is the difference between the way linguists view language in general and the way a speaker views his or her own language. Keren Rice aptly summarizes this difference when she characterizes the linguist's view of languages as "objects of beauty and awe," and then quotes a statement by the Assembly of First Nations: "Our languages are the cornerstone of who we are as people. Without our languages, our cultures cannot survive."[7] As Jane Simpson points out in a blog post, "Bound up with language as property are the ideas of *respect for ownership,* and *denial of access to the language.* Respect seems to matter to speakers of many small languages, regardless of how strong the language is. It's their language; they have the right to say how it's spelled, what the words of the language are, when and where it's used in public."[8] For "outsider" linguists committed to academic freedom, respect for ownership rights can come into conflict with strongly held views about the importance of free access to intellectual property. But the concept of ownership with respect to language has more to do with ethical responsibility and personal relationships than with legal property rights. Many linguists agree with Pullum that making language materials widely available is "not a threat to, or a theft of, cultural patrimony," but nonetheless refrain from doing so out of respect for the beliefs of the communities they work with. Moreover, when linguists are working on a language that they do not speak, they are dependent on speakers of the language for the knowledge on which their research depends. When a group like the Mapuche say that only they can safeguard, maintain, and develop their language, they mean that any uses of the language outside of the community of speakers are based at best on partial knowledge, and so they have the right, and even the responsibility, to be consulted by anyone who plans to produce a product and call it Mapudungun.

Academic linguists often go into the field assuming that a well-meaning eagerness to respect the views of everyone will be enough to direct them toward work that will be useful to the people whose language they study. Most linguists these days are eager to avoid exploitative relationships with the people they work with, and to reject research models in which "people are treated as 'data generators,' and little attention is paid to their needs or desires."[9] They are aware that many cases of language endangerment are the direct result of policies and attitudes of the dominant culture toward indigenous languages, and do not want to repeat the atrocities of the past. Programs have been developed to address "the issues of power inequalities that arise when members external to the language community engage in linguistic projects," and a number of linguists have exhorted their colleagues to move beyond linguist-centered models of research and toward "initiative(s) from within the community, relying on internal resources, and with minimal input from outside advisers"—in other words, "schemes [that] can be self-sustaining given sufficient motivation."[10] There are some success stories involving partnerships between linguists and language activists within speech communities, as well as cases where efforts that are entirely community-based have been encouraged or aided by linguists.[11] Currently, however, there are more accounts of pitfalls and problems, and warnings that power imbalances and mis-matched goals can engender "anger, resentment, volatile feelings of being ripped off because the researcher, like the Colonialists, has taken what they wanted but not lived up to the community's expectations of continu-ity and reciprocity."[12] This gap between linguists' ideals and current reality is attributed by linguists to factors such as differences in language ide-ologies that are "grounded in the social distribution of both indigenous social inequality and the differential impact of colonial and postcolonial contact experiences," the need for "a deliberate, focused effort to rethink paradigms for research and Western methodologies," and the fact that "the ambiguity and manipulation in Navajo-Anglo relations promote misunderstanding and mistrust, of motive and message."[13]

Ultimately, it is clear that "in order to be successful, a revitalization program must be driven by the community of people who do or will use the language."[14] This means that there are obvious limits on the role to be played by outsider linguists, which in turn means that it is not unusual for there to be at least some community members who feel that linguists could help most by leaving them alone. More often, community members are glad to have people who are eager to help, but the kind of help that linguists offer is not what the community feels they need most. This, of course, is the history of contact between "helpful" Euro-Americans and Native Americans in a nutshell. Outsiders decide what Native communi-ties need—boarding schools, haircuts, a "civilized" language, a "civilized" religion—and proceed to empower them to get these things, hearing nothing of what the people say they actually need.

In the case of language revitalization, however, there is a fundamental power imbalance that is rarely mentioned in the literature on empower-ment models of research: outsider linguists simply do not have the power to create a new generation of speakers. No matter how much linguists set aside research on "arcane matters" that have "minimal application" in favor of community-oriented work, and no matter how successful linguists are at rethinking paradigms and overcoming their neocolonialist tendencies, the success of any language revitalization program crucially depends on the extent to which a community's families insist that their children hear and acquire the language.[15] This power imbalance means that linguists who are eager to help will almost always risk providing something that does not meet the community's core needs. I do not mean to say that language endangerment is the "fault" of communities. And there are plenty of situations where a community decides on goals other than total fluency of the next generation, and finds skills in language documentation useful. Rather, I want to suggest that linguists must recognize that communities, not linguists, have the power over the central factor in language revitalization. It's not just that we must empower communities; it's that we must recognize the limits of our own power.

Recognizing this power imbalance is a key to overcoming the gap between linguists and speech communities that Keren Rice calls "two solitudes." Rice concludes that there need not be two solitudes "if there is mutual recognition that a linguist cannot on their own save a language."[16] This does not mean that linguists should ignore the needs of the people they work with or go back to the "helicopter" model of research. On the contrary, it means that it is not up to us to decide among ourselves what kind of help a community needs, nor is it up to us to "rais[e] community awareness about the impact of colonial and hegemonic language ideologies on local thinking about language and communication," or to "convince the community that there is a problem of language loss, that the responsibility lies with the community."[17] It means that linguists cannot decide in advance what will be needed, or even if language revitalization is advisable. Margaret Field and Paul Kroskrity note that "American Indian language ideologies not only are historically very different from each other, but today, *even within a single community* are typically complex, heterogeneous, contradictory and even contentious." Moreover, as Lise Dobrin points out, linguists also cannot decide in advance that they should just stand back and withdraw from the community. She describes her experience in Papua New Guinea, where village leaders taught her that "the outside acknowledgment I provided was precisely what was needed for a community-wide language project they were engaged in to succeed."[18] Finally, linguists should not be surprised to find that their most valuable contributions are nonlinguistic.

On Being Coauthor of a Navajo Textbook

My own involvement has been with the Navajo language. It began when I was a student at the University of Arizona and had a linguistics professor who was a Navajo speaker. I went on to study for my PhD with

Kenneth Hale at the Massachusetts Institute of Technology. Ken Hale was renowned for his research on understudied languages and for his dedication to providing the speakers of these languages with the training to carry out their own research. I was inspired by Hale's exhortations to give back to the communities whose languages we study, although the extent to which I have done so is decidedly meager compared to many other linguists.[19]

Many speakers of Navajo are concerned that the survival of their language is threatened. Like many other groups, they were subjected to the destructive boarding school experience, where they were punished for speaking their heritage language. With the high rates of unemployment and poverty on the Navajo reservation, it is not surprising that the majority of families see English as the language of power, necessary for success. As of 2005, it was estimated that Navajo still had perhaps 178,000 speakers. Navajo dictionaries and grammar descriptions have been widely available since the 1970s, and bilingual programs have existed on the Navajo reservation since the 1960s.[20] In an article published in 2001, however, Paul Platero found that the number of children who speak Navajo is declining rapidly.[21] With considerable community interest in the Navajo language and even several Navajo speakers with PhDs in linguistics, it is still not clear whether the language will survive into the next century.

From 2004 to 2008 I worked with a Navajo educator to coauthor a textbook for teaching Navajo at the high school and college level.[22] In this section I would like to discuss some ways in which this experience illustrates some of the issues of power, ownership, and listening that outsider linguists need to deal with, and describe the book itself, which is quite different from the kind of textbook that a linguist would write.

The primary author for the textbook was Evangeline Parsons Yazzie, who grew up on the Navajo reservation, earned a doctorate in education, and is currently a professor at Northern Arizona University. She has been teaching Navajo for over twenty years. After she had worked with me on linguistics projects for a number of years, Parsons Yazzie asked me join her in producing an introductory Navajo textbook based on her college-level curriculum. My role was to explain—without getting bogged down in too much linguistic detail—a few important grammar concepts in a way that would be accessible to high school or college students and to help with prose editing and continuity.

Many people assume that if a Navajo and a European-American are coauthors, the Euro-American must be the "real" author, with the Navajo being some kind of assistant. We found that people would sometimes persist in this belief even after being told that Parsons Yazzie was the primary author. In part this reflects the prejudice that minority scholars routinely encounter. Even when the actual authorship was known, I was accorded what I call "gratuitous prestige," and people would assume that a book written with a professional linguist must be of a higher quality than one written solely by a Navajo. The pervasiveness of this kind of prejudice is not news to any member of a minority group, but it is worth mentioning, because for reasons I will outline the resulting book could not possibly have been written by a non-Navajo academic linguist. Parsons Yazzie wrote the book to reflect the voice of Navajo elders, or of a Navajo parent teaching a child, using personal examples, repetition of important concepts, and admonitions to students. Despite the strong commitment of our publisher to supporting Navajo authors, our copy editor often pressed us to revise the text to a more "neutral" (that is, non-Navajo) style. One of my contributions to the project was to act as a go-between in working with the editor, explaining why we were using devices such as repetition and admonition. Because the editor accorded me gratuitous prestige, she would accept explanations of the style when they came from me rather than from Parsons Yazzie, even though I know next to nothing about the speaking style of Navajo elders or parents and was simply repeating what Parsons Yazzie had already told her.

The assumptions that some people made about my role in the book also reflect the fact that when outsider linguists coauthor books or papers with speakers of endangered languages, the research agenda is virtually always set by the linguist. Even if the project is a grammar, dictionary, or other nontheoretical work, the outsider linguist is almost always the one who decides on the topics, organization, and voice for the work. Of course, there is nothing wrong with this when a community asks a linguist to produce a dictionary or grammar for them; presumably the community expects the linguist to advise them on the appropriate topics and organization. They may even expect and need the gratuitous prestige accorded the "expert."[23] But before I became involved in this textbook, it had never occurred to me how rare it is to find a collaboration in which the community member rather than the linguist really controls the intellectual agenda.

The textbook that Evangeline Parsons Yazzie and I produced together is different in many ways from the kind of book that a linguist would write. It has been extremely well received, and I believe that this is *because* it was conceived, organized, and written by a nonlinguist who knew the community thoroughly. First of all, as a linguist I believe that the most important thing about learning a language is learning to speak, but I am not at all concerned with whether the learner's accent is precisely correct. Parsons Yazzie designed her curriculum with the first two lessons (spanning a minimum of four weeks) devoted entirely to the Navajo alphabet and phonemes. This would be shocking to most linguists, who would generally explain the sound system within a few pages and then move on. For example, one linguist, Clay Slate, reports that when he first team-taught a class with Tony Goldtooth, a Navajo scholar and teacher, "I insisted that from the first, in the reading and writing courses . . . we use entirely whole-language activities, eschewing Goldtooth's tried-and-true phonics coverage. . . . Thereafter, throughout the program, some students had difficulty with [certain features of pronunciation and writing]." Slate attributes his error to being "caught up in the controversy of whole language versus phonics," and advises that linguists learn to "see beyond such false oppositions."[24] As I see it, the problem is not one of being caught up in a theory; it is a problem of failing to listen to the person who best knows the audience. As Parsons Yazzie explained to me, Navajo elders emphasize how essential they feel it is for learners to pronounce Navajo correctly, and she knew how important it was for the community that the textbook reflect and respect the attitudes of Navajo elders. Moreover, most high school and college Navajo classes combine students who have had little or no exposure to Navajo with students who have heard Navajo and may even speak it quite a bit but can't write it. Those who have no experience with the way colloquial Navajo is pronounced often have an easier time learning the writing system, because they have not heard how the sounds actually blend together in casual speech. This can be very discouraging for the Navajo speakers. Spending a substantial amount of time on the sound system at the beginning of the course gives the Navajo speakers a chance to get used to the writing system, and it gives the nonspeakers a chance to learn from the students who already can pronounce the Navajo phonemes.

Second, a linguist would be likely to organize a textbook in terms of linguistic structure rather than conceptual topics, and would include information on culture as a supplement to the language lessons rather than as a basis for them. Language teachers who are not linguists are more likely to organize material around themes like clothing, weather, food, and so forth. One important goal of our textbook was to teach Navajo culture as a living set of values rather than a list of foods, clothing, and customs or a description of traditional ceremonies and beliefs. A substantial number of Navajo parents who are Christian are very wary of allowing their children to take Navajo classes, because they worry that culture lessons will teach traditional Navajo religion. Organizing the lessons according to conceptual topics made it clear how many facets there are to Navajo culture that can be made relevant to young people today. For example, the chapter about clothing begins with the story of an elder whom Parsons Yazzie interviewed; the elder talks about the contrast between the attitudes people had toward clothing when she was young and the attitudes today. The chapters on family and kinship discuss the role that each family member plays in the upbringing of a child, and the chapter on the body includes information about Navajo views of health. Parsons Yazzie worked with Navajo elders on all chapters, and as I mentioned earlier, she tried to write the culture sections to sound like a Navajo elder or mother teaching.

Third, linguists are analytical and interested in discovering generalizations. My preference as a linguist would be to explain grammar points once and expect students to discover how the grammar patterns apply to new examples. This is not the approach that Parsons Yazzie believes to be the most effective with her students. In a joint article, Anna Ash, Jessie Little Doe Fermino, and Ken Hale report similar experiences in constructing Wampanoag language materials; Little Doe Fermino's Wampanoag students did not find it helpful to analyze verbal paradigms or syntactic structure.[25] Parsons Yazzie designed the Navajo textbook to reflect a Navajo teaching style, which includes repetition of important points and emphasizes observation rather than generalization. I have to admit that it was sometimes difficult for me to believe her when she explained that my succinct analytical explanations were not appropriate for the book's audience. It was hard for me to imagine the importance of reinforcing the material in a way her students found comfortable, rather than revealing what I thought of as the fascinating patterns of the language. I also will confess that I was anxious about what my linguistics colleagues would think about a book that does not conform to their conception of the linguistically informed language textbook. But since Parsons Yazzie knew her audience and I did not, the resulting book is one that is highly accessible to Navajo young people.

One final property of the book that a linguist would not have paid attention to is its graphic design and production values. Linguists are not noted for their refined sense of style, and we generally would assume that excellence in a book comes solely from its content. Parsons Yazzie knew that it was important that the book look elegant. We had a Navajo graphic designer, who laid out the pages so that the material looks approachable and attractive. In the end, the fact that the book looks like a "real" book on a valued language is one of the things that Navajo students appreciate the most.

Parsons Yazzie believes that the book was enhanced by my expertise and analytical tendencies, and I think I was helpful in negotiating with the editors. But the real basis of the book's success was her ability to keep me aware that I did not have the power to convey her language to young people in a meaningful way. I am not arguing that linguists should withhold their expertise or abandon their convictions about language, but if we truly want to be helpful to a community whose goal is to stabilize their language, we must keep in mind that our expertise just may not be what that community really needs. In the following section I will look at some of the ways that linguists' knowledge, while valid, can come up against the real-world situations that communities find themselves in.

Linguists, Language Analysis, and Language Learning

Linguists receive a very specialized training in the analysis of language and are generally fascinated by languages, but as I noted earlier, it is not clear that their skills are those that a community needs for revitalizing a language.[26] Linguists are interested in what all languages have in common and in what the properties of language can tell us about how the human brain works. Linguists are often very good at taking language apart and putting it back together, but just as you can be an excellent driver without knowing how your car's engine works, you can be an excellent language teacher without knowing how to do a linguistic analysis.

In fact, the knowledge and perspective that one gets on language from studying it linguistically leads to a view of language that is at odds with the view of society in general. For example, most Americans believe that casual speech is illogical and disregards rules. Linguists who have studied casual speech carefully find that in fact even the most informal speech is an instantiation of a complex system of linguistic patterns. Many Americans believe that a child who is brought up speaking two languages will have special trouble learning the dominant language, but as we will see, this is simply not true. The average undergraduate comes into Linguistics 101 holding these misconceptions about language, and linguists see it as their job to teach them the truth.

This point is important because discussions of the gap between linguists and language communities often claim that the viewpoint of academic linguists is a Western or "colonizing" ideology. This leads some to suggest that we take "a language ideological approach for those searching for a 'decolonizing methodology' for conducting linguistic research in indigenous communities."[27] In other words, researchers should help community members to see through the Western ideology promulgated by linguists. But the linguist's view of language is not the ideology of the dominant Western culture, as I am reminded each fall by the undergraduate students in Linguistics 101. Since the ideology of linguists is in some ways quite distinct from that of American society as a whole, linguists are susceptible to believing that their ideology counts as a decolonizing one, and they may be at a loss when community members explain that they plan to bring up their child speaking English so she will not have trouble in school.

Most linguists are trained as cognitive scientists and (to return to my earlier analogy) are more skilled at engine mechanics than at driving. It is not that what linguists do is misguided or useless; on the contrary, I have spent my life as a linguist because I think that linguistic analysis has led to fascinating insights about the human mind. I also believe it is important not to assume that people with an "indigenous ideology" can never be interested in theoretical linguistics. My mentor Ken Hale spent his life training speakers of indigenous languages to be linguists. He didn't think you had to be a linguist to pass on your language—he just found that there are people in every community who are interested in linguistics, and he believed that his knowledge of the subject wasn't esoteric learning that only Anglos can have. In fact, as I mentioned earlier, one of my first linguistics professors was Navajo. Most people in Western culture aren't inherently interested in linguistic analysis and do not find it natural to pull languages apart. But learning to speak a language does not depend on conscious knowledge of grammar and linguistic analysis. As the Blackfoot educator Darrell Kipp puts it, "The most sophisticated computer program cannot mimic the genius of a child speaking their tribal language." His experience with efforts to revitalize the Blackfoot language has taught him that the "basic formula" is "a room, a teacher and some children."[28]

I would like to look in a bit more detail at some of the views that linguists have found to be misconceptions about language. I think it is worthwhile to look at the grain of truth behind each of these misconceptions, in order to clarify the relationship between linguists and the communities they work with.

To begin the discussion, we can look at two Stabilizing Indigenous Languages (SIL) roundtables held in 1994 and 1995. I assume that these symposia were quite productive and successful, judging by the papers collected in the proceedings and many interesting talks at SIL conferences over the subsequent years.[29] These meetings raised issues that have been echoed in numerous other conferences, such as the UNESCO conferences on Indigenous Languages in 2003 and 2009. According to Gina Cantoni, who edited the collected proceedings, the SIL symposia identified barriers to language revitalization, such as the perception that English is a better vehicle for success, teachers' criticism of those who speak a minority language at home, and the tendency to teach isolated vocabulary items instead of complete language. The participants also identified some "widespread misconceptions" that impede language revitalization efforts:

- You have to give up your own language in order to master another one.
- You need special training to teach your own language to your children.
- Schools can take over the job of teaching a language if families do not teach it.
- Writing a language is what keeps it alive.[30]

Most linguists would agree that these are misconceptions, and that they impede efforts to stabilize endangered languages. In fact, linguistic research has led to these conclusions:

- Children can easily learn two languages if both are spoken around them as they are growing up. Bilingual children are superior to monolinguals in many cognitive tasks, and by about age 9 are completely equivalent to monolingual children in their skills in the school language.
- Children learn a language naturally, without special instruction, just by hearing it spoken around them.
- By age 12, which is when most schools begin teaching second languages, children are already beyond the "critical period" for naturally learning languages.
- Spoken languages are living languages, and writing is not essential for keeping a language alive.

Thus the viewpoint that results from studying language as a linguist is at odds with the usual viewpoint of the general public. Linguists are often very earnest in trying to inform the public (or at least the members of it in their college classrooms) of the truth as they see it, but this habit can lead to conflict when a linguist goes to into another community to help with language issues. Naturally, people in Native communities often hold some of the same ideas about language and bilingualism as the general Anglo population, along with their own culture-specific views about their own languages, and the well-meaning linguist may see her task as teaching them the truth as she sees it. In order to show why it is not always helpful to zealously correct the "misconceptions" of speakers of endangered languages, in the next section I will examine why these misconceptions are so widespread, and consider how the grain of truth within them is relevant to the role of linguists in language stabilization efforts.

Some Popular Misconceptions about Language

The first common misunderstandings that I would like to look at have to do with bilingualism. As I noted earlier, it is popularly believed in America that a child who is brought up bilingual will be behind her monolingual peers in school, will be confused by input from two languages, and may have trouble achieving proficiency in any one language. For this reason, it is not uncommon for parents who speak a minority language to decide to bring up their children speaking the majority language.

Linguists know that studies of bilingual children tell a different story. For example, a recent University of Miami study of Spanish/English bilingual children conducted by Barbara Pearson found that bilingual first-graders have a larger vocabulary than monolingual first-graders, that by the fifth grade bilingual children's English reading test scores were no different from those of monolinguals, and that bilingual children are better than monolinguals in cognitive tasks involving metalinguistic awareness, divergent thinking, and selective attention. In fact, Pearson reports that to her knowledge there exist no nonlinguistic cognitive tests in which bilinguals do worse than monolinguals.[31] Doesn't this mean, then, that there is a pressing need for linguists to disabuse speakers of endangered languages of their misconceptions about bilingualism, so that they will not bring up their children speaking only English?

Maybe there would be in a world where speakers of minority languages were not socially stigmatized and school systems waited until fifth grade to give children language tests. In the real world, bilingual parents in America know that school systems care only about English skills, and minority languages are not widely valued. Their children will be tested in kindergarten or first grade, and their knowledge of the home language will be generally ignored. A six-year-old who knows 16,000 words, 8,000 of English and 8,000 of Navajo, will be considered "behind" a monolingual child who knows 10,000 words of English.[32] The child will be given special English language instruction, and will be expected to be behind in other subjects. It is well known that teachers' expectations have a significant effect on performance, and that children's attitudes toward their own abilities and teachers' attitudes toward the children are formed well before fifth grade. A child could be treated as "deficient" based on her first-grade scores, and this could have an irreversible effect. In short, parents are not deluded to worry about the effects of bringing their child up bilingual. It takes a very strong parent with ample time to advocate for her children to counteract these effects.

A related misconception is that you need special training to teach your language to your child. It can be very frustrating to a linguist to observe that some parents come to them hoping for training that will help them pass along their language, when the linguist knows that linguistic training will not help. How can parents expect linguists to help them if they aren't speaking the language with their own children? But as with the issue of bilingualism, the desire for training comes from real-world pressures that make it extremely difficult to construct the environment for natural language learning.[33] Children are bombarded by messages that the dominant language is the language of power. Moreover, if their friends don't speak the heritage language, then it isn't cool, and they risk humiliation if they speak it. Often parents will try to bring up children speaking the heritage language, only to find the children answering back in the dominant language. Teresa McCarty and her colleagues found that the level of proficiency among Navajo children seemed to be higher than the level they displayed in public. They conclude that these factors lead to a loss of opportunities for children and adults to interact naturally in Navajo. It is far from a misconception to hope for some training that could teach you how to deal with this kind of situation.

Since many families do not find themselves in a situation where natural acquisition of the heritage language is possible, some communities put energy into developing curricula for middle school, high school, and college-age students, who may be realizing that their parents' language has value that they hadn't recognized when they were younger. Linguists may worry that the community fails to understand that language learning should not be put off until middle school. But chances are the community is well aware of the home situations of its children during the "critical period" years, and developing this kind of curriculum may be the best choice that is practical for them.

Finally, the issue of writing is complex, and community views are widely disparate. Some communities prefer not to write their language; others feel that writing is crucial. Linguists may worry that focusing on writing diverts energy from the enterprise of bringing up fluent speakers of the language. But given that the dominant culture clearly holds writing of their own language to be a crucial component of education, we should expect strong views among speakers of an endangered language.

The point is that clearing up misconceptions may not be the best task for an outsider linguist who wants to be helpful to a community. For linguists like me who are not trained in writing dictionaries, collecting texts, or developing pedagogical materials, this might mean that imparting our central area of expertise is not the most useful thing we can do. As Marianne Mithun points out, "Where language use is widespread and vigorous, it is natural to follow the interests of both the speakers and the fieldworker. Where the speech community is fragile, however, time with skilled speakers is a finite resource."[34] This point echoes suggestions by Donna Gerdts, Collette Grinevald, and Keren Rice, among others, who offer suggestions of other tasks that linguists might take on, such as helping to secure funding, acting as a liaison between communities and universities, acting as an advocate for the language, soliciting donations of needed supplies, and arranging access to media.[35] Being helpful to a community also means accepting the community's views about what will constitute the "success" of a program. There are many vibrant programs within communities today that might never result in large numbers of children learning the language fluently, but may be enormously successful in reinforcing the community's values in a world where their children face prejudice and economic disadvantage.

As long as linguists restrict what they are willing to do to things that directly involve their linguistic expertise, they are extremely likely to be doing what *they* think the community needs rather than what community members say they actually need. In retrospect, I think that the things that have made me most useful as an outsider have been independent of my linguistic wisdom. For example, one summer I babysat for a woman who was working as a consultant for me so that she could have time to pursue her own studies. I volunteered to be treasurer of the Navajo Language Academy, which organizes summer workshops for Navajo bilingual teachers. With me doing bookkeeping and paperwork, the Navajo speakers have more time for their own language work.[36] Members of the dominant culture have resources that might be more valuable than their linguistic expertise. We have access to people who would not listen to people from a stigmatized group. We have experience in expressing ourselves in the way that grant panels, college professors, legislators. and school principals expect. We have jobs that allow us a significant amount of freedom to pursue our own activities. These things are at least as valuable as our knowledge about the true nature of human language. They put us in a position to clear up the misconceptions about endangered languages in our own culture, to work for change in the role of testing in schools, to seek grant resources for community members, and to take on tasks that community members do not have the time or resources to do, such as getting coffee for meetings, bookkeeping, lobbying legislators, finding materials and supplies, setting up archives, and mailing out flyers.

Since the early 1990s an increasing number of linguists have become interested in contributing to language revitalization efforts and have been trying to avoid destructive ways of interacting with speakers of endangered languages and to address (or at least acknowledge) the power imbalances that arise when outsiders try to be "helpful" to a minority community. My own experience suggests that as we train the next generation of linguists it is important to teach them that one key power imbalance is that they simply do not have the power to pass along someone else's language. Because of this imbalance, what they have to offer to the communities they work with might not involve "clearing up misconceptions" or even developing materials that make direct use of their training as linguists. It is clear to all who work on endangered languages that only community-based projects have any hope of success, and linguists who are committed to language revitalization must be willing to help meet the goals that communities decide to set, rather than telling communities what needs to be done.[37] Fortunately, as Ash, Little Doe Fermino, and Hale write, "There is reason for optimism because local language communities all over the world are taking it upon themselves to act on behalf of their imperiled linguistic traditions in full understanding of, and in spite of, the realistic perception that the cards are stacked against them."[38]

NOTES

1. Letter of August 12, 2005, www.mapuche.info/mapu/ctt050812.html.
2. The quotation is from Nora Marks Dauenhauer and Richard Dauenhauer, "Technical, Emotional and Ideological Issues in Reversing Language Shift: Examples from Southeast Alaska," in *Endangered Languages: Language Loss and Community Response,* ed. Lenore Grenoble and Lindsay Whaley (Cambridge: Cambridge University Press, 1998), 60.
3. For one study that particularly addresses issues of ownership, see Judith Maxwell, "Ownership of Indigenous Languages: A Case Study from Guatemala," in *Indigenous Intellectual Property Rights: Legal Obstacles and Innovative Solutions,* ed. Mary Riley (Walnut Creek, CA: AltaMira, 2004), 173–217.
4. Michael Krauss, "The World's Languages in Crisis," *Language* 68.1 (1992): 4–10; Leanne Hinton, "Language Revitalization: An Overview," in *The Green Book of Language Revitalization in Practice,* ed. Leanne Hinton and Kenneth Hale (New York: Academic Press, 2001), 5; UNESCO Ad Hoc Expert Group on Endangered Languages, "Language Vitality and Endangerment," document submitted to the International Expert Meeting on UNESCO Programme: Safeguarding of

Endangered Languages, Paris, March 10–12, 2003, available at www.unesco.org /culture/ich/doc/src/00120-EN.pdf; Jane Hill, "'Expert Rhetorics' in Advocacy for Endangered Languages: Who Is Listening, and What Do They Hear?," *Journal of Linguistic Anthropology* 12.2 (2002): 119–33.

5. I. Wayan Arka, "Local Autonomy, Local Capacity Building and Support for Minority Languages: Field Experiences from Indonesia," in *Documenting and Revitalizing Austronesian Languages,* ed. D. Victoria Rau and Margaret Florey (Honolulu: University of Hawai'i Press, 2007), 66.

6. ASEDA (Aboriginal Studies Electronic Data Archive) FAQ, www1.aiatsis.gov.au /ASEDA/faq.html; Geoff Pullum, blog post on *Language Log,* November 24, 2006, http://itre.cis.upenn.edu/~myl/languagelog/archives/003820.html.

7. Keren Rice, "Must There Be Two Solitudes? Language Activists and Linguists Working Together," in *Indigenous Language Revitalization: Encouragement, Guidance and Lessons Learned,* ed. Jon Reyhner and Louise Lockard (Flagstaff: Northern Arizona University College of Education, 2009), 37–60, quotations on 41. For an excellent exploration of these issues within the Northern Athabaskan community of Kaska speakers in the Yukon, see Barbara A. Meek, *We Are Our Language: An Ethnography of Language Revitalization in a Northern Athabaskan Community* (Tucson: University of Arizona Press, 2010).

8. Jane Simpson, "Sovereignty over Languages and Land," posted on *Transient Languages & Cultures,* November 25, 2006, http://blogs.usyd.edu.au/elac/2006/11/ sovereignty_over_languages_and_1.html.

9. Raquel-Maria Yamada, "Collaborative Linguistic Fieldwork: Practical Application of the Empowerment Model," *Language Documentation and Conservation* 1.2 (2007): 258.

10. The first quotation is from Elena Benedicto, "Participative Research: The Role of the Linguist in the Development of Local Researchers," unpublished manuscript, Purdue University, 2008; the second and third are from Lise Dobrin, "From Linguistic Elicitation to Eliciting the Linguist: Lessons in Community Empowerment from Melanesia," *Language* 84.2 (2008): 307 (quoting linguist Geoff Smith). See also, among others, Deborah Cameron et al., *Researching Language: Issues of Power and Method* (London: Routledge, 1992); Deborah Cameron et al., "Ethics, Advocacy and Empowerment in Researching Language," in *Sociolinguistics: A Reader and Coursebook,* ed. Nikolas Coupland and Adam Jaworski (London: Macmillan, 1997), 145–62; Eva Czaykowska-Higgins, "Research Models in Linguistics: Reflections on Working with Canadian Indigenous Communities," unpublished manuscript, University of British Columbia, 2007; Collette Grinevald, "Language Endangerment in South America: A Programmatic Approach," in Grenoble and Whaley, *Endangered Languages,* 124–59; Marianne Mithun, "Who Shapes the Record: The Speaker and the Linguist," in *Linguistic Fieldwork,* ed. Paul Newman and Martha Ratliff (Cambridge: Cambridge University Press, 2001), 34–54; Keren Rice, "Ethical Issues in Linguistic Fieldwork: An Overview," *Journal of Academic Ethics* 4 (2006):

123–55; and Clay Slate, "Promoting Advanced Navajo Language Scholarship," in Hinton and Hale, *Green Book of Language Revitalization,* 389–410.

11. See in particular the accounts in Hinton and Hale, *Green Book of Language Revitalization.*

12. Patricia Shaw, "Negotiating against Loss: Responsibility, Reciprocity, and Respect in Endangered Language Research," in *Lectures on Endangered Languages: 4,* ed. Osama Sakiyama, Fubito Endo, Honoré Watanabe, and Fumiko Sasama (Osaka: Endangered Languages of the Pacific Rim [ELPR], 2004), 181–94, quotation on 188.

13. Margaret Field and Paul Kroskrity, "Introduction: Revealing Native American Ideologies," in *Native American Language Ideologies: Beliefs, Practices and Struggles in Indian Country,* ed. Kroskrity and Field (Tucson: University of Arizona Press, 2008), 6; Lenore Grenoble, "Linguistic Cages and the Limits of Linguists," in Reyhner and Lockard, *Indigenous Language Revitalization,* 61; Slate, "Promoting Advanced Navajo Language Scholarship," 389.

14. Grenoble, "Linguistic Cages and the Limits of Linguists," 64.

15. The quotations are from Slate, "Promoting Advanced Navajo Language Scholarship," 389.

16. Rice, "Must There Be Two Solitudes?," 56.

17. Christopher Loether, "Language Revitalization and the Manipulation of Language Ideologies: A Shoshoni Case Study," in Kroskrity and Field, *Native American Language Ideologies,* 239; H. P. Valiquette, "Community, Professionals, and Language Preservation: First Things First," in *Endangered Languages—What Role for the Specialist?,* ed. Nicholas Ostler (Bath, UK: Foundation for Endangered Languages, 1998), 107, quoted in Rice, "Must There Be Two Solitudes?," 48.

18. Field and Kroskrity, "Introduction," 6; Dobrin, "From Linguistic Elicitation to Eliciting the Linguist," 310.

19. I was trained essentially as a theoretical linguist/cognitive scientist, and my research on Navajo would be characterized by some as arcane. I cannot claim to be a specialist in language documentation, and my involvement with the Navajo community has been largely limited to Navajo linguists and educators.

20. See in particular Robert Young and William Morgan, *The Navajo Language* (Albuquerque: University of New Mexico Press, 1980). This work is an extension of Young and Morgan, *The Navaho Language: The Elements of Navaho Grammar with a Dictionary in Two Parts containing Basic Vocabularies* (Phoenix Indian School, 1943), a version of which was published in 1972 by the Deseret Book Company, Phoenix. The figure for remaining speakers is taken from AnCita Benally and Denis Vin, "*Diné Bizaad* (Navajo Language) at a Crossroads: Extinction or Renewal?," *Bilingual Research Journal* 29 (2005): 85–108, cited in Teresa McCarty, Mary Eunice Romero-Little, and Ofelia Zepeda, "Indigenous Language Policies in Social Practice: The Case of Navajo," in *Sustaining Linguistic Diversity: Endangered and Minority Languages and Language Varieties,* ed. Kendall King, Natalie Schilling-Estes, Lyn Wright Fogle, Jia Jackie Lou, and Barbara Soukup (Washington, DC: Georgetown University Press, 2008), 159–72.

21. Paul Platero, "Navajo Head-Start Language Study," in Hinton and Hale, *Green Book of Language Revitalization,* 87–100.

22. Evangeline Parsons Yazzie and Margaret Speas, *Diné Bizaad Bínáhoo´aah (Rediscovering the Navajo Language)* (Flagstaff, AZ: Salina Bookshelf, 2008).

23. See Dobrin, "From Linguistic Elicitation to Eliciting the Linguist."

24. Slate, "Promoting Advanced Navajo Language Scholarship," 395.

25. Anna Ash, Jessie Little Doe Fermino, and Ken Hale, "Diversity in Local Language Maintenance and Restoration: A Reason for Optimism," in Hinton and Hale, *Green Book of Language Revitalization,* 19–35.

26. In addition to the studies cited earlier, see also Rice, "Must There Be Two Solitudes?"; Donna Gerdts, "The Linguist in Language Revitalization Programmes," in Ostler, *Endangered Languages—What Role for the Specialist?,* 13–22; and Grenoble, "Linguistic Cages and the Limits of Linguists."

27. Field and Kroskrity, "Introduction," 25–26.

28. Darrell Kipp, "Encouragement, Guidance and Lessons Learned: 21 Years in an Immersion School," in Reyhner and Lockard, *Indigenous Language Revitalization,* 2.

29. The proceedings were published in Gina Cantoni, ed., *Stabilizing Indigenous Languages* (Flagstaff: Northern Arizona University College of Education, 1996), available at http://jan.ucc.nau.edu/~jar/SIL/.

30. Ibid., vii.

31. Barbara Pearson, *Raising a Bilingual Child* (New York: Living Languages, 2008).

32. See Slate, "Promoting Advanced Navajo Language Scholarship."

33. Many of these pressures are clearly explained in McCarty, Romero-Little, and Zepeda, "Indigenous Language Policies in Social Practice."

34. Mithun, "Who Shapes the Record," 34.

35. Gerdts, "The Linguist in Language Revitalization Programmes"; Grinevald, "Language Endangerment in South America"; Rice, "Must There Be Two Solitudes?"

36. Some information on the Navajo Language Academy can be found in Margaret Speas, "Someone Else's Language: On the Role of Linguists in Language Revitalization," in Reyhner and Lockard, *Indigenous Language Revitalization,* 23–36.

37. For useful advice about language planning that can be implemented by community members on their own, but is also a good blueprint for an outsider linguist because it lays a framework for the community to articulate its goals, see Leanne Hinton, "Language Planning," in Hinton and Hale, *Green Book of Language Revitalization,* 51.

38. Ash, Little Doe Fermino, and Hale, "Diversity in Local Language Maintenance and Restoration," 20.

5
ARCHAEOLOGISTS,
INDIGENOUS INTELLECTUAL PROPERTY,
AND ORAL HISTORY

H. Martin Wobst

THIS CHAPTER FOCUSES on interactions between professional arch-aeologists and members of Indigenous populations, in the traditional lands of Indigenous people. The world's Indigenous people as defined here are not neatly or categorically different from other descendant groups, and they are not a racial category. Instead, they are culturally and politically defined, and they are quite different from each other. I have chosen them as my topic primarily because the cultural differences between many Indigenous people and archaeologists are often quite massive, particularly when it comes to cultural patrimony and intellectual property.[1] Pragmatically, that makes it easier to think about potential problems that the interaction between archaeologists and descendant populations might generate when archaeologists work with another population's intellectual property.

While my discussion logically applies to all descendant populations, it is focused particularly on Indigenous ones, that is, those who were subject to colonization and now occupy minority status in the nation-states that were established following decolonization, including Native Americans and First Nations, the Australian aborigines, the people of the North in Russia, and similar groups.[2] These are the kinds of populations that fall under the purview of the United Nations Secretariat of the Permanent

Forum on Indigenous Issues, which also provides a very legalistic and detailed definition of the term "Indigenous."[3] I consider Indigenous intellectual property to consist, very broadly, of a group's language and lore, art and music, history and material record, ritual and religion, custom and knowledge, and the like. I am not concerned here with the "intellectual property" of archaeologists, as in the copyrighted publications archaeologists may generate for themselves, their institutions, or their sponsors, on Indigenous intellectual property.

In the sections that follow, I first sketch how a more professional archaeology became logically separated from the descendants whose ancestors produced the artifacts (that is, the Indigenous intellectual property that constitutes the databases of the archaeological profession). I then survey some developments, beginning in the 1970s, that are generating a rapprochement between archaeology and Indigenous populations. In the final section, I suggest that the most well-meaning attempts to decolonize relations between archaeologists and Indigenous populations, in themselves, are often deeply problematic when it comes to intellectual property. I illustrate that with "oral history," a method championed by archaeologists and, often, the Indigenous populations themselves, to work together toward shared goals again. Yet often such a collaboration introduces as many problems as it seeks to overcome.

The Profession of Archaeology Constitutes Itself as "Archaeological"

Before the middle of the nineteenth century, interest in the past seamlessly integrated the many ways of knowing about it. Before there was an archaeology, that is, before the latter half of the nineteenth century, antiquarians would illuminate the past of the people in their surroundings from many different angles. For example, they would record written and oral histories and literatures, carry out language and dialect work, and report on myths and folklore, standing ruins, and (fairly rarely) "archaeological" (subsurface) finds. For antiquarians, access to the past could be gained in a number of different ways, and often the same antiquarian reported about it in several different modes. Many of these modes of access involved direct interactions with the living descendants of the pasts in which the antiquarians had an interest.[4] Antiquarians, broadly speaking, were neither hard scientists nor social scientists, though their interests covered the width and breadth of these later branches of inquiry, but they were broadly interested humanists.

Over the course of the nineteenth and twentieth centuries, against this background of a considerably more integrated and holistic access to the past, archaeology gradually established itself as a profession.[5] It saw its niche increasingly as bringing the material past to the attention of scientists and the public, and it developed a set of methods for uncovering, documenting, conserving, and analyzing material remains, and relating them to the events, actions, processes, and behaviors that had generated them in the past. In short, archaeologists became the professionals who used information from artifacts to scientifically unravel human histories, human evolution, and past human behavior.[6]

Yet in contrast to the savants who preceded them, this disciplinary niche essentially closed archaeologists off from interactions with the modern descendants of the people whose past they tried to elucidate. The very starting point of most archaeological problem solving, the excavation unit, can be located only where no people are currently living. Thus excavation, professional archaeologists' core methodology of data acquisition, separates them from the descendants whose patrimony the archaeological data represent. Archaeological expertise was to connect the contents of excavation units with the social variables in which they once were embedded, and archaeologists did that with archaeological methods, not by interacting with actual people in the present. On the contrary, the less archaeologists depended on the word of living descendants in linking material remains of the past to past social behavior, and the more they achieved that linkage by purely "archaeological" data and methods, the higher their standing within the profession.[7] In the post-antiquarian age, to work with descendants on their myth, lore, or language was seen by archaeologists, wanting to distinguish their new field from much older humanities and sciences, as being outside of their professional niche. If they didn't assess such interaction with living descendants as altogether scientifically soft or irrelevant, they happily gave it up to other disciplines, such as folklore, mythology, linguistics, ethnohistory, and oral history, that is, to disciplines that used interaction with living people to gain information about the past.

Most steps in archaeological method that follow the removal of artifacts from the ground only tended to increase the separation of archaeologists from descendant populations, and thus the distances, both logical and spatial, between archaeologists and "their" data on the one hand, and the descendants who considered these data to constitute important parts of their own material patrimony and intellectual property on the other hand. Be it by laboratory analysis, preservation, curation, display, or publication, the collections entered realms beyond the control of the descendants, physically and logically remote from their reach.[8]

This accelerating crystallization of a new set of archaeological practices with material remains from the past happened in the face of the time-honored practices of most descendant populations, particularly many of the world's Indigenous populations, relative to their material (and nonmaterial) cultural patrimony. Most of these descendant populations differentiate between the heuristics of "the past" and "the present" significantly less than professional archaeologists. To many of them, the past, present, and future are not logically separated at all. Moreover, many Indigenous people consider themselves fully knowledgeable about all aspects of their pasts, or at least they acknowledge that some individuals or groups among them have that full knowledge. They also know that their people who hold that knowledge about the past (or less ethnocentrically, that domain which archaeologists tend to call "the past") did not acquire it through archaeological method, but by a long process of *social* interactions with those group members who have more, or more authoritative, knowledge than they themselves currently have. They learn about it in the present, by interacting with other group members. To them, both that knowledge about the past and the processes through which group members acquire it are daily reminders of the vitality of their sociality, at the same time that they help to construct or (re)constitute that sociality, and contribute to shaping the social positioning of all of its members.[9]

Thus, during archaeology's history, an ever-widening logical chasm has developed between professional archaeology (and its self-understanding and practices related to the pasts of others) and the self-understanding and practices that many if not most Indigenous and other descendant populations have about their own pasts. To many archaeologists, Indigenous knowledge of Indigenous pasts prompted reactions like "not my department," or "there are other professions that deal with that," or epithets such as "unprofessional," "metaphysical," or "unscientific." If such knowledge were admitted as the equal of the knowledge of archaeology, it would weaken the very expertise of that profession, that is, the cleverness with which archaeologists connected the material remains of the past "archaeologically" with the present. On the other hand, if any Indigenous people were to admit the equivalence of their own and archaeological methods of accessing their past, that would disempower Indigenous ways of constituting the Indigenous sociality, the individual's positions within that sociality, and the authority of all the group members who had painstakingly acquired those Indigenous forms of knowledge (and the important ranks, roles, and statuses that often accompany its possession), together with everything that they know and hold dear about themselves.

The divide between archaeologists and Indigenous populations was exacerbated because archaeologists, as scientists, tended to hold themselves responsible for generating knowledge about the "human" past, or about "national" pasts, and they considered the generation of that knowledge to be in the interest of all humans, or at least all citizens of a nation-state. They thus viewed all of their archaeological fieldwork as being in the common interest and for the common good, and their entire profession as serving pan-human or national universals, rather than simply the needs of the archaeological profession as I have outlined them. Such a worldview made it easy for archaeologists to interpret Indigenous desires to keep their buried past buried as expressions of sectarian interests or of local self-interest, as blocking the road to human progress, negating basic pan-human needs, and reeking of lack of education and general backwardness.[10]

On the other side, many Indigenous populations considered the claim of archaeologists in pursuit of the human past to be irrelevant to their own situation. To them, archaeologists are simply hiding their own self- or sectarian interest (making sense out of people's past with the help of archaeological methods) behind the smokescreen of speaking about all humans, or all of a nation's citizens. To the contrary, many Indigenous cultural custodians considered their own desire to keep their cultural patrimony buried, and to control what people could or could not do with it, to be basic human rights. To them, invoking the universal knowledge goals of science did nothing to affect, much less invalidate, these basic human rights.[11] As Joe Watkins's chapter elsewhere in this volume documents in detail, such "professional" conduct was even encouraged by laws that had empowered the nation (and its archaeological professionals) to be the custodians of Indigenous remains on federal lands.

The same professional archaeologists who would have defended themselves vigorously if they had seen outsiders taking away or defiling their own ("historical") heritage and intellectual properties rode the high horse of scientific detachment in their interactions with the intellectual properties and cultural patrimony of Indigenous others. Even in the face of the laments and loud protests of cultural custodians and other descendants, archaeologists felt free to continue mining Indigenous sites, collecting their artifacts, excavating their cemeteries, and violating their sacred ground in search of archaeological remains. In archaeological laboratories, museums, and repositories, Indigenous cultural properties were completely alienated from their Indigenous cultural contexts, decoupled from their cultural trajectories, and disembedded from the social relations within which they had been embedded. In the power scenario of late colonialism and early post-colonialism, archaeologists could violate Indigenous human rights and intellectual properties with little fear of legal consequences, since they had the power of the law and the might of the state backing them. This constitutes the painful background to the federal legislation that finally granted Native Americans some recourse and partial remediation only well after the middle of the last century.

The Archaeology of Other Peoples' Intellectual Property Becomes a Social Science Again

After the Second World War, the power scenario for archaeology shifted. First, independence movements and decolonization unshackled the people in the colonies. Second, as more and more people in the Third World, at least nominally, gained their civil rights, it became ever harder to justify withholding civil rights from segments of the population in the settler societies of North America, South Africa, Australia and New Guinea, Russia, and China. Third, the Indigenous populations in these settler societies themselves actively mobilized to politicize and resist their colonial status quo, and used the media, public demonstrations, and the law for their defense and liberation. This set in motion a process in which the Indigenous populations have been able to get some of their grievances heard, stop some of the worst civil-rights violations against them, and gradually achieve some recognition in the law to control their cultural patrimony and intellectual resources in the law.

These processes began to have an effect in a number of the settler societies, such as the United States, Canada, Australia, and New Zealand, in the 1960s. In these countries, certain laws were passed, or court cases decided, in favor of Indigenous rights and Indigenous control over their cultural resources and intellectual properties of interest to archaeologists. For example, in the United States a number of laws were passed already in the first half of the twentieth century to help safeguard archaeological sites on public lands from destruction, such as the Antiquities Act of 1906 and the Historic Sites Act of 1935.[12] It was not until after the Second World War, however, that laws began to be passed that gave descendant populations some legal standing over their own intellectual properties. They included, among others, the National Historic Preservation Act of 1966, the Archaeological Resources Protection Act of 1979, the American Indian Religious Freedom Act of 1978, and finally the Native American Repatriation Act of 1990 (NAGPRA).[13] NAGPRA for the first time gave federally recognized American Indigenous groups a legal mechanism for righting previous injustices to their skeletal remains, associated archaeological remains, and items of cultural patrimony.[14]

Legal developments in Canada, Australia, New Zealand, and South Africa (after the collapse of the apartheid regime) were parallel to those in the United States.[15] All four of these countries now have laws in place that recognize that Indigenous populations (at least those that are federally, state, or provincially recognized) have valid legal standing in many questions related to their cultural and "archaeological" resources.

If archaeologists want to work with such remains, the law in many countries now requires them to obtain the permission of the modern descendants connected to those remains before they carry out their fieldwork, and both the fieldwork and what happens to the remains thereafter must respect the wishes of the descendant populations. Frequently, the law also requires archaeologists to ascertain that collections acquired before these laws took effect are in harmony with the newly passed laws, that is, that their continued curation by archaeologists does not violate important human rights or vital interests of the descendants whose past the collections represent.[16]

In other words, whether archaeologists want to or not, in many countries the law now requires them to work closely with descendant populations, at least as long as they seek to acquire new data. At the same time, a number of developments within the discipline of archaeology itself have brought archaeologists and descendant populations closer together again. Many of these came to the fore in the same decades that the laws forced archaeologists to pay closer attention to the descendant populations whose data they had been processing.

There had been a long tradition of learning, from well-published sites or those still in use by Indigenous populations, about how to interpret the sites that preceded them, an archaeological methodology known as "the direct historical approach."[17] This methodology, at the least, encouraged archaeologists to familiarize themselves with the published record about the descendant populations whose earlier history they were interested in. Yet often the publications that resulted from this approach did not actually testify to close interaction between the archaeologists and descendants' knowledge about their past, instead bypassing those avenues in favor of collating what had already been published by scientists, or what was contained in the historic record about that past (parallel to the archaeologists' own predilection). In addition, there was the danger of freezing earlier societies into the straitjacket of the behavior of their descendants.[18]

Ethnoarchaeology became more central to the discipline, as a respected part of the new theoretical approach known as processual archaeology, to give the discipline a more explicitly scientific bent.[19] It may be defined as the use of contemporary ethnographic data and contexts for archaeological purposes, usually to make graspable in a scientifically controlled manner aspects of behavior that are considered significant for understanding what went on in a given archaeological context, but are not directly graspable in archaeological data. For example, Bill Longacre studied modern Indians in the U.S. Southwest (and populations in the Philippines) to determine how their ceramics articulated with other cultural variables to help with interpreting prehistoric ceramics and societies. Lewis Binford lived with an Inuit community to enrich methodologies for interpreting forager archaeological remains. Polly Wiessner looked at the !Kung San hunter-gatherers of Botswana for behaviors linked to exchange goods (and thus to improve archaeologists' ability to interpret prehistoric forager exchange systems). And John Yellen studied the same group to learn from their modern settlement behaviors about forager settlement behavior in prehistory.[20]

Clearly, ethnoarchaeology requires intense social interaction between archaeologists and ethnographic (and thus descendant) populations. Yet in the logic of processual archaeology, where this approach reached its fruition, the ethnographic populations were not considered important bearers of knowledge about their own pasts as much as data exemplars (like the standard "archaeological sites") against which to develop "archaeological method" or "archaeological theory" in a controlled fashion. This method and theory could then be used anywhere, to make better sense of archaeological data (and thus, again, enable the archaeologists to bypass descendant knowledge in interpreting the material culture that the antecedents of the modern descendants had left behind). If not handled carefully, such an ethnoarchaeology actually may devalue descendant knowledge at the cost of "scientifically" developed knowledge and thus, in the long run, pull descendants and archaeologists further apart.[21]

The theoretical inroads of postmodernism have been more effective in bringing about constructive interactions between archaeologists and descendant populations concerning Indigenous intellectual properties. In archaeology, such postmodern approaches are usually defined as "post-processual archaeology," a term that loosely circumscribes an internally varied, not very clearly bounded set of theory and methods.[22] Yet its practitioners, on the whole, share a number of assumptions about the world and humans. Ironically, the first card-carrying post-processual monograph in archaeology, *Symbols in Action* by Ian Hodder, used ethnoarchaeology as its basic method.[23] It attempted to show that the law-like generalizations archaeologists had championed in the processual archaeology approach were not of much help when it came to making sense of the material culture of descendant populations. The decisions with which East African populations made and distributed artifacts were instead deeply grounded in their local, historically grown cultural logic. Quite conveniently, their rationales often strongly contradicted the interpretations scientific archaeologists would have offered on general theoretical grounds, or made them look altogether irrelevant. In the context of Indigenous cultural properties, that kind of result has been often repeated since then. It makes fine-grained communication with descendant groups, as a fount of cultural knowledge about the past, an important axis of archaeological research.

In another important dimension, it was post-processual archaeologists who realized that "artifacts" are not just the *products* of human behavior, but significantly channel, control, and bring about such behavior. Moreover, artifacts, under the post-processual gaze, are seen to be very important in helping to constitute individuals and social groups, and instrumental in realms well beyond feeding and reproductive behaviors.[24] The very science of "material culture" was an outgrowth of this realization.[25] Where before most archaeologists had concentrated their method and theory on explaining artifacts in their interaction with each other and with variables of the natural environment, this new focus on "material culture" caused a shift in interest toward the contexts of meaning in which artifacts were embedded. It called for illuminating exactly those realms of behavior, such as myth, folklore, religion, ritual, place name, sound, smell, symbols, and so forth, that antiquarians had studied along with artifacts, while archaeologists had lost interest in all but the "archaeological" core, the material artifact. These dimensions of information about past human behaviors are not easy to read in past human artifacts, however clever the method, though they provide rich information about the contexts in which the artifacts functioned and their relationships to, and embeddedness within, nonmaterial domains. The richest and most proximate source of information resides in the cultural custodians and other cultural practitioners of the descendant populations. To gain access to that kind of information about past materialities, archaeologists needed to establish positions of trust and cooperation with Indigenous societies.[26]

Post-processual archaeology also became a trendsetter for research into the history of archaeology.[27] Much post-processual research documented the close ties between previous archaeological practice and colonialism, and how much Indigenous groups had suffered from the ways archaeologists had constructed their pasts and their cultural evolution. That kind of archaeological theory and method made it easier for the colonial powers to rule Indigenous people, and to feel good about their colonial roles, while giving archaeologists the sense that they were engaged in an important civilizing mission.[28] With this ugly history emerging, many archaeologists realized that their past attitudes toward Indigenous populations had been quite colonial: archaeologists had become the producers of, and spokespeople for, Indigenous histories, in the interest of archaeological method and theory, rather than attempting to answer the questions of the descendants about their history. In the post-processual milieu, this has motivated much archaeological work to be collaborative with Indigenous cultural custodians, and to give voice to Indigenous knowledge, aspirations, and long-term plans for their intellectual property from the past.[29]

In a similar vein, many archaeologists could not fail to notice that they occupied positions of privilege and prestige, and had access to significant financial and institutional resources in the context of their own work, while few of these resources trickled down to the Indigenous populations with whose data they worked. Lest archaeologists be branded as parasites on Indigenous populations, shouldn't more of these resources flow into the Indigenous populations whose pasts those funds were designed to unearth? Shouldn't more archaeological work be accessible to the descendant populations (in their language, in museums within their reach, at sites in their homelands)? Shouldn't archaeologists provide training for members of descendant populations so that they might end up with well-paying jobs akin to those that the archaeologists held? Shouldn't archaeological work on Indigenous pasts be in the hands of Indigenous archaeologists, since Indigenous data are the focus of study?[30]

Post-processual archaeologists began to acknowledge that different stakeholders, in the same context, could have different, though internally entirely consistent and reasonable, interpretations or explanations for the same material artifacts or contexts. This had long been acknowledged by Marxians, anarchists, and adherents of some other social philosophies.[31] When archaeologists internalized the multitude of reasonable but different stakeholder interpretations for the same archaeological contexts, they realized that their scientific pedestal was not categorically different from the pedestals from which other stakeholders pronounced their positions. In such a scenario, points of contention could not be resolved simply through the intervention of the scientist; rather, they had to be negotiated, and such negotiation required developing long-term social relationships with Indigenous groups.[32] For archaeologists who had felt most comfortable interacting mainly with material artifacts in the close confines of their excavations, labs, and museums, that realization was a difficult one to put to work. Post-processualism had made it obvious that archaeology was a social practice, and it had become a sine qua non of the discipline, in a number of settler countries anyway, to acknowledge Indigenous cultural custodians as the ultimate referees for access, and disputes over, the Indigenous cultural heritage.

Unfortunately, the time has not yet come when Indigenous human rights are respected worldwide and Indigenous populations can realize their aspirations concerning their past and present intellectual property. In many parts of the world, Indigenous people still live in colonial conditions when it comes to their material cultural patrimony, and some still die in defense of their cultural patrimony. But today, archaeologists have no excuse for persisting with their inherited colonial practices. Archaeology's previous sins are well published in accessible places. Best practices (I actually prefer the terms "improved" or "improving" practices) for the interaction with Indigenous populations have been adopted by many of the national professional organizations of archaeologists as well as by the international World Archaeological Congress, a banner-carrier for decolonizing archaeology vis-à-vis the Indigenous intellectual property.[33] Archaeologists should know better! And it behooves all of us to bring that point to bear on the places where Indigenous populations today continue to suffer severe abuses at the hands of archaeologists interested in their cultural patrimony.

Given archaeology's previous track record with the pasts of Indigenous populations, we need to be doubly cautious that our present "best practices" themselves will not have created, in hindsight, more problems than they were intended to solve. We cannot be vigilant enough to ensure that our interaction with Indigenous cultural heritage will really be in their best interests in the long run. It would be ideal if all work that dealt with the archaeological past of Indigenous populations were subject to rigorous Human Subjects Review, to ensure that it was designed and executed in the best interests of, and to avoid or obviate both short-term and long-term harm for, the Indigenous population concerned.[34] Indeed, what is needed would go well beyond Human Subjects Reviews as they are conducted today, to include the review and revisiting of such projects at intervals after completion, to validate that what was thought to have been beneficial or, at least harmless, actually turned out that way.

After a long period of logical separation, archaeologists and Indigenous people are reenergizing their social relations in many parts of the world. The goal of many of these relationships is to give Indigenous populations access to basic human rights, and to decolonize archaeological practice vis-à-vis Indigenous intellectual property. Archaeologists are rediscovering many access roads to the archaeological record which they had given up to other fields early in their history, such as ways of knowing about the past through folklore, religion, myth, oral history, place name study, and so forth. A considerable amount of archaeological practice is designed for the benefit of Indigenous populations. Nevertheless, even the most well-meant archaeological practice may generate serious problems for Indigenous populations over the long run. In the next section I will illustrate that dilemma with the example of oral history.

Oral History as an Artifact

One avenue of access to the Indigenous past that has seen a particularly massive increase in attention, from archaeologists and Indigenous populations alike, is oral history, which may be defined as information about the past that is passed on through word of mouth across generations, and then gathered, in recordings and transcriptions and the like, by archaeologists or historians, to be written down and turned into an artifact. To differentiate the history that is orally passed along from its artifact as recorded by archaeologists or historians, I will refer to the former as Indigenous oral history, and the latter as artifactualized oral history.[35] To the archaeologist, Indigenous oral history offers access to the cultural contexts of artifacts in the past, and to aspects of the past that are not well tracked in the material traces that archaeologists traditionally consider their data base. Many Indigenous populations appreciate such interest, since the archaeologist may help them preserve something that they highly value but know to be fleeting and vulnerable to permanent loss. When speakers give up their Indigenous mother tongue, when Indigenous contexts of making and doing things are alienated by imported commodities and non-Indigenous media, and when people sense their Indigenous specificities disappearing one after the other, it is not surprising that an archaeological offer to record their oral history would be received very positively.

At the same time, even the most well-meaning interaction between descendants and archaeologists, with artifactualized oral history as the outcome, carries potential risks and dangers for the Indigenous group. Both archaeologists and Indigenous cultural custodians need to be aware of these dangers so that they can avoid, or control, the potential damage that may result if they throw themselves uninformed into collaboration over the preservation of orally transmitted knowledge.

In many Indigenous contexts, oral history is part and parcel of social relations, a process by which Indigenous cultural custodians learn about their group's history and through which they release information about the past to others within the community. Gaining access to that knowledge, being known as a person who has that knowledge, and releasing that information to others are all immensely social, and help to shape individuals and social groups, and their roles, ranks, and positions. Indigenous oral history keeps that memory alive without artifacts (such as writing down or otherwise recording it). Thus it implies communication, social interaction, relationships of trust and access, and differentials in access and distribution of knowledge. In a given group, in its oral history pipeline, vast amounts of information about the past circulate, are kept in memory, and are created, passed down, modified, and authenticated by social process. At the same time, that social process helps to construct the social group, its distribution of social roles and access, and its internal mechanics and dynamics.

That Indigenous oral history is valuable and should be kept going is reasonable, since it is so closely tied to the social self-understanding of the group (and so rich in information about a group's past). Let us assume that archaeologists and Indigenous cultural custodians agree (for their own reasons) that such knowledge should be recorded, in order to help archaeologists enrich their sense of the Indigenous past and to provide everlasting preservation of its history to the Indigenous group. Looking at these benefits, and the care with which Indigenous interests promise to be respected in this interaction, there is little doubt that the project would pass Human Subjects Review (although in point of fact, Human Subjects Review is not required for most oral history projects). Yet recording and archiving for the good of archaeologists and descendants the Indigenous oral history of a given group has potentially very serious implications for the group and for its cultural custodians, even when they freely agreed to this release of their intellectual property.

In recording Indigenous oral history for posterity, a social process is turned into artifacts (written-up notes and publications, recordings, CDs, documentaries, and the like), and such artifactualized oral history can seriously transform the group in question. Artifactualized oral history potentially preempts the entire social dynamic that had been Indigenous oral history. Before, history was communicated in the group in a social process that was based on its unequal distribution, continuous learning and communication, and other social interaction. People gradually acquired (or released) their knowledge, with no way to establish what was right or wrong except by means of long-term interaction within the social group, particularly with the cultural custodians, and the gradual evolution of bona fides resulting from these interactions.

Once what was oral is artifactualized, everybody can short-circuit the interaction by going directly to the artifactual record. Access to artifactualized oral history is potentially more even and egalitarian, but it is removed from the web of social relations in which it had been embedded. Similarly, social roles, positions, and contexts that were supported by the gradual acquisition and release of information about the past are destabilized, since people now have more direct ways of acquiring it. The entire enculturating process, of learning more through time and becoming more valued by becoming more knowledgeable, has been preempted. Anyone, even those with little or no knowledge of the Indigenous oral history, can now go the artifactualized oral history and access it in its entirety. The youngest learner and the most knowledgeable cultural custodian are thus equalized in their (potential) knowledge. It is obvious that this will destabilize or deflate social positions tied into the Indigenous oral history process, including those of the traditional cultural custodians.

Truth about the past, in this intervention, has become an artifact—the artifactualized oral history. That truth is, in part, alienating for the Indigenous group—it is contained in an artifact that an outsider, the archaeologist, in consultation with the cultural custodians who released the information, considered to be the essential oral history. In the first place, taking down such orally transmitted knowledge itself is a social process. This social process originated because of the archaeologists' questions about Indigenous pasts. In that context, the archaeological goal is usually to learn as much as possible about the articulation of material variables with ones that are not as easily read into (or out of) archaeological records. In contrast, in many Indigenous populations Indigenous oral history is a social practice made possible by, and facilitating, a less object-focused discourse about the past and its social milieus. It is very likely that archaeologists as elicitors of oral history will transform that mode of interacting about the past, explicitly non-artifact-embedded as it was, to one that is disproportionately linked with material references, if only to satisfy their disciplinary interests. In short, the danger is great that what ends up as artifactualized oral history in this context is not oral history the way it had been when it was oral, but a recorded version of that historical knowledge biased in the direction of the material fetishism of archaeology.

Since Indigenous oral history is so heavily embedded in social relations, its "historicizing," that is, turning it into documents, potentially sets in motion both centripetal and centrifugal processes in the Indigenous societies. Centripetal, because one version of Indigenous oral history will usually be preserved by this cooperation between archaeologists and Indigenous populations. That preserved version will validate the story of the Indigenous oral history informant, at the cost of other stories. It easily may give the appearance that what was in process was actually complete and finished and right and accurate and, thus, endow that informant's story with considerable authority, authenticity, and the possibility of authentication against the artifact thus produced. If the informants actually are the traditional cultural custodians, the archaeologists' intervention would validate and strengthen them.

The impact of artifactualizing oral history will, however, in the main be centrifugal, that is, by diffusing information to others. For example, because it is outsiders who tend to document the oral history, they deflect from the traditional cultural custodians, and the "right" version of oral history now turns into a readily accessible document rather than residing in the social web. Also, archaeologists do not usually have access to all members of a given society, but primarily only to those who are prepared to handle the group's foreign relations. These highly acculturated individuals, rather than the most knowledgeable cultural custodians (who might actually be the most inwardly centered members of the group), may get their story to fossilize in the resulting document. Finally, artifactualized oral history, even under the best of circumstances, is always a sample of the prevailing oral communication about the past. In communities, that communication web is community process. To release (parts of) that knowledge for publication would usually require the agreement of all community members. If individual community members testify about their knowledge to generate a record of that history, they affect everybody's knowledge, and everybody's social articulations.

Indigenous oral history across a given ethnographic population may be different by subgroup, gender, age, and location. It is probable that some such subgroups do not even know of the others' knowledge, or may explicitly keep their knowledge hidden from others.[36] Retelling such subgroup knowledges in carefully considered settings and at marked occasions is often central to the self-understanding of its members. Subgroup insiders might suffer if they are exposed to such information outside of its traditionally ritualized contexts. Explicit taboos and fear of great harm may prevent subgroup members from releasing their oral histories to other members of the groups. If the latter, for whatever reason, gain access to the previously tabooed oral histories, they might also feel violated and hurt. To non-group members, their lack of access to the hidden oral histories from what has become the artifactualized oral history makes such groups appear more integrated and internally homogeneous than they actually are. Thus "artifactualized" oral history tends to flatten the rich tableau of orally transmitted knowledge.

In Lieu of Conclusions

Ironically, and most likely even with the most careful controls in force, the results would not be massively different for an Indigenous group if the historization of the group's oral history were handled completely within the group, under the careful eyes of all of the group's members. The living social process "oral history" would be significantly different, before and after its recording; the web of social relations would change and the social position of every member of the group would be affected. It is tragic that social interventions in the interest of revitalizing a group (preserving their historically grown knowledges about the past) may actually destabilize these very processes and even stop them altogether. On the one hand the irreplaceable loss of historic substance; on the other the potential sabotage of social process.

The archiving of oral history is just one of many instances where strategies of decolonization and remediating colonialist harm may themselves generate trajectories of irreversible and massive change. Where these impacts can be anticipated in advance, they might be avoided, mitigated, or buffered. Similarly severe dilemmas, for example, may be set in motion by language revitalization (as discussed in the chapter by Margaret Speas elsewhere in this volume), or by repatriation as it is presently legislated in the United States (as discussed in the chapter by Joe Watkins). With reference to repatriation, the law differentiates Indigenous populations into those that are recognized by the State, and those that are not. These groups tend to be corporate in ways that make them easy for the State to recognize. Thus along the range of Indigenous social and political entities, those that get disproportionately rewarded look most statelike to the State. The State is (or has become) the arbiter. Such a procedure could be considered colonial in and of itself, with serious implications for Indigenous social structure. In addition, the very process of repatriation of cultural property rearticulates originally distributed Indigenous remains with Indigenous central authority and central places for depositing those repatriations, a significant centripetal force for Indigenous spatial process, independent of where the items are ultimately curated or re-interred.

This is not the place to spell out, for the Indigenous cultural custodians or for archaeologists who engage with them, optimal resolutions for the dilemmas I have outlined, or to dispense advice on how one can be proactive in order to optimally safeguard Indigenous intellectual property and Indigenous social process. Instead, the point of this essay is to encourage the most careful review of intended and actually realized impacts at each step along the way of archaeological work, to help Indigenous populations toward recovery from the forces of colonialism. Before it is taken, each step needs to be understood in all its potential impacts, analyzed for how well it is working while it is being implemented, and carefully reviewed for its actual impacts long after it has been implemented. Such impact assessment goes well beyond what is presently required under the law, what is presently considered best scientific practice, and what safeguards most Indigenous communities have been able to develop.

Archaeologists interested in any aspect of Indigenous intellectual property need to realize that their science inescapably is a social one, with serious implications for human rights. Archaeology extends to all dimensions of the descendant populations' social process, not just to those that are directly tied to their cultural patrimony from the past. Archaeological practice exposes descendant populations to serious risks, even if the archaeologists are fully committed to remediating previous wrongs and improving the population's conditions in the present, and even with the full support of the Indigenous cultural custodians. Archaeology thus requires a commitment to, and taking responsibility for, the long term, in a spirit of mutual trust and respect. There should be only one ultimate criterion for the success or failure in archaeological interactions with Indigenous populations: the population's well-being and sense that conditions have improved as a result of archaeologists working with them.

NOTES

Without the gentle prodding of the editor of this volume, my chapter would not have seen the light of day. I also would like to acknowledge the help of the Closet Chickens (see Sonya Atalay, "Decolonizing Archaeology," *American Indian Quarterly* 30.3–4 [2006]: 269–79) in helping me to learn how archaeologists need to rearticulate their practice. As usual I learned much from discussions with the graduate students and colleagues at the University of Massachusetts Amherst. Since I worked on this essay in the early days of my retirement, I need to make amends to Jude and Kutya for letting me steal away from them to complete it. Any shortcomings in logic are entirely my own.

1. The following works provide a good sense of the interface between Indigenous populations and archaeologists: Sonya Atalay, *Community Based Archaeology: Research with, by, and for Indigenous and Local Communities* (Berkeley: University of California Press, 2012); George P. Nicholas, ed., *Being and Becoming Indigenous Archaeologists* (Walnut Creek, CA: Left Coast, 2010); Stephen W. Silliman, ed., *Collaborating at the Trowel's Edge: Teaching and Learning in Indigenous Archaeology* (Tucson: University of Arizona Press, 2008); Claire Smith and H. Martin Wobst, eds., *Indigenous Archaeologies: Decolonizing Theory and Practice* (London: Routledge, 2005); and Margaret M. Bruchac, Siobhan M. Hart, and H. Martin Wobst, eds., *Indigenous Archaeologies: A Reader on Decolonization* (Walnut Creek, CA: Left Coast, 2010).

2. I have defined these Indigenous groups at greater length in H. Martin Wobst, "Indigenous Archaeologies: A World-Wide Perspective on Human Materialities and Human Rights," in Bruchac, Hart, and Wobst, *Indigenous Archaeologies: A Reader on Decolonization*, 17–28.

3. United Nations Secretariat of the Permanent Forum on Indigenous Issues, "The Concept of Indigenous Peoples," Background Paper, Workshop on Data Collection and Disaggregation for Indigenous Peoples, PFII/2004/WS.1/3, January 21, 2004, available at www.un.org/esa/socdev/unpfii/documents/workshop_data_background.doc.

4. See, for example, Amy Gazin-Schwartz, "Constructing Ancestors: Archaeology and Folklore in Scotland" (PhD diss., University of Massachusetts Amherst, 1999); Amy Gazin-Schwartz and Cornelius Holtorf, eds., *Archaeology and Folklore* (New York: Routledge, 1999); and Joe L. Watkins, *Indigenous Archaeology: American Indian Values and Scientific Practice* (Walnut Creek, CA: AltaMira, 2000).

5. See Glyn Edmund Daniel, *The Origins and Growth of Archaeology* (Harmondsworth: Penguin, 1967); Bruce G. Trigger, *A History of Archaeological Thought* (Cambridge: Cambridge University Press, 1989); and Gordon R. Willey and Jeremy A. Sabloff, *A History of American Archaeology* (New York: W. H. Freeman, 1993).

6. Observe the contrast between the dilettanti in Jason M. Kelly, *The Society of Dilettanti: Archaeology and Identity in the British Enlightenment* (New Haven: Yale University Press, 2009) and the professional archaeologists in a book like Don Brothwell and Eric S. Higgs, eds., *Science in Archaeology* (London: Thames & Hudson, 1969).

7. H. Martin Wobst, "Power to the (Indigenous) Past and Present! Or: The Theory and Method behind Archaeological Theory and Method," in Smith and Wobst, *Indigenous Archaeologies: Decolonizing Theory and Practice*, 17–32.

8. H. Martin Wobst and Claire Smith, "Unothering Theory and Practice in Archaeology," in *Indigenous People and Archaeology: Honouring the Past, Discussing the Present, Building for the Future*, ed. Trevor Peck, Evelyn Siegfried, and Gerald A. Oetelaar (Calgary, AB: The Archaeological Association, 2005), 211–25.

9. Johannes Fabian, *Time and the Other: How Anthropology Makes Its Object* (New York: Columbia University Press, 2002).

10. The increasing logical distance between many archaeologists and Indigenous people during the period in which archaeology turned professional is well covered for many regions. See Margaret M. Bruchac, "Historical Erasure and Cultural Recovery: Indigenous People in the Connecticut Valley" (PhD diss., University of Massachusetts Amherst, 2007) for a particularly powerful investigation of historic scientists helping to make living Native Americans invisible with their work.

11. See Vine Deloria Jr., *Custer Died for Our Sins: An Indian Manifesto* (New York: Macmillan, 1969).

12. Thomas F. King, *Cultural Resource Laws and Practice: An Introductory Guide* (Walnut Creek, CA: AltaMira, 1998); see also the discussion in Joe Watkins's chapter in this volume.

13. Advisory Council for Historic Preservation, *The National Historic Preservation Act of 1966 (as Amended through 2006) with Annotations*, www.achp.gov/docs/nhpa%202008-final.pdf; U.S. Department of the Interior, National Park Service, *Archaeological Resources Protection Act of 1979 as Amended*, www.nps.gov/history/local-law/fhpl_archrsrcsprot.pdf; U.S. Department of the Interior, National Park Service, *The American Indian Religious Freedom Act of 1978*, www.nps.gov/history/local-law/fhpl_indianrelfreact.pdf; U.S. Department of the Interior, National Park Service, *Native American Graves and Repatriation Act*, www.nps.gov/nagpra/mandates/25usc3001etseq.htm.

14. The National Park Service website provides detailed information about the history, context, and present reach of NAGPRA: www.nps.gov/nagpra.

15. On Canada see, for example, Brian Kiers and Catherine Bell, *Canadian Legislation Relating to First Nation Cultural Heritage* (Edmonton: University of Alberta, 2004), www.law.ualberta.ca/research/aboriginalculturalheritage/CanadianLegislation.pdf; on Australia see Claire Smith and Gary Jackson, "Decolonizing Indigenous

Archaeology: Developments from Down Under," *American Indian Quarterly* 30.3–4 (2006): 311–49; on New Zealand see New Zealand Ministry for Culture and Heritage, *Protected Objects Act 1975 No. 41,* www.legislation.govt.nz/act/public/1975/0041 /latest/DLM432116.html; and on South Africa see Sven Ouzman, "Another World: Archaeology and Intellectual Property," *The Digging Stick* 22.2 (2005): 16–17.

16. See George P. Nicholas et al., "Intellectual Property Issues in Heritage Management—Part 1: Challenges and Opportunities Relating to Appropriation, Information Access, Bioarchaeology, and Cultural Tourism," *Heritage Management* 2.1 (2008): 261–86.

17. The approach uses the later periods to help make sense of the periods preceding them, in a kind of reversal of the arrows of history. Its origins go further back than I can discuss here, with an important and relatively early proponent being Waldo R. Wedel; see Wedel, *The Direct-Historical Approach in Pawnee Archaeology,* Smithsonian Miscellaneous Collections 97.7 (Washington, DC: Smithsonian Institution, 1938). It was picked up again in the 1970s and 1980s within the so-called New Archaeology, with many of the participants in Lewis Binford, ed., *New Perspectives in Archaeology* (Chicago: Aldine, 1968) applying it to their data.

18. See Timothy Earle, "Cultural Anthropology and Archaeology: Theoretical Dialogues," in *Handbook of Archaeological Theories,* ed. R. Alexander Bentley, Herbert D. G. Maschner, and Christopher Chippindale (Lanham, MD: AltaMira, 2006), 187–202.

19. "Processual archaeology," or "New Archaeology" as it was often called, is an explicitly scientific (rather than humanist) archaeology that became dominant in the field beginning in the early 1960s, following publications by Lewis R. Binford such as, for example, Binford, "Archaeology as Anthropology," *American Antiquity* 28. 2 (1962): 217–25, and Binford, "A Consideration of Archaeological Research Design," *American Antiquity* 29.4 (1964): 425–41.

20. William A. Longacre, ed., *Ceramic Ethnoarchaeology* (Tucson: University of Arizona Press, 1991); Lewis R. Binford, *Nunamiut Ethnoarchaeology* (New York: Academic Press, 1978); Polly Wiessner, "Hxaro: A Regional System for Reducing Risk among the !Kung San" (PhD diss., University of Michigan, 1977); John E. Yellen, *Archaeological Approaches to the Present: Models for Reconstructing the Past* (New York: Academic Press, 1977).

21. This point is very succinctly supported by the ethnoarchaeological papers in Lewis R. Binford, ed., *For Theory Building in Archaeology: Essays on Faunal Remains, Aquatic Resources, Spatial Analysis, and Systematic Modeling* (New York: Academic Press, 1977).

22. For reviews of early post-processualism in archaeology, see Ian Hodder, "Postprocessual Archaeology," in *Advances in Archaeological Method and Theory,* vol. 8, ed. Michael B. Schiffer (New York: Academic Press, 1985), 1–26; and Mark P. Leone, "Symbolic, Structural, and Critical Archaeology," in *American Archaeology Past and Future: A Celebration of the Society for American Archaeology, 1935–1985,* ed. David

J. Meltzer, Don Fowler, and Jeremy J. Sabloff (Washington, DC: Smithsonian Institution Press, 1986), 415–38.

23. Ian Hodder, *Symbols in Action* (Cambridge: Cambridge University Press, 1982).

24. See H. Martin Wobst, "Artifacts as Social Interference: The Politics of Spatial Scale," in *Confronting Scale in Archaeology: Issues of Theory and Practice*, ed. Gary Lock and Bryan Molyneaux (New York: Springer Verlag, 2006), 55–64.

25. Daniel Miller and Christopher Tilley, "Editorial," *Journal of Material Culture* 1.1 (1996): 1–4.

26. See Chip Colwell-Chanthaphonh and T. J. Ferguson, eds., *Collaboration in Archaeological Practice: Engaging Descendant Communities* (Lanham, MD: AltaMira, 2008); and Claire Smith and Gary Jackson, "Living and Learning on Aboriginal Lands: Decolonizing Archaeology in Practice," in Smith and Wobst, *Indigenous Archaeologies: Decolonizing Theory and Practice*, 336–49.

27. For examples see Ian Hodder, ed., *Archaeology as Long-term History* (Cambridge: Cambridge University Press, 1987); Peter R. Schmidt and Tom Patterson, eds., *Making Alternative Histories: The Practice of Archaeology and History in Non-Western Setting* (Santa Fe, NM: School of American Research, 1995); Alain Schnapp, *The Discovery of the Past* (New York: Harry N. Abrams, 1997); and Trigger, *A History of Archaeological Thought*.

28. See Jane Lydon and Uzma Rizvi, eds., *Handbook of Postcolonial Archaeology* (Walnut Creek, CA: Left Coast, 2010); Ian J. McNiven and Lynette Russell, *Appropriated Pasts: Indigenous Peoples and the Colonial Culture of Archaeology* (Lanham, MD: AltaMira, 2005); and Linda Tuhiwai Smith, *Decolonising Methodologies: Research and Indigenous Peoples* (London: Zed Books, 1999).

29. One of the major banner-carriers for this effort has been the Intellectual Property Issues in Cultural Heritage: Theory, Practice, Policy project, an international collaboration catalyzed by George P. Nicholas (Simon Fraser University), Julie Hollowell (Indiana University), and Kelly Bannister (University of Victoria). Its website, www.sfu.ca/IPinCulturalHeritage, is a rich source of information on what has been accomplished and what yet needs to be done.

30. See H. Martin Wobst, "Descendant Populations and Their Parasites," discussant's comments at the symposium "Current Issues in the Practice of Archaeology in Puerto Rico," at the annual meeting of the Society for American Archaeology, San Juan, Puerto Rico, 2006.

31. See Maria Franklin and Robert Paynter, "Archaeology and Inequality," in *Voices in American Archaeology*, ed. Wendy Ashmore, Dorothy T. Lippert, and Barbara J. Mills (Washington, DC: Society for American Archaeology Press, 2010), 94–30; and Randall H. McGuire, *Archaeology as Political Action* (Berkeley: University of California Press, 2008).

32. For an excellent exposition of this negotiation and give-and-take, see Siobhan B. Hart, "High Stakes: A Poly-communal Archaeology of the Pocumtuck Fort, Deerfield" (PhD diss., University of Massachusetts Amherst, 2009).

33. For an example of a national professional organization's code, see the Australian

Archaeological Association's "Code of Ethics" (2004), www.australianarchaeo logicalassociation.com.au/ethics. The World Archaeological Congress's *Vermillion Accord on Human Remains* (1989) and its *First Code of Ethics* (1990) are available at www.worldarchaeologicalcongress.org/site/about_ethi.php.

34. The Office of Human Subjects of the National Institutes of Health maintains a detailed website on the applicable laws, regulations, and procedures as they apply to the United States; see http://ohsr.od.nih.gov/guidelines/index.html.

35. The website of the Oral History Association (a U.S. organization), at www.oralhis tory.org, maintains a rich collection of information on all aspects of oral history.

36. This caused considerable pain in the Hindmarsh Island case in South Australia, where female secret knowledge resulted in the destruction of Ngarrindjerri sacred sites; see Steven J. Hemming, "Inventing Ethnography," in "Secret Women's Business: The Hindmarsh Affair," ed. Richard Nile and Lyndall Ryan, special issue, *Journal of Australian Studies* 48 (1996): 25–39.

III

NEGOTIATING THE BOUNDARY

6

RE-OWNING THE PAST

DNA and the Politics of Belonging

———⟨∞⟩———

Banu Subramaniam

> Those who do not have power over the story that dominates
> their lives, the power to retell it, rethink it, deconstruct it, joke
> about it, and change it as times change, truly are powerless,
> because they cannot think new thoughts.
>
> —Salman Rushdie, "One Thousand Days in a Balloon" (1991)

THE ESSAYS IN this volume highlight the complexities of ownership and belonging in a world where contested definitions of ownership and commodification loom large, and where multiple histories, colonization, shifting national boundaries, and inequities in wealth and power have created vastly unequal players. The many issues that the authors bring to the table—from the controversies over very material objects like bones and historical objects and artifacts, to more abstract questions of the ownership of intellectual property such as ideas and creative works—force us to examine what we mean by culture as well as ownership, revealing the deep disciplinary differences in these ideas.

This chapter developed out of my interest in the growing industry of genetic genealogical studies—using DNA to tell family, cultural, and national histories. In particular, I was fascinated by a recent controversy in India raised by genetic studies that purported to establish a link between race and caste. These studies reignited old contestations on the country's origin stories. Who are Indians? Where do they come from? Who are the original inhabitants of India? Who are the ancestors of contemporary Indians? The genetic studies added to this long-enduring debate on the origins of the people of India.

As we will see, DNA as an object proves to be both similar and different from the other objects of inquiry discussed in this volume, and as a result raises some new questions about our conceptions of culture, ownership, and belonging. My essay begins with a brief description of the controversy, followed by an exploration of DNA as an object of inquiry and the particular problems it raises for issues of cultural belonging and ownership. I conclude with some insights on the question of DNA and the politics of belonging.

Origin Stories We Tell

I grew up on stories: Indian mythological stories and more "real" stories about the nation and its beginning—about British colonialism, about the horrors of partition, about heroic Indian kings and queens. And there were stories about the history of the subcontinent's origins. One of these stories involved the invasion of the Aryans. As with Indian mythologies, there are many versions of this story—in the public imagination, among politicians and activists, and among academic scholars in the humanities, the social sciences, and the biological sciences. Does the current population of India represent the descendants of an ancient people who arrived there millennia ago? Or do they represent the descendents of many different migrations into South Asia? After all, there have been many incursions into South Asia, the British being the most recent.

The most prevalent narrative, and certainly the one I grew up with, was the orientalist version. It went something like this: The Indian subcontinent was peopled by Dravidians and other aboriginal groups and tribes. The first invasion, and the one with the greatest impact, came from the northwest as Aryans invaded India around 3000–1000 BCE. With them came Sanskrit, which belongs to the family of Indo-European languages. These Aryans are believed to have ushered in the grand Vedic tradition and fueled the development of a distinguished scientific, technological, and philosophical tradition. Many other invasions followed: Persians in 500 BCE, Greeks in 150 BCE, Arab traders in 712 CE, Portuguese in 1510 CE. Finally, of course, were the British in 1610, who came to rule the country for over three hundred years.

Now, the invasion of the Aryans is crucial to the orientalist history, which sees the Aryans as having the greatest impact on Indian history. In the south of India, where I grew up in part, these historical origins and the

Aryan invasion were an important part of explaining the variation in skin color among the population. The south of India, the state of Tamil Nadu in particular, is populated with people who are distinctly dark (indeed some darker than in most parts of Africa), as well as those with much fairer skin, and all possible hues in between. Popular explanations racialized the skin color differences we saw around us. The Aryans, the story went, were fair people, the Dravidians dark-skinned; and Indians from the north of India are generally considered fairer than those from the south. Thus it was said that the Aryans, seen as a superior people, dominated the Dravidians, driving them southward and into the margins of the subcontinent. These groups are seen as the contemporary indigenous peoples in India categorized, for political purposes, as "scheduled" castes and tribes. For someone like me, coming from the south of India and the land of Dravida, speaking the Dravidian language Tamil (which is unrelated to Sanskrit or the Indo-European group of languages), these stories were relevant and deeply personal. The orientalist version also quite skillfully incorporated the caste system and social privilege: upper-caste Tamils are lighter-skinned because they have some Aryan blood in them.

While there is, in fact, plenty of variation if you look around, these stories or mythologies remain strong in the public imagination. But it is important to understand that there is an alternate view of the Aryan invasion/migration theory, one which sees this as a Western construct invented by Europeans and used primarily to lend a scientific rationale to colonial policies, to a racism central to the British colonial empire. For example, the historian Romila Thapar argues that "the notion of the Aryans being a physical people of a distinct biological race, who moved *en masse* and imposed their language on others through conquest, has generally been discarded."[1] The Hindu nationalist movement, in particular, used this line of argument with great enthusiasm.[2] According to this argument, Indians are endogenous to South Asia and there was never any significant Aryan invasion into South Asia. Both versions circulate in the culture's public imagination, and these competing stories are neither trivial nor innocent. They are deeply political, culturally critical threads that weave national identities—of where we came from, of who we are, and of where we want to go. Of whether we are different, and if we are, what meaning we give that difference.

Such stories endure. Scholars in the humanities and social sciences claim evidence of the Aryan invasion—the emergence of the motif of the horse and the chariot—while linguists stress the Indo-European linguistic group that includes English and Sanskrit. How else could we explain these historical facts? But the links between race and caste that have haunted the public imagination since British colonialism have been largely discredited. In its broadest sense, race is said to include any essentializing of groups which are claimed to display inherent, heritable, persistent, or predictive characteristics and which thus had a biological or quasi-biological basis. But any perusal of the genetics of this biological or quasi-biological entity we call "race" will leave most people unconvinced. Historians of science have traced the dubious science of race and caste and the links between race and caste that permeated much of British colonialism. They note the profound political opportunism of the discourse of race and caste that helped the British recruit upper-caste Indians, on the grounds that they were racially and intellectually superior, to govern the rest of their country. The success of the British in India, most historians argue, was their ability to rule India through Indians. Manipulating the complex sociologies of caste and race was part of their strategy to success.

DNA: Telling "Natural" Histories of Our Times

"People are trapped in history and history is trapped in them," James Baldwin wrote in 1955 in *Notes of a Native Son*. Certainly DNA, a material that links all life on earth, is part of the history hidden within us. It is a chemical with remarkable influence—a deoxyribonucleic acid, a double helix with a backbone of sugar and phosphate and a nitrogen base attached to its sugar molecule. It has four nucleobases: adenine, guanine, cytosine, and thymine (A, T, C, G). And it has also emerged as a cultural icon, the hero or heroine of our times, called the "holy grail," the "book of life," the "blueprint of life," or the "secret of life." Its power and influence span most spheres of our existence.

There is a copious literature on DNA and its emergence as the idiom of our times, as the "essence" of individuals, cultures, and nations.[3] We routinely talk metaphorically about the DNA of nations and corporations. In analyzing what Dorothy Nelkin and Susan Lindee call the "DNA mystique," feminist scholars have traced the dense thicket of meaning that develop in the traffic between natures and cultures.[4] Narratives of DNA and genes, they argue, cannot be understood purely within the realms of real or abstract, as material or semiotic, natural or cultural, but must be understood as co-constituted entities and as co-productions. We need to understand objects that are very material, such as our bodies or our DNA, as co-productions of natures and cultures. For example, different human bodies have had very different scientific and cultural understandings at various times in history. Certain groups, such as women, communities of color, and third-world communities, were considered inferior beings because of purported differences in human biology: skulls, brains, or other anatomical, physiological, or behavioral differences.[5] Such sexual, racial, and other differences translated into very real consequences in terms of rights and liberties. Women's perceived inferiority, for example, kept them from the right to vote, own property, and access higher education. Coverture laws denied women the right to their own personhood after marriage.[6] Slavery and colonization were intricately interconnected with scientific theories of racial and sexual difference.[7]

The history of science teaches us that science must be understood as an institution embedded in its historical, economic, and cultural contexts and that knowledge is always socially embedded (see also the chapters by Margaret Speas and H. Martin Wobst in this volume). Furthermore, objects such as DNA have another level of complexity. As Donna Haraway suggests, we need to think of such objects as "naturecultures" rather than as natures *and* cultures.[8] DNA is a material object that is passed down through generations. But its passage is a deeply social story. Who reproduces with whom? Which communities have the resources to reproduce? What is the quality of survival and health in different groups? Which communities succumb to illnesses or epidemics? Who dies in wars and battles? Each of these "social" factors shapes the histories of DNA; we cannot separate the biological history from its social history.

These complex circulations of DNA are deeply apparent in the emergence of migration stories rooted in the evidence in our DNA. Using DNA sequences, scientists have begun to narrate stories about the origins and migrations of humans. The international Genographic Project launched by the National Geographic Society, the HapMap Project, and the now discontinued Human Genome Diversity Project all sought to trace human migrations through DNA. The most popular of these have been two public-television documentaries, Spencer Wells's *Journey of*

Man (2003) and Henry Louis Gates's miniseries *African American Lives* (2006 and 2008). Indeed, there has emerged a cottage industry of personal genealogy companies—you send them off a cheek swab and they return with your genealogical roots. These have proved popular and led to the emergence of the field of "recreational genetics." These scientists would contend that our DNA sequences are living histories—remnants of the story of our historical migrations, couplings, exterminations, and proliferation.

The Genetics of Race and Caste

In June 2001, the following headline graced the pages of *Frontline: India's National Magazine*: "New Genetic Evidence for the Origin of Castes Indicates That the Upper Castes Are More European Than Asian."[9] The same summer, the United Nations sponsored the World Conference against Racism, Racial Discrimination, Xenophobia, and Related Intolerance, held in Durban, South Africa, from August 31 to September 7. A controversy involving India's participation surrounded this conference, bringing the purported links between caste and race to the fore of Indian politics. Dalits, members of an oppressed group of the caste system in India, wanted to take the matter of the continuing brutality of the caste system to the World Conference against Racism. They argued that caste discrimination against Dalits (the word literally means crushed and broken) has continued to the present day, affecting over 160 million in India, and that the Indian government must be held accountable through international attention and monitoring. According to Smita Narula of the international group Human Rights Watch, caste discrimination was a "hidden apartheid" that affected more than 250 million people in India, Nepal, Sri Lanka, Bangladesh, Pakistan, and Japan.[10] The Indian government disagreed. They argued that caste was not race and therefore ought not to be discussed at the UN conference on racism. Hindu nationalist leaders closely associated with the party then in power, the Bharatiya Janata Party (BJP), "added fuel to the fire by declaring that caste was a part of India's ancient traditions—and could not be discussed at international fora."[11]

    Science has long played a critical role in the development of the idea of race and racial ideology (see for example, Joe Watkins's essay in this volume). In keeping with the long history of scientific studies on race, scientific evidence (as cited in the *Frontline* headline, for example) became an important part of this controversy over the purported link between race and caste. A group of scientists led by Michael Bamshad of the Eccles Institute of Human Genetics at the University of Utah, along with other scientists from Estonia, India, the United Kingdom, and the United States, had published a joint article just a few months before reporting evidence that upper castes in India were more closely related to Europeans and lower castes more closely related to West Asians.[12] As one of the authors, Lynne Jorde, put it, "Groups of males with European affinities were largely responsible for this invasion 3,000–4,000 years ago."[13] Dalit groups used this scientific study to argue that caste was analogous to race and therefore merited a hearing at the World Conference. Extending the long history of controversies on the biological significance of race, we have in the new millennium yet another claim about science's incontrovertible evidence in deciding an issue, in this instance to bring attention to the suffering of an oppressed group.

The controversy highlights the difficulties of viewing DNA evidence as an easy binary of natural versus unnatural, scientific versus unscientific. The transmission of DNA down the generations is literally implicated in the complex histories of gender, race, class, caste, and sexuality. Who reproduces, how many children they have, who survives, who migrates, who lives and who dies—these are all deeply social and political questions. Biological transmission of DNA across the generations is therefore deeply implicated in the social histories of groups. In the next section, I explore why and how the natural and cultural intertwine in narratives of cultural ownership and belonging of DNA. In order to understand the ensuing controversies on the genetics of caste and race, it is important to appreciate the complexities of the history of India, of religious nationalism, secularism, and the histories of race, caste, and genetics—all of which are intertwined in the material body of DNA.

(Un)Natural Histories: Reading Race and Caste in DNA

Developing origin stories of a nation through "reading" the DNA of its population is a quintessential interdisciplinary project. It reveals the common goals and methods across fields as well as the many synergies and confluences. After all, multiple fields have the same goal—producing an origin story for a nation. Donna Haraway puts this eloquently in arguing that "biology is inherently historical, and its form of discourse is inherently narrative":

> Biology as a way of knowing the world is kin to Romantic literature, with its discourse about organic form and function. Biology is the fiction appropriate to objects called organisms; biology fashions the facts discovered from organic beings. Organisms perform for the biologist, who transforms that performance into a truth attested by disciplined experience; i.e., into a fact, the jointly accomplished deed or feat of the scientists and the organism. Romanticism passes into realism, and realism into naturalism, genius into progress, insights into fact. Both the scientist and the organism are actors in a story telling practice.[14]

As genetic studies have continued to proliferate, from biopharmaceutical invocations of race-based medicine, to recreational genetics, through markers that have spanned the mitochondrial and nuclear DNA, researchers have begun to reweave new stories of identity and belonging. Many scholars and activists are deeply troubled by the primacy and uncritical acceptance of a "new regime of biologism" emerging through genetics, which is similar to the scientism discussed by Wobst and Watkins in this volume.[15] We have "mitochondrial Eve" and "Y chromosomal Adam," the invocation of a common humanity "out of Africa," and the promise of a "global genome" with tantalizing similarities and significant differences rife with the politics of gender, race, class, colonialism, and nationhood, speeding up the stories of our genomic era faster than we can process them.

One of the particular challenges of DNA as an object, and one that distinguishes it from others, is that DNA is inherited and shared with "blood" relatives, families, and communities; the closer the relationship, the greater the similarities. Furthermore, DNA and its parts (genes/sequences) can be commodified, patented, and owned. The challenges and consequences of the commodification of DNA have been explored elsewhere, but they raise important questions—who has a right to DNA when it is shared by many?[16] Scholars have highlighted the limits of a liberal individual-rights framework in questions of rights and ownership.[17] Indeed, the Human Genome Diversity Project collapsed in part because of the difficulties of consensus on defining ownership and rights to the DNA.[18] This controversy, however, focused less on issues of ownership and rights, and more on the way different groups deployed the Bamshad study's conclusions for political ends, both domestic and international.

In analyzing the controversy, it seems critical to first understand what the Bamshad study claimed and more importantly what it *could* claim. What can DNA research show us about human migration patterns and about our belonging to various groups and nations? DNA is a material-semiotic object par excellence. DNA is indeed passed down through generations and is therefore a real material link to history. Yet how scientists go about studying it—the methodological and especially statistical assumptions they need to make—are significant. Furthermore, DNA is unique in that it is not passed down without social context; the politics of gender, race, class, and nation are literally written into the history of DNA. In the next section, I outline some of the challenges in using DNA as an object of study.

The Process of "Reading" DNA

Scientists follow a standard protocol in genealogical studies. Typically they take a cheek swab of an individual, and the DNA is then sequenced. The idea is to sample the individuals alive today in order to ascertain whom they are most closely related to, as well as to develop a history of human migration. In studying human history through genes, scientists examine particular sequences of DNA—markers—and in general focus on three main sources of DNA: nuclear, mitochondrial, and Y chromosomes. The latter two have proved particularly invaluable to genealogical studies. Mitochondrial DNA (mtDNA) is maternally inherited, although some evidence questions this strict inheritance.[19] The mutation rate of mtDNA is ten times that of nuclear DNA; therefore there are more genetic differences at the individual level. Since it is maternally inherited, there is believed to be no recombination (although some dispute this claim).[20] A mutation that arises is therefore passed on to the next generation, and such changes can be traced across the generations. The Y chromosome in contrast is paternally inherited; it is considered to be one of the sex chromosomes and is usually present only in males. The Y chromosome is quite small, with very few functional genes, and for this reason there is little selective pressure or known recombination with the X. As a result, it is passed down the male line exclusively and, again, has proven to be a useful source. Markers in the nuclear DNA are also often included in addition to the other two. Scientists use the variation in these loci and sequences to reconstruct family trees and genealogies of individuals, families, and populations.

Tracing the history of DNA sequences is a nifty technological technique. But as with most scientific studies, the discourses and implications within the published scientific realm and the political-social realm can be quite disparate. Carefully constructed and often narrow results are frequently transformed into sensational and more generalized headlines in popular journals, and they are often sensationalized by the same scientists.

Methodological Issues: The Invisible Assumptions

A close examination of the unspoken methodological and statistical assumptions that underlie studies like the one conducted by Bamshad and his coauthors reveals several areas of concern.

Sample sizes: Studies of genealogy often have very small sample sizes for the grand histories they attempt to tell. The Bamshad study sampled only 265 men. The size of one caste population, the Kshatriyas, in one comparison is as small as 10.[21] Writing grand narratives from such small samples is troubling. This is not atypical; grand claims and attempts at rewriting national histories rest on surprisingly tantalizing and slim evidence.

Population biology and alternate hypotheses: Extrapolating thousands of years of history from varying sources of DNA often leads to contradictory data. What are the histories of these populations? Were they homogeneous? How large were they at different times? Were there significant migrations? Were there any major natural disasters or diseases that might have wiped out particular populations? As Alan Rogers argues, in order to interpret the DNA of the living, we must make assumptions about population biology and history, the actions of natural selection, population size, genetic drift, and migration timelines, to name just a few variables.[22] It is not often easy to tell them apart. Making sense of migration histories through genetics requires many such assumptions, making it a particularly contentious field. What are we reading in this history? Historical artifact or a legitimate interpretation?

Determining the "correct" family tree: The construction of family trees and genealogies is largely a statistical process. Depending on which markers one considers, different family trees are possible, and different genealogies emerge. Determining the "correct" tree often involves making assumptions and decisions about which variables are studied, which markers are most significant, the degree to which the loci are variable, and so forth. Often there is no consistent use of the same markers across genetic studies. As a result, it is common to find multiple genealogies and narratives of migrations emerging, each of which is prone to contest. In the Bamshad study, the researchers used multiple loci and multiple sources of DNA to develop their reconstructed genealogies. They compared mtDNA and Y chromosomes of 265 males from eight different caste ranks to 750 individuals—Africans, Asians, Europeans, and other Indians. Collectively, their data show "a trend towards upper castes being more similar to Europeans, whereas lower castes are more similar to Asians." Their conclusion was that "Indian castes are most likely to be of proto-Asian origin with West Eurasian admixture resulting in rank-related and sex-specific differences in the genetic affinities of cases to Asians and Europeans."[23] It is this conclusion that began the controversy. Dalits used the genetic evidence to make claims for a global citizenship—a global brotherhood among blacks across the world. It must also be noted that the categories used here— "Europeans," "Asians," "Africans"—are used very uncritically. Researchers work with databanks already in existence to find base populations they can compare their studies with. Often the comparisons are across categories of analysis that are not analogous; for example, a caste population from Andhra Pradesh in India is compared to a population from an entire continent, such as "Europe." Yet such comparisons and conclusions are unfortunately ubiquitous in genealogical literature.

Partial histories: Because they are exclusively maternally and paternally inherited, mtDNA and Y chromosomes provide a unique methodological benefit. But this characteristic creates its own problems, in particular in questions of sampling, since mtDNA and Y chromosomes each trace only one genetic line on a family tree. As Carl Elliot and Paul Brodwin note, "Y chromosome tracing will connect a man to his father but not to his mother, and it will connect him to only one of his four grandparents: his paternal grandfather. In the same way, it will connect him to one of his eight great grandparents and one of his 16 great great grandparents. Continue back in this manner for 14 generations and the man will still be connected to only one ancestor in that generation. The test will not connect him to any of the other 16,363 ancestors in that generation to whom he is also related in equal measure."[24]

Sampling such a genealogy gives us partial histories. It can tell us about the presence of an ancient ancestor, but what it does not to tell us about is the absences: the ancestors who, through the vagaries of history, are not retained in the individual DNA's material history. Such partial data, such partial evidence, cannot and should not stand for the truth of history. We should also note which markers are being used, namely the mtDNA and Y chromosomes. Y chromosomes, for example, represent only 1 percent of a person's DNA. Rewriting national histories on the basis of a small section of the DNA (when other markers give alternate histories) is troubling.

Disciplinary Issues: The Tangles of Nature and Culture

How can you do disciplinary research with an interdisciplinary "boundary" object such as DNA? This is fundamentally a problem that such research raises. Nature and culture are so intertwined, so embedded in each other, that producing a narrative of one without considering the other proves problematic if not nonsensical. The histories of genetics, race, and caste add further complications to this narrative.

Essentializing/naturalizing social constructs: In each of these genetic studies, the researchers begin with socially constructed categories—caste, race, nation, and so forth. By the end of the study, these categories have been reified and rendered "natural" through science. This is particularly problematic in a context like India. India as we know it today is a recent invention, created in 1947, after gaining independence from British colonial rule. Before colonialism, the Indian subcontinent was home to a heterogeneous and diverse collection of rulers and kingdoms, with no common religions, traditions, cultures, languages, or ideologies. In the context of South Asia, a site of tremendous political mobility, transience, and conflict for many centuries, the uncritical use in genetic studies of such categories—which are not homogeneous, and present unique histories and complexities—requires closer examination. By ignoring these complexities, studies like Bamshad's ultimately reinforce the social categories as natural and biologically significant.

What is a caste? One of the recurrent problems in the literature is the use of the term "population." In the Bamshad study, the researchers compared mtDNA and Y chromosomes of 265 males from eight different caste ranks in one southern state, Andhra Pradesh. The researchers used these samples to claim something unique about caste patterns in one region of India and of a certain caste population. Yet in their conclusion and in subsequent papers and reports, these results have been used to make larger claims about caste in India, such as in the *Frontline* headline mentioned earlier, where the claims are now made for the caste system all over India. Are caste and caste hierarchies in one region of India similar to those all over India?

Social scientists studying caste in India present a much more complex picture. Indeed, the system is as complicated as it is contested.[25] The term "caste" is believed to have been introduced by the Portuguese in the sixteenth century.[26] It is an elaborate system with a complex and long history. Overall, it has two elements: *Jathis,* the endogamous community often defined by occupation, geography; and *Varna,* a broader category of contemporary caste. The varnas include four main castes: *Brahmin,* the priestly caste; *Ksatriya,* the warrior class; *Vaisya,* the merchant class; and *Sudra,* the lowest of the four classes. The system further splinters into subcastes; India is said to have about 3,000 or so subcastes. The Dalits, often called the untouchables, represented individuals who were considered outside the caste system. In some schemes, they are included as a fifth class, the *pancham.*[27]

The caste system is considered the "largest social system ever designed," one that has produced distinct inbreeding communities.[28] In practice, it has been the defining factor that affects individual and groups in India throughout their lives. It affects all aspects of life—religious, social, economic, and political. The caste system is believed to have evolved as populations grew, and become more and more intricate and elaborate by being rigidly defined and perpetuated by division of labor and specialization of profession on the one hand, and religious and commensal practices and marriage rules (endogamy) on the other. There are innumerable theories on the origins of caste—about when, where, and how. But most historians seem to believe that caste predated the British colonial rule, although that period certainly shaped and consolidated the hierarchical nature of the caste system that we see in modern India in very particular ways.[29] The consolidation and practice of caste in the recent past must be understood within such a colonial interpretation and legacy.

But while the caste system permeates all of India, it is less clear what "caste" means. Is someone of lower caste in the south of India analogous to someone in a northern state? Caste, according to Dipanker Gupta, is a much more fluid, mobile system than popular and even academic mythography would have us believe. As Gupta writes, "It is more realistic to say that there are probably as many hierarchies as there are castes in India. To believe that there is a single caste order to which every caste, from Brahman to untouchable, acquiesces ideologically, is a gross misreading of facts on the ground. . . . As the 'book view' of the caste system is derived largely from sacerdotal Hindu texts, members of the upper castes find it extremely agreeable. . . . Nevertheless, the difference between the book view and what actually happens on the ground is quite remarkable." The Brahminical dictum of the established four castes that has disciplined all Indians into submission, Gupta argues, is patently false. Instead he maintains that we have seen throughout history both caste revolts and caste mobility.[30] Given the complex realities on the ground, the uncritical use of caste populations is troublesome and misleading.

Genetic natures/genetic cultures: Our inability to understand the interrelationship between nature and culture permeates genetic discourse. There were strong reactions both from supporters and opponents in the debate over bringing the case of caste discrimination to the UN's conference on racism based on the genetic evidence. I argue that both sides conflated genetic natures and cultures. This conflation of nature and culture comes from a long history of biological determinism. After all, for both race and caste, science has played a central role in translating cultural privilege into biological superiority. Conversely, the vast history of colonialism and racism shows how claims of biological superiority in turn translate into claims of social superiority and privilege. Those who balk at the conclusions of the Bamshad study and the analogy it sets up between race and caste are troubled by the way the two are historically enmeshed. Racial histories get written onto caste histories. The strong strain of biological determinism that undergirds the ways in which genetic research is publicized lies at the heart of the trouble. When the British or upper-caste Indians claim Aryan ancestry, are they not implicitly claiming racial superiority? Adding racial superiority to the problem of caste superiority compounds the problem. Since genealogical studies of DNA focus on non-coding regions of the DNA, they cannot and should not be connected to any claims of behavioral, intellectual, or physiological functions. Class and race are biologically problematic categories, but socially potent forces.

One of the striking features of contemporary Indian politics is the centrality of caste politics. Dalit activists have worked for a long time to create international alliances and highlight the oppressive nature of the caste system. Even before the rise of Hindu nationalist parties such as the BJP, secular parties have unashamedly infused religion into national politics. In the name of secularism and the support of minority communities, they have pitted religious communities against each other and courted minority groups—only to fail them once in power. Religious and secular parties have used casteism, sexism, and classism in their efforts to secure power. This has led to the rise in caste- and religion-based politics. As a result, Dalit and other minority groups have mobilized to create political parties of their own and now wield considerable power in an increasingly fragmented national government. Such regional and small parties have grown in power and stature and their support has proved crucial to various governing coalitions. Thus the rise of Dalit and other caste-based parties has become a phenomenon to be reckoned with in contemporary India.[31] Whether these groups are strategically using essentialist ideas to create a more potent political international movement, or are making these claims because of a belief in such analogies between race and caste, is up for debate. But the analogies of race and caste continue, now bolstered by the authority accorded to DNA studies like Bamshad's.

The strategy of claiming links between race and caste also goes back decades. Dalit groups continue to build a transnational movement as they internationalize the struggle against caste oppression by calling themselves "the black untouchables of India" and building solidarity with black resistance movements across the world.[32] A group called the Dalit Panthers are "south Asian branch of the Black Panthers of America." By aligning themselves with the Black Panthers and with black social movements around the world, Dalit groups are attempting to create a global black brotherhood/sisterhood that resists a common oppression. These alliances are not new. African American political activists in the 1930s and 1940s spoke out strongly in favor of Indian independence and drew direct connections between anticolonial nationalism in India and the elimination of racial discrimination and the demand for full citizenship of African Americans in the United States. A group of African American and Dalit scholars are at work in creating an "Afro-Dalit" literature that draws on the similarities in the histories and lives of African and Dalit peoples.[33]

The History and Reemergence of the Politics of Race and Caste

In 1901 the colonial government of India undertook what a modern writer calls "the greatest ever exercise in human nose-counting": the third complete census of its Indian provinces:

> Her Majesty's Indian subjects were being counted, sifted and sorted. The Census of India was on. Census commissioner Sir Herbert Risley noticed that upper caste Hindus were fair and had sharp noses. Since these are among the distinguishing features of the "white man"—caucasoids—he figured there may be a relationship between the two. To make this scientific, he took a few measurements. The methodology: measure nose length, divide by nose breadth, and call the number arrived at the "nasal index." The conclusion, of course, was that upper caste Hindus are distant relatives of Englishmen who have been out in the sun a few centuries.[34]

Within the context of South Asia, studies and conceptions of race include anthropological, linguistic and philological, and ethnolinguistic analyses addressing such characteristics as skin color, language, body type, religious identity, and caste. Modern genetic studies are but the newest incarnation in a history of race and caste classification. One can see that the idea of race at various times is used to explain these differences. Perhaps it is not surprising, as Gail Omvedt suggests, that because the British colonized India at a time when racist concepts were flourishing, when they were confronted with the puzzling phenomenon of caste they interpreted it in racial terms.[35] The links between caste and race thus have a long and tortuous history.

At the time of the UN conference on racism in 2001, newspaper headlines trumpeted "Casteism Is the Mother of Racism" and "Caste Is a Variety of Race." One of the difficulties of analogizing caste with race is that race has its own sets of histories and meanings. Race means many things in many contexts. Indeed, all kinds of social hierarchies have been "racialized." Science has played a central part in the development of racial theories; craniometry, morphology, facial characteristics, skin color, skeletal structures, and blood have all been used to define and consolidate racial differences. Twentieth-century U.S. history shows twenty-six different racial terms or categories used to identify populations in the U.S. census.[36] Such racial analyses remind us of both the limits of power and the dominance of science. For despite decades of refutations of the scientific evidence, decades of critiques and denunciations, decades of declarations of the "biological insignificance" of race, race lives on as a potent social, political, cultural, and economic category. We see this in the recent revival of "ethnic drugs" tailored for different races and in the resurgence of biological claims that some racial groups are genetically predisposed to diseases such as hypertension, diabetes, and heart disease.[37] Race is back again in the scientific and medical imagination with renewed vigor. To me, this is a reminder that nature and culture are not binary opposites, but rather always co-constituted and co-produced.

The tensions of race as a biological versus a social category persist in the debates on the relationship of race and caste. On the one hand, the social anthropologist Andre Beteille, a member of India's National Committee on World Conference against Racism, reifies race in some comments he made during the pre-conference controversy: "Race is a biological category having distinctive physical markers whereas caste is a social category. The consequences of this proposed inclusion of caste at the UN conference will be to add more divisions in Indian society. We have enough divisions based on language, religion and caste, which we have to address. So we don't need to fabricate or invent yet another based on race."[38] Here race is defined as biological and caste as social.

On the other hand, many theorists and social activists, including Dalit activists, point to both race and caste as potent systems of social stratification. As Ambrose Pinto observes, "Prejudice and discrimination are both a part of caste and race. And what is worse is that such prejudice and discrimination are not merely personal but institutional, a part of the structure and process of the whole society. In both caste and race theories, the so-called higher or superior groups take the attitude that their culture is superior to all other cultures, and that all the other groups should be judged according to their culture. What is the difference between the claims made by the white race in Europe and the upper castes in India?"[39] Others, like Dipanker Gupta, instead stress the many differences between race and caste, such as the way the idea of pollution is central to the caste system, but is largely absent from race. Similarly, race is a "global" construct that categorizes people across continents, whereas caste is much more localized.[40] An illustrative example Gupta cites is endogamous marriage, where caste loyalties gain in strength the more localized and particularized they get. It is not enough, he argues, to be a "Brahman," but rather a Brahman of a certain "endogamous jati," and in many cases even further subdivisions and localized identities become critical. The broad categories of caste that are highlighted in the studies do not capture the lived realities and are not analogous across the country.

It is within this cauldron of contested meanings—India, religion, race, caste, science, genes—that the genetic study by Bamshad and his colleagues emerged. While the Dalits fought to include caste discrimination in the conference and the government fought against its inclusion, intellectuals on both sides of the case joined the debate. Some argued the position of the government, others that of the Dalits, and yet others pointed out that while caste discrimination was a horrendous practice, we must be intellectually honest and not confuse "race," already a biologically dubious concept, with caste. Andre Beteille resigned from the National Committee on World Conference against Racism in protest over this issue. He suggested that treating caste as a form of race is "politically mischievous and scientifically nonsensical," adding, "Not content with condemning racism and racial discrimination, the UN now wants to take on racialism, racial discrimination and xenophobia and related intolerance. It has in its wisdom decided to expand the meeting on racial discrimination to accommodate exclusion or preference 'based on race, colour, descent, or national or ethnic origin.' In doing so it is bound to give a new lease of life to the old discredited notion of race that was current a hundred years ago." He concluded, "We cannot throw out the concept of race by the front door when it is being misused for asserting social superiority and bring it again through the back door to misuse it in the cause of the oppressed."[41]

The Politics of History and the Challenges of Interdisciplinarity

This controversy demonstrates the way that new genetic technology gets embroiled in the old politics of race and caste as well as in longstanding debates that pit the sciences against the humanities. Yet we need to remember that biology and society, science and politics, are not binary opposites but rather co-constituted. As Donna Haraway reminds us, "We need the power of modern critical theories of how meanings and bodies get made, not in order to deny meaning and bodies, but in order to live in meanings and bodies and have a chance for a future."[42]

Instead of answering the question of the relationship between race and caste, genetic studies like Bamshad's prompt still more questions. What seems most significantly lacking in this discussion is why these questions are important. If the Aryan invasion did indeed take place, does that justify millennia of caste prejudice? And what bearing should such an age-old event have on the future of South Asian culture and politics? Does the proving or disproving of the genetic basis of caste serve to justify inequality, inequity, and a disproportionate access to power and education for fair-skinned Indo-Aryans over their darker Dravidian neighbors?

Within the academy, the old politics of disciplinarity have reemerged in two different areas. First, disciplines seem to have to compete to produce the "correct" history. Science, and in particular genetics, the contemporary currency of scientific modernity, help valorize certain political positions. Humanists and social scientists counter with their critiques of science and the salience of their own disciplinary work. To me, this controversy displays perhaps most importantly the limits of disciplinary research. While I am resolutely critical of the new biologism, what is striking is that there is little room for multiple histories, for multiple disciplines to provide correct answers. After all, genetic histories may not correspond with linguistic or archaeological histories. Languages may diffuse differently and leave different marks on history than genes might.[43] As long as they are methodologically rigorous, might not each of these partial histories give us useful information? There is very little in the disciplinary debates that leaves room for such a possibility. Yet DNA seems the ideal object through (or with) which to consider the interconnections of nature and culture, of the biological and the social. This in turn raises the question broached earlier—how to conduct disciplinary research on an interdisciplinary object like DNA. Ultimately, it would seem that our meaning lies not only in our genes, our politics, our identity, or our history, but in all of them.

Fundamentally, these debates on the relationship of race and caste point to contestations of the relationship between nature and culture. They also point to the conflation of our genetic natures and cultures, of the ways in which genetic and cultural arguments get pulled into old and familiar political debates. Who we are depends on what authority we give nature or culture, what authority we give to our interpretations of nature and culture, and what meanings we choose to give those in our lives and our world. Genetic technologies have moved out of research laboratories into public life, and with them arise necessary debates about their proper use and interpretation.[44] We see genetic technologies used in forensic medicine, in predicting disease susceptibility, and more recently in tracing ancestry. Many companies already "sell" genetic genealogies. One such company, DNA PrintGenomics, says its tests will be useful "for people interested in their own origins as well as for more practical purposes," such as "to validate your eligibility for race-based college admission or government entitlements."[45] Given what we know about these technologies, what if a person whose family has lived as "white" for generations finds that she has African ancestry? Is she now "African American"?

These cutting-edge genetic technologies ignore the complex understandings that questions of race and caste require.[46] Yet, as the case of caste and the World Conference against Racism demonstrates, there may be little control over how these results are interpreted, used, understood, and deployed, no longer just by geneticists and population biologists, but also by political activists as well as those individuals claiming inclusion in a particular ethnic, racial, or national group. Who decides to accept or reject their claims? Genetic marker claims purport to reveal long-term generational connections, but people have always used a knowledge of ancestry to illuminate social connections with the present. Paul Brodwin uses the example of the Lemba, a tribe in South Africa and Zimbabwe who believed they were descendents of Semitic peoples. Genetic studies supported these claims, and the Lemba interpreted the findings as confirmation of their oral tradition of Jewish descent.[47] But does this mean that they are Jews?

Such claims of identity and ancestry cannot be reduced to genetic or biological simplifications but must necessarily be complex, grounded in the multifaceted lived realities of our histories. To understand migration and identity, we need interdisciplinary research in which genetic research is grounded in complex political and historical contexts. After all, despite all the power of science, the Indian State won in the fight over the inclusion of caste in the World Conference against Racism: caste was not included.

But I doubt this will be the end of this story. Tracing claims of ownership tells us about the complex machinations of power. As the essays in this volume demonstrate, cultural ownership, like the helical spirals of DNA, is intertwined and enmeshed in the complexities of biology, history, and culture. The helix winds on, to weave and reweave the complexities of life, identity, ownership and belonging in the twenty-first century.

NOTES

1. Romila Thapar, "The First Millennium B.C. in North India," in *Recent Perspectives of Early Indian History*, ed. Thapar (Bombay: Popular Prakashan, 1995), 87–150, quotation on 95–96.

2. See Edwin Bryant, *The Quest for the Origins of Vedic Culture: The Indo-Aryan Migration Debate* (Oxford: Oxford University Press, 2001).

3. See, for example, Elizabeth Parthenia Shea, *How the Gene Got Its Groove: Figurative Language, Science, and the Rhetoric of the Real* (Albany: State University of New York Press, 2008).

4. Dorothy Nelkin and Susan Lindee, *The DNA Mystique: The Gene as a Cultural Icon* (Ann Arbor: University of Michigan Press, 2004).

5. Londa Schiebinger, *The Mind Has No Sex? Women in the Origins of Modern Science* (Cambridge: Harvard University Press, 1991); Sandra Harding, ed., *The "Racial" Economy of Science: Toward a Democratic Future* (Bloomington: Indiana University Press, 1993).

6. Mary R. Beard, *Woman as Force in History* (New York: Macmillan, 1946).

7. Sally Markowitz, "Pelvic Politics: Sexual Dimorphism and Racial Difference," *Signs* 26 (2009): 389–414.

8. Donna Haraway, *How Like a Leaf: An Interview with Thyrza Nichols Goodve* (New York: Routledge, 2000).

9. R. Ramachandran, "New Genetic Evidence for the Origin of Castes Indicates That

the Upper Castes Are More European Than Asian," *Frontline* 18.12 (June 9, 2001).

10. Smita Narula, "Caste Discrimination," in *Exclusion: A Symposium on Caste, Race, and the Dalit Question,* December 2001, www.india-seminar.com/2001/508/508%20 smita%20narula.htm.

11. Ranjit Devrag, "Study on Caste's Origins in Race Undercuts Government Stance," www.ipsnews.net/2001/08/rights-india-study-on-castes-origins-in-race-undercuts -govt-stance/.

12. Michael Bamshad et al., "Genetic Evidence on the Origins of Indian Caste Populations," *Genome Research* 11.6 (2001): 994–1004.

13. Quoted in Robert Cooke, "Genetic Studies Confirm an Aryan Invasion of India," *Seattle Times,* June 13, 1999.

14. Donna Haraway, *Primate Visions: Gender, Race, and Nature in the World of Modern Science* (New York: Routledge, 1989), 4–5.

15. See, for example, David Skinner, "Racialized Futures: Biologism and the Changing Politics of Identity," *Social Studies of Science* 36.3 (2006): 459–88.

16. See Kimberly TallBear, "DNA, Blood, and Racializing the Tribe," *Wicazo Sa Review* 18.1 (2003): 81–107.

17. David Resnik, *Owning the Genome: A Moral Analysis of DNA Patenting* (Albany: State University of New York Press, 2004); Mario Biagioli, Peter Jaszi, and Martha Voodmansee, eds., *Making and Unmaking Intellectual Property: Creative Production in Legal and Cultural Perspective* (Chicago: University of Chicago Press, 2011).

18. Jenny Reardon, "Democratic Mis-haps: The Problem of Democratization in a Time of Biopolitics," *BioSocieties* 2 (2007): 239–56.

19. Andrew Morris and Robert N. Lightowlers, "Can Paternal mtDNA Be Inherited?," *The Lancet* 355 (April 15, 2000): 1290–91.

20. Ibid.

21. Bamshad et al., "Genetic Evidence on the Origins of Indian Caste Populations."

22. Alan Rogers, "Order Emerging from Chaos in Human Evolutionary Genetics," *Proceedings of the National Academy of Sciences* 98.3 (2001): 779–80.

23. Bamshad et al., "Genetic Evidence on the Origins of Indian Caste Populations," 994.

24. Carl Elliott and Paul Brodwin, "Identity and Genetic Ancestry Tracing," *BMJ* 325 (2002): 1469–71, quotation on 1470.

25. My discussion draws on Rama S. Singh, "The Indian Caste System," in *Thinking about Evolution: Historical, Philosophical, and Political Perspectives,* ed. Rama S. Singh, Costas B. Krimbas, Diane B. Paul, and John Beatty (Cambridge: Cambridge University Press, 2000), 152–83.

26. Stephan Palmié argues that the "caste" concept in India came with the Portuguese, who transferred the Latin American usages of the term *casta* to the Indian subcontinent. See "The 'C-Word' Again: From Colonial to Postcolonial Semantics," in *Creolization: History, Ethnography, Theory,* ed. Charles C. Stewart (Walnut Creek, CA: Left Coast, 2007), 78n11.

27. Joanna L. Mountain et al., "Demographic History of India and mtDNA-Sequence Diversity," *American Journal of Human Genetics* 56 (1995): 979–92, esp. 979.

28. Singh, "The Indian Caste System," 152.

29. Nicholas Dirks, *Castes of Mind: Colonialism and Making of Modern India* (Princeton: Princeton University Press, 2001).

30. Dipanker Gupta, *Interrogating Caste: Understanding Hierarchy and Difference in Indian Society* (Delhi: Penguin, 2000), 1–2.

31. Celia W. Dugger, "Why Governments Tumble: India's Poorest Are Becoming Its Loudest," *New York Times,* April 25, 1999.

32. See V. T. Rajshekar, *Dalit: The Black Untouchables of India* (Atlanta: Clarity Press, 2009).

33. Vijay Prashad, "Afro-Dalits of the Earth, Unite!," *African Studies Review* 43.1 (April 2000): 189–201.

34. Supriya Bezbaruah and Samrat Choudhury, "White India," *India Today,* July 30, 2003, 64–66.

35. Gail Omvedt, "The UN, Racism and Caste II," *The Hindu,* April 10, 2001; see also *Dirks, Castes of Mind.*

36. American Anthropological Association, "Response to OMB Directive 15: Race and Ethnic Standards for Federal Statistics and Administrative Reporting," at www .aaanet.org/gvt/ombdraft.htm.

37. Dorothy Roberts, *Fatal Invention: How Science, Politics, and Big Business Re-create Race in the Twenty-First Century* (New York: New Press, 2011).

38. Quoted in Subhash Gatade, "Durban and the Indian Elite," *Himal South Asian,* July 14, 2001, www.dspace.cam.ac.uk/retrieve/533060/HSA_14_07_2001.pdf.

39. Ambrose Pinto, "Caste Is a Variety of Race," *The Hindu,* March 24, 2001.

40. Dipankar Gupta, "Case, Race, Politics," *Seminar* 508 (December 2001), www.india-seminar.com/2001/508/508%20dipankar%20gupta.htm.

41. Quoted in Naunidhi Kaur, "Caste and Race," *Frontline* 18.13 (June 23, 2001).

42. Donna Haraway, *Simians, Cyborgs, and Women: The Reinvention of Nature* (New York: Routledge, 1991), 187.

43. Thapar, "The First Millennium B.C. in North India"; Bryant, *Quest for the Origins of Vedic Culture.*

44. See Paul Brodwin, "Genetics, Identity, and the Anthropology of Essentialism," *Anthropological Quarterly* 75 (2002): 323–30.

45. Quoted in Amy Harmon, "Seeking Ancestry, and Privilege, in DNA Ties Uncovered by Tests," *New York Times,* April 12, 2006.

46. See Abha Sur and Samir Sur, "In Contradiction Lies the Hope: Human Genome and Identity Politics," in *Tactical Biopolitics: Art, Activism, and Technoscience,* ed. Beatriz da Costa and Kavita Philip (Cambridge: MIT Press, 2008), 269–87.

47. Brodwin, "Genetics, Identity, and the Anthropology of Essentialism"; Elliott and Brodwin, "Identity and Genetic Ancestry Tracing."

7
DIGITAL COMMONS
The Rise of New Models of Collaborative Ownership

David Bollier

O UR UNDERSTANDINGS OF ownership—the value associated with
private-property rights—are changing profoundly in the emerging
networked environment. Although markets remain a powerful force for
creating certain types of wealth, a new social institution that combines
productive activity with self-governance and new forms of property
rights is starting to emerge: *the commons.*

In many respects, there is nothing new about the commons; it has been
a paradigm for managing resources communities from time immemorial.
But now that the commons is becoming a robust model for production
and governance in Internet contexts, it is attracting attention as a form
of social order and management beyond market and state. As this chapter explains, the drama now under way in virtual spaces is how the new
forms of bottom-up cooperation and social organization will transform
our ideas about property rights, the organization of production, and the
functioning of markets.

We are accustomed to speaking about "intellectual property" as if the
value of a song or an image were essentially fixed and physical. Copyright
holders often liken their ownership to the possession of a car or a tract of
land. But if there is anything that the Internet has demonstrated since the
birth of the World Wide Web in the early 1990s, it is that the singular
private possession of "intellectual property" can *limit* the creation of value.

This is because the existing owners of "intellectual property" have sought to extend the rights associated with their copyrights, trademarks, and patents, at the expense of the social, cultural, and civic interests and rights traditionally enjoyed by the public and future creators.[1] These interests include the right to excerpt portions of copyrighted works for educational, cultural, and political purposes and to make new creative works ("fair use" or "fair dealing"), the right to resell a purchased copyright work without authorization by or payment to the copyright holder (the first-sale doctrine), and the expectation of a robust public domain as a reservoir of material for future creativity, free expression, and democratic culture.

Copyright and its kindred bodies of law seek to convert knowledge and culture into artifacts of property (songs, texts, images, videos) so that they can be owned and sold. But there is a built-in tension to this act of propertizing culture, because the very existence and meaning of these works depend in great measure on their unrestricted social circulation. Works are meaningful only because they are part of a shared cultural context. Bottling up a work as a proprietary commodity can help convert that work into money (by enabling its ownership and sale), but it can also—especially in the Internet age—*diminish* the value of a work (by making it less known and less accessible to society). Or as the copyright scholar Siva Vaidhyanathan succinctly puts it, with apologies to Oscar Wilde, "The only thing worse than being sampled on the Internet is *not* being sampled on the Internet."[2]

In other words, value is not necessarily intrinsic to a cultural artifact, but rather arises from its social circulation, uses, and ascribed meanings. The actor Jack Nicholson put it nicely: "Only that audience out there makes a star. It's up to them. You can't do anything about it. . . . Stars would be Louis B. Mayer's cousins if you could make 'em up."[3] The strange, counterintuitive truth is that exclusive possession of a song, film, visual image, or text in an Internet context may actually diminish its market value. This is a key lesson of new genres such as open source software, Wikipedia and other wikis, remix music, collaborative archives, open access scholarly journals, and social networking, among many others. The common denominator of these forms is that each is generating enormous reservoirs of intangible value by eschewing strict private-property controls and instead inviting mass participation and shared access and collaboration. As the conventional boundaries of property law blur in online contexts, the terms of participation, access, and collaboration are wide open to negotiation and innovative hybrid structures that blend sharing and control.

"What we are seeing now," writes Yochai Benkler in his landmark book, *The Wealth of Networks*, "is the emergence of more effective collective action practices that are decentralized but do not rely on either the price system or a managerial structure for coordination." Benkler's preferred term is "commons-based peer production." By that, he means online systems that are collaborative and nonproprietary, and based on "sharing resources and outputs among widely distributed, loosely connected individuals who cooperate with each other."[4]

This emerging sector of self-organized community resource management is *the commons*. The term has long been associated with the "enclosure movement" in English history, the period from the fifteenth through the nineteenth centuries in which the landed gentry conspired with Parliament to privatize forests, pastures, and other natural resources that commoners collectively relied upon for subsistence.[5] For the past generation, the commons has been widely associated with the "tragedy of the commons," a term introduced by the biologist Garrett Hardin. In a famous 1968 essay, Hardin argued that the overexploitation and ruin of a resource is more or less inevitable when the resource is shared.[6]

The rediscovery of the commons as something more positive and generative began in 1990 when the political scientist Elinor Ostrom, in her pioneering work *Governing the Commons*, demonstrated that the commons is an eminently viable and even ingenious social system for managing shared resources.[7] Ostrom, who won the Nobel Prize for economics in 2009 for her studies of common-pool resources and cooperation, amassed persuasive historical evidence to rebut the "tragedy" thesis, which over the past generation has come to be seen as an economic truism in conservative political circles. She showed how communities can in fact sustainably manage fisheries, irrigation waters, wildlife, and other depletable natural resources without overexploiting them and causing a "tragedy." Hardin's error was in conflating an *open access regime*, in which anyone can overuse a collective resource without impediment or sanction, with a *commons*, which is a defined social community that acts as a steward of a resource by enforcing certain rules, maintaining a certain transparency of decision making, and punishing "free riders."

With the rise of the Internet, there has been a resurgence of interest in the commons paradigm as an alternative to market forms of property, wealth creation, and resource management. The interest has been fueled by the rise of highly effective, versatile online regimes for creating information and social community. It can be seen in the thousands of people who have built Wikipedia into the leading reference source of our time (more than 22 million user-written articles in 285 languages by mid-2012), in the thousands of hackers who have made Linux a highly respected computer operating system that now competes with Microsoft's Windows and enterprise software systems, and in homegrown social collaborations such as Crisis Commons, a global community of volunteers who use networked digital technologies to coordinate responses to disasters such as the Haiti earthquake.[8] Informal, self-organized social relationships, working in the unregimented, free space of open platforms, are changing the dynamics of economic production and culture. The commons is a powerful new social modality that is developing new spaces for self-governance and resource management beyond the conventional relationships ordained by markets and the state.

The classic economic narrative launched by the eighteenth-century philosopher Adam Smith holds that human beings are rational, self-interested creatures who invariably maximize their material, utilitarian interests. This is alleged to be the engine that drives economic life. But life on the Internet is proving this premise to be problematic. Benkler argues that on the Internet, "behaviors that were once on the periphery—social motivations, cooperation, friendship, decency—move to the very core of economic life."[9] Money and markets do not necessarily animate creative activity and wealth creation. In many online communities, enormous value is being created by large numbers of people coming together to negotiate their own worlds on open platforms.

In each instance, a community must come to agree on shared rules and norms for managing their collective resources. Rather than assign exclusive property rights, these collectives must figure out who will be allowed access to the resource and under what terms, what forms of hierarchy and authority will prevail with the consent of the governed, how violations of rules will be monitored and reported, how rules-violators will be sanctioned or excluded, and so on. These are some of the classic social negotiations identified by Ostrom and many of her colleagues as essential to the management of natural resource commons.

Perhaps the key difference in establishing viable commons in "digital spaces" is that digital information and culture are essentially infinite in nature; for all practical purposes, they can't be "used up" and they can be reproduced and shared at virtually no (incremental) cost. This differs from natural resource commons in which land, water, wild game, and other resources tend to be finite and "rivalrous" (that is, one person's use precludes another's and the resource can be depleted). Because of these differences, the social management of digital commons is less about "managing scarcity" than about "curating plenitude." The chief social issue to be negotiated is not how to thwart free riders, but rather how to organize information intelligently, protect it from private appropriation, and minimize community disruptions.

New Genres of Creativity

The universe of online commons is still a grossly undertheorized realm, and its most powerful archetypes are not familiar to the layperson. So it is useful to briefly describe some of the leading online commons and explain how they are creating value and governing shared resources in radically new ways.

Open source software (also known as "free software," meaning "free to use," not "no cost") has been profoundly influential in developing new sorts of online commons that show impressive technical creativity, flexibility, and popularity. This type of software is developed by communities of programmers who share the source code—the otherwise inaccessible design architecture and binary code—with anyone. This in turn allows the software to be subject to open inspection, modification, improvement, and sharing by large communities of volunteers (many of whom, interestingly, are employees of companies that find it advantageous to support such software). Remarkably, this process has proven competitive against conventional software whose source code is closed and proprietary.

The ability to access and share software code without restriction—while preserving it as a shared resource—stems from a legal innovation developed by a software hacker, Richard Stallman, in the late 1980s—the General Public License, or GPL. The GPL is a legal license based on copyright ownership that lets a programmer legally guarantee that his or her work will remain in the commons and not be appropriated by any private party. The license authorizes anyone to use the work (the software code) for free, without permission, so long as any derivative works are also made available under the same terms. This self-replicating legal provision encourages people to contribute to a shared pool of code, and to enter into enduring communities of collaboration, because everyone knows that their work will not be "taken private."

In this fashion, the GPL enables the emergence of a stable commons of shared software code. With the assurance that free riders will not be able to appropriate their work, volunteers have contributed their energies to the building of Linux and countless open source software applications since the GPL was developed. Many of these programs are key software systems for the Internet and popular desktop applications.

Wikipedia is another signature commons of our times. Although this user-generated and user-curated encyclopedia is the most famous wiki in existence, there are dozens of offshoots that rely on the same software and similar social dynamics. Wikispecies is a collective that is compiling an inventory of the world's species. Wikiquote is a site for amassing notable quotations. Wikitravel is a growing collection of user-written travel guides to hundreds of locations around the world. OpenWetWare is a wiki for biological researchers. Wookiepedia is a wiki for *Star Wars* fans. There is even a Conservapedia, an online encyclopedia of conservative political thought, and Intellipedia, an online resource for the U.S. government's intelligence agencies.

Creative Commons is a nonprofit organization that has helped provide legal tools for people to create their own commons of digital works. In 2002 a group of law professors, computer scientists, and artists developed a suite of standardized licenses for copyright owners that lets creators signal to the public that their works are freely available to anyone, without permission or payment. The licenses enable copyright owners to stipulate certain conditions for the reuse of their works, such as requiring that authorship is attributed, that the work not be used for commercial purposes, and that no derivative use is made.

The Creative Commons licenses represent a significant legal innovation because they enable authors to forgo the strict terms of copyright protection, which automatically treats any creative work, upon its creation, as private property. Copyright law makes no provision for affirmatively committing works to the public domain so that they may be legally shared. The CC licenses were expressly developed to let creative works exist in a legal "middle zone" between private property and the public domain—the commons—without forcing authors to surrender their copyrights.

What may seem like a rather mundane legal innovation has in fact given rise to countless online communities whose members are committed to sharing their works with each other. The photo-sharing website Flickr, for example, has more than 100 million user-contributed photos that are "tagged" with Creative Commons licenses. This means that anyone can use those photos consistent with the CC license terms. There are also communities of remix musicians, video mashup artists, book authors, and filmmakers who use the CC licenses to promote their works, their reputations, and cultural sharing.[10]

Academics and scientists are among the most frequent users of CC licenses because they enable authors to retain control over their works. Rather than surrender their copyrights to commercial journals as a condition of publication (which enables publishers to restrict access to Web-published articles, for example), academics can self-archive their works or publish them in "open access journals." In an attempt to confront soaring subscription prices and restricted access to published works, academic disciplines, learned societies, and universities have launched more than 8,800 open access journals whose articles are freely available for copying in perpetuity.[11] There are usually no copyright restrictions, payments, or permissions needed except to provide credit to the author. By creating their own online commons, academic specialties are bypassing commercial journals while fostering greater access and circulation for their research.

The CC licenses are also used by many communities devoted to remix music, video mashups, graphic design, and, of course, the "blogosphere" of tens of millions of blogs. For members of these communities, the CC licenses are helping to transcend the conventional legal limitations of copyright law while building new oeuvres of sharable content. Usage of the licenses is also something of a cultural statement, one that says, in effect, "I believe in the sharing economy, and I reject the Big Brother–style copyright intimidation of creators shown by Hollywood studios and the major record labels."

Open education, open science, and open business: The CC licenses have become widely used, as well, in education and science. In higher education especially, the open educational resources movement, or OER, is developing new bodies of freely shareable textbooks, curricular materials, databases, scholarly journals, collaborative digital archives, and much else. MIT's pioneering OpenCourseWare initiative, which put the curricular materials for hundreds of its courses online, for free, is now being emulated by more than 250 educational institutions in some 57 nations and regions, who have constituted themselves as the OpenCourseWare Consortium. The Connexions project at Rice University is the host of more than 20,000 "learning modules" woven into 1,200 collections that can be freely used, modified, and improved by anyone. The materials, now in many languages, are used by more than two million teachers and students a month, from 194 countries.

The Science Commons, a project of Creative Commons, is now working with leading scientific institutions to overcome legal and technological barriers that impede easy sharing of research and scientific literature. Besides the open access scholarly publishing movement, many scientific disciplines and organizations are supporting work to develop "Semantic Web" protocols, an evolving set of computer standards that will help researchers identify highly specific literature and data from the vast ocean of scientific research that is created every day. The Neurocommons project, for example, is a project that aims to use Semantic Web tools to hasten the interoperability of specialized knowledge from different fields that is currently isolated. Because large databases are becoming increasingly important to scientific inquiry, many scientists are also participating in efforts to develop "database commons" so that disparate pools of data can be shared without encountering copyright restrictions of technical barriers. In each of these instances, the goal is to break down the "transaction costs" that inhibit the flow of knowledge, so that scientists can accelerate the cycles of research, discovery, and innovation.

Social Networking and the Rise of the Commons

Nearly a decade ago, a new generation of Web-based software programs arose whose chief goal was to allow richer, more interesting types of social interactions online. There are many terms used to describe the social behaviors made possible by the new software: "smart mobs" (Howard Rheingold), "the wisdom of crowds" (James Surowiecki), and "wikinomics" (Don Tapscott and Anthony D. Williams) among others. But the terms that have gained the most widespread usage are "social networking," and "Web 2.0" (the tech publisher Tim O'Reilly popularized the latter term in a celebrated 2005 essay).[12]

Social networking has come to mean the body of software and open Web platforms that leverage people's natural social proclivities and give them new tools for interacting socially. Blogs, wikis, social networking websites, and other open, collaborative platforms all embody Web 2.0 principles. They are all oriented toward user freedoms and the ability to reuse and share other people's work.

What makes Web 2.0 platforms so significant is that they empower social communities to incubate value in new ways. Self-selected communities can create distinctive types of value that may elude conventional market players who are likely to regard a new idea as too quirky, underdeveloped, or niche to be commercialized. After all, participating in the marketplace requires a costly apparatus of business overhead: buildings, management systems, lawyers, advertising, and so on. Many Web 2.0 commons are more competitive than the market itself because they manage to create value at much lower costs, more rapidly, and in more socially responsive ways. Instead of formal legal relationships, commons leverage informal relationships of reciprocity and trust. Freed from the high barriers to participation in conventional markets, commons give space to serendipity, idiosyncratic ideas, personal passions, and community need, and then allow open networks to validate attractive ideas, without necessarily relying on market exchange or proprietary ownership. The Internet inverts the familiar process of "edit first, then publish," making it a "publish first, then edit" process.

The inner metabolism of online social communities constitutes a growing challenge to the conventional seller-driven economy. It enables people to develop valuable bodies of information and creative work, and to sustain them, in ways that are user-driven and autonomous from existing markets. In this sense, the commons is becoming a new kind of competitor to conventional markets. Alternatively, the commons can serve as a "staging area" for new types of markets. Facebook, for example, has become a hugely popular website because software meta-tagging has enabled people to identify like-minded people with great ease. A person can "tag" her personal profile with "Bob Dylan" and then locate other aficionados of the musician. In countless other venues, people can use tags to more easily find each other and build their own identity-based collectives, which in turn are becoming the basis for new niche markets. Advertisers may wish to buy ads to reach that particular demographic of users, or a company may be able to monetize some of the content produced by the community. For example, Wikitravel publishes books based on the travel reports and advice contributed by users, and Facebook generates a gold mine of social data that is used by marketers.

Eric von Hippel, a professor at MIT, has explored how user communities are increasingly seen by many companies as valuable sources of innovation. By blending social commons with commercial goals, some companies are blurring the lines that have historically separated "production" from "consumption." "Communities of interest are morphing into communities of creation and communities of production," according to von Hippel, who writes about this theme in his book *Democratizing Innovation*.[13] The cutting-edge participants of snowboarding, for example, came up with improved boot and binding designs; adventurers who climb canyon walls developed a method for cutting loose a trapped rope. Alert companies that have earned the loyalty and trust of key user communities can capitalize on these relationships to identify promising new ideas for product development.

We do not yet have well-developed theoretical models for understanding this new "socioeconomic space"; the online environments are still relatively new, and too much is still in flux. But it has not escaped the notice of major corporations that online social dynamics offer some radically more effective models for organizing employees and engaging with customers. In business, "crowdsourcing" has become a new template for work as companies find that they can solve problems and do research more rapidly and effectively if they invite mass collaborations or competitions. So, for example, InnoCentive has become a highly successful company by acting as a broker between "seekers" with research and development problems and "solvers" who propose solutions that meet the desired criteria.[14] In a similar vein, Hewlett-Packard has created a virtual stock market among its staff to gather collective estimates that have improved sales forecasts.[15] *The Economist* has written about the "fortune of the commons" that can result when there are open technical standards, and business professors like Henry Chesbrough have examined new "open business models."[16] The point is that distributed problem-solving via open platforms is an increasingly effective way to access unidentified talent and develop innovations.

The rise of these many new commons suggest that, in many circumstances, greater value is created by works being openly available than by being exclusively controlled. A recurring lesson is that economic and social value cannot necessarily be encased in an airtight bubble of property rights, especially copyrights, without incurring huge "opportunity costs," or forgone economic gain. This is a new kind of open marketplace that thrives by loosening proprietary controls and inviting the widest possible participation, free of charge.[17] Instead of trying to consummate a market transaction (such as a subscription or a product purchase), open business sites aim instead to cultivate user loyalty to the site and its content and to the people who congregate there. It then tries to "monetize" user and community relationships indirectly, for example through advertising and the sale of aggregated personal information to marketers. This business model requires a greater degree of respect for the user community, whose members are, after all, free to move on to other sites if a site host imposes obnoxious conditions (such as too much advertising or invasions of personal privacy). This is a built-in tension for companies such as Facebook and Twitter, whose business models depend on monetizing personal information about their users (by selling the data to advertisers) while somehow retaining their users' social trust.

The value generated by the online community, alternatively, can be captured by a commons, a bounded, self-governed social community that tends to exist outside of the marketplace. A commons illustrates that a business enterprise may or may not be necessary to generate value on Web 2.0 platforms. For example, a community of fans originally created the Internet Movie Database, which has since become a preeminent source of historical information about thousands of films. The site might have remained a commons, but its founders decided to convert it into a business and sell it to Amazon.com. Craigslist, a free online advertising service in dozens of cities, has long functioned as a commons as a deliberate choice by its founder, Craig Newmark. Despite the huge price he could obtain for selling the site and turning it into a business (it is run as a nonprofit), Newmark has insisted on preserving the site as a commons so that it would be a useful, noncommercial haven for ordinary people.

The decision to manage an online community as a commons is only possible because "commoners" (as many in fact call themselves) are acquiring the sophistication and tools to develop their own technological platforms, legal protections, and social norms. They can defend and preserve the value they create without relying on a corporation or a marketplace as a means to collective provisioning. At least in online spaces, the commons is an eminently viable option with few barriers to entry and use.

The Void in Economic Discourse

There is a conspicuous lacuna in market discourse for talking about this sort of value creation, however. Conventional economic analysis has no way of understanding how social communities of trust, shared purpose, and altruism can generate enduring value. After all, conventional economics envisions people pursuing their own rational, materialistic self-interests separately and individually. The idea of group identities, collective purpose, and collaboration having economic consequences is not taken as seriously. Economists who focus on "rational," "utility-maximizing" activity, as conventionally understood, fail to see that people might consider it rational and utility-maximizing to share with their online neighbors and participate in something larger than themselves. Historically, too, social collectives have not generally had the resources or legal structures for meeting group needs. (Cooperatives have trouble obtaining capital and capable management, for example, and niche interest groups have not had the communications tools to locate like-minded peers and nurture a shared community ethos and history.)

There is another reason why the value generated by the commons is easily overlooked by conventional economics: its resources cannot be privately owned or (generally) turned into money. Value in the commons is a shared, intangible resource that "hovers in the air," so to speak, and is not strictly owned by anyone. It consists of stable, enduring social relationships yoked to a shared resource. The circulation of the "wealth" (access to Wikipedia, use of a free software program, copying of an open access journal article) is not governed by money. And yet the commons nonetheless is highly generative. This is confounding to conventional economists who assume that one needs private-property rights, contracts, and markets in order to produce useful resources. But open platforms have shown impressive results in productive innovation as more people participate in a project, without restrictions on access. A related form is the semi-closed community—a commons—which manages a shared resource for the benefit of "members in good standing" who voluntarily adhere to a set of community norms.

A commons is more likely to grow if the value generated by a community is not monetized and it is legally protected from private appropriation through such mechanisms as the GPL or Creative Commons licenses. By making software code inalienable—something that cannot be taken private—the GPL assures that the hacker community will have guaranteed access to its code without anyone appropriating it and privatizing it attracted.[18] By guaranteeing that companies cannot take exclusive control of Wikipedia content, for example, Wikipedia has attracted tens of thousands of volunteers around the world who have been willing to contribute their talents to a shared enterprise.

What makes the new online commons so interesting is that they do not pose a mere rhetorical challenge to the worldview embodied by copyright law and late-capitalist discourse; they represent a *functional* challenge. They can often accomplish specific tasks with greater speed, creativity, and social satisfaction than markets can. They are frequently more efficient, innovative, and robust than conventional market-based enterprises. Wikipedia has played a significant role in out-competing Encyclopedia Britannica's long-standing business model, for example. (It was so successful that in March 2012 Britannica announced that it would no longer produce a print edition.) Similarly, Craigslist has provided a far cheaper, more flexible venue for want ads than conventional newspapers.

Neoliberal industrial societies are accustomed to seeing value as something that is monetized and privately owned by companies. The *market* is seen as the only significant source of wealth creation, and the contributions of government, nature, and social community are secondary if not negligible. But increasingly, as my brief tour of the commons shows, people are developing new technological, legal, and social vehicles to protect *socially created value*. The standard narrative of "individual originality" that is the justification for copyright privileges is being subverted by modes of creation that are derivative, collaborative, and context-based. The traditional narrative of intellectual property is under siege. As the commons sector grows, so do the variety of forms of social negotiation and organization. Networked communities are learning that if they can protect their online resources and relationships from market appropriation, they can use this freedom to develop innovative governance models that advance their self-interest in ways that neither markets nor governments can.

The socially created value generated within commons is starting to have serious micro- and macro-economic effects. Mainstream media corporations are starting to wake up to the fact that their most formidable adversary may not be piracy—illicit copying of their movies and music—but the diversion of people's attention from the commercial media marketplace to their own non-market commons and Web 2.0 social spaces. The popularity of blogs, wikis, social networking sites, and a host of other amateur, participatory websites means that the commercial media can no longer aggregate large audiences with such ease. Their advertising base is migrating elsewhere—to online media—a reality that has a lot to do with the sagging economic fortunes of the newspaper industry.

The commons is not likely to supplant markets any time soon, but it is an inescapable fact that it is becoming a serious alternative sector for creating value (monetized and otherwise). It bears noting that the new commons are not necessarily incompatible with markets per se. But commoners do insist on their own non-market identities and sense of inalienable value. Rather than summarily surrender the value they create for market purposes, or let businesses appropriate that value, commoners in many instances can assert control over their own resources. They are able to manage themselves and their collectively generated content (code, music, text, video) according to their own priorities, which may or may not involve the marketplace.

The Commons as a Fledgling Type of Democratic Polity

In a brilliant essay published in 2006, the Internet scholar David R. Johnson declared that online commons represent a new kind of social/biological metabolism for creating "law."[19] By that, he meant that commons have their own internal systems for managing their affairs and for interacting with their environment. They can repair themselves and define their own persistent identity. They have a moral legitimacy and social trust that "competes" with the declining sense of trust and legitimacy in markets and government. As I describe in a paper written with John H. Clippinger, open platforms are spurring a movement away from *government* and toward new forms of online *governance* as a more effective alternative: "As more of life and commerce are mediated by digital technologies and Internet platforms, the tensions between legacy institutions (centralized, hierarchical, control-based) and emergent social practices on open networks (distributed, participatory, emergent) are intensifying. For years, such tensions have been deliberately ignored or finessed—but that approach may no longer be possible. The structural deficiencies of existing online systems are spurring the search for better, more practical approaches to governance, law and policymaking [than that provided by government]." Denizens of the digital commons tend to believe that their open, participatory, self-governed communities can produce better results than outcomes mandated by legislatures, government bureaucracies, or courts.[20]

In this sense, the Commons Sector represents a great leap forward in citizenship—a reimagining of civil society in the digital age. In the United States in the eighteenth century, citizens had the right to affirm the decisions of the landed elite. In nineteenth-century America, citizenship was all about joining large, centralized political parties. In the twentieth century, citizenship was mostly about becoming an "educated voter" and working to achieve good government.[21] The Commons Sector takes citizenship to an entirely new level. It enables and honors the principles of open access, transparency, the freedom to participate, and social equity in ways that previous versions of citizenship—and the official democratic polity itself—cannot or will not fulfill. This is not to say that the commons paradigm is an ideological or political construction in any conventional sense. It is, rather, a new vehicle for self-directed production and self-governance, as I describe in my book *Viral Spiral: How the Commoners Built a Digital Republic of Their Own*.

One could argue, as some do, that the new digital citizenship is "only in virtual spaces," and so can be safely ignored as interesting but not that consequential. But the migration of commerce and culture to online spaces is proving this assumption to be incorrect. The power of bloggers to initiate news stories, challenge errors in the mainstream press, root out stories of corruption in government, and in other ways participate directly in democratic life is remarkable.[22] The presidential candidacy of

Barack Obama in 2008 was driven in large measure by his ability to tap into the enthusiasm and money of Internet users; he raised over $650 million from more than 2.5 million Americans, with about half in amounts of less than $200. The "crowdfunding" website Kickstarter now raises and distributes more money for artistic projects—a sum estimated to exceed $150 million in 2012—than the entire fiscal budget of the U.S. National Endowment for the Arts ($146 million).[23]

If there is one overriding lesson from the rise of new digital commons, it is that ownership of private property (at least in digital contexts) is not what it used to be. The market individualism associated with property is beginning to erode and mutate in the burgeoning Internet culture. In truth, the absolute dominion over a resource implied by private property has always been something of a fiction; property rights have always needed to make concessions to the needs of the community, nature, and custom. But digital commons are not just lurking on the outskirts of property law; they are transforming it. Digital commons are forcing a new recognition that property law in modern, liberal states is deeply embedded in the life of social communities. This means that communities can make property law more accountable to them.

The productive energies and innovation of online collectives are eclipsing those of the individual at the heart of property law. The sheer generative power of Internet communities is eclipsing the self-made man valorized by John Locke and his modern successors—and along with it, the idea of fixed, inviolate rights that inhere in individuals. Thus the very character of property rights—individual vs. collective, formal vs. informal, static vs. evolving—is subject to negotiation. And if the terms dictated by large market players are seen as too onerous (privacy violations, excessive advertising, bad functionality), Internet users are free to develop their own commons-based alternatives. Hence the bright future for this new form of social governance and order. Digital commons are likely to expand and diversify in coming years as the limitations of conventional institutions—centralized, inflexible, bureaucratic, distrusted—become less tolerable and as the virtues of "commoning" become more evident.

NOTES

1. See, for example, Lawrence Lessig, *Code and Other Laws of Cyberspace* (New York: Basic Books, 1999); and David Bollier, *Brand Name Bullies: The Quest to Own and Control Culture* (New York: John Wiley & Sons, 2005).

2. Siva Vaidhyanathan, remarks, in Norman Lear Center, "Ready to Share: Fashion and the Ownership of Creativity," conference proceedings, ed. David Bollier and Laurie Racine, Los Angeles, 2005, p. 142, available at www.learcenter.org/pdf/RTStranscript.pdf.

3. Quoted in Jib Fowles, *Starstruck: Celebrity Performers and the American Public* (Washington, DC: Smithsonian Institution Press, 1992), 84.

4. Yochai Benkler, *The Wealth of Networks: How Social Production Transforms Markets and Freedom* (New Haven: Yale University Press, 2006), 60.

5. See Raymond Williams, *The Country and the City* (New York: Oxford University Press, 1973), especially chap. 10; and W. E. Tate, *The English Village Community and the Enclosure Movement* (London: Victor Gollancz, 1967).

6. Garrett Hardin, "The Tragedy of the Commons," *Science* 162 (December 13, 1968): 1243–48.

7. Elinor Ostrom, *Governing the Commons: The Evolution of Institutions for Collective Action* (New York: Cambridge University Press, 1990).

8. Two overviews of this trend can be found in Clay Shirky, *Here Comes Everybody: The Power of Organizing without Organizations* (New York: Penguin, 2008); and Lawrence Lessig, *Remix: Making Art and Commerce Thrive in the Hybrid Economy* (New York: Penguin, 2008).

9. Yochai Benkler, remarks at the iCommons Summit (Dubronik, Croatia, June 15, 2007), quoted in David Bollier, *Viral Spiral: How the Commoners Built a Digital Republic of Their Own* (New York: New Press, 2009), 126n10.

10. Bollier, *Viral Spiral*, chap. 5.

11. For a complete list see the Directory of Open Access Journals at www.doaj.org/.

12. Tim O'Reilly, "What Is Web 2.0: Design Patterns and Business Models for the Next Generation of Software," O'Reilly Media website, September 30, 2005, http://oreilly.com/web2/archive/what-is-web-20.html. The terms referred to here are discussed at great length in Howard Rheingold, *Smart Mobs: The Next Social Revolution* (New York: Perseus, 2003); James Surowiecki, *The Wisdom of Crowds* (New York: Doubleday, 2004); and Don Tapscott and Anthony D. Williams, *Wikinomics: How Mass Collaboration Changes Everything* (New York: Portfolio, 2006).

13. Eric von Hippel, *Democratizing Innovation* (Cambridge: MIT Press, 2005).

14. David Bollier, *The Future of Work: What It Means for Individuals, Businesses, Markets and Governments* (Washington, DC: The Aspen Institute, 2011), available at www.aspeninstitute.org/publications/future-of-work.

15. Robert D. Hof, "The Power of Us: Mass Collaboration on the Internet Is Shaking Up Business," *Business Week,* June 20, 2005, 73–82.

16. "The Fortune of the Commons," *Economist*, May 8, 2003, www.economist.com/node/1747362; Henry Chesbrough, *Open Business Models: How to Thrive in the New Innovation Landscape* (Cambridge: Harvard Business School Press, 2006).

17. See Chris Anderson, *Free: How Today's Smartest Businesses Profit by Giving Something for Nothing* (New York: Hyperion, 2010).

18. Interestingly, derivative works that use free software and open source software can legally be commercialized; they just cannot be privatized. No business can withhold the code from general use. Red Hat, for example, is a commercial vendor of Linux, the computer operating system, despite the fact that the code is freely accessible to anyone. Red Hat makes money by selling prepackaged "distributions" of Linux and by providing technical support to business users.

19. David R. Johnson, "The Life of the Law Online," *First Monday* 11.2 (February 2006), http://firstmonday.org/issues/issue11_2/johnson/index.html.

20. John H. Clippinger and David Bollier, "The Social Stack for New Social Contracts" (January 2013), available at http://idcubed.org/open-platform/socialstack. See also David Bollier, "Digital Common Law: Moving from Government to Governance" (blog post, June 25, 2012), at www.bollier.org/blog/digital-common-law-moving-government-governance.

21. This scenario is sketched by Michael Schudson in *The Good Citizen: A History of American Civil Life* (New York: Free Press, 1998).

22. See, for example, Dan Gilmor, *We the Media: Grassroots Journalism, by the People, for the People* (Sebastopol, CA: O'Reilly Media, 2005).

23. Carl Franzen, "Kickstarter Expects to Provide More Funding to the Arts Than NEA," Talking Points Memo (February 24, 2012), http://idealab.talkingpointsmemo.com/2012/02/kickstarter-expects-to-provide-more-funding-to-the-arts-than-nea.php.

OWNERSHIP AND THE BOUNDARY

———— ∞∞∞ ————

Stephen Clingman

THE ESSAYS IN this volume cover a broad range of topics, from questions of open source access on the Internet, to issues of heritage and ownership among native and aboriginal communities, to questions of who owns our genes, to claims on artworks, papers, languages, and archaeological finds in national and international contexts, and more. The settings range from North America to Italy to India to Spain to—if we take the Internet or the genetic landscape as our model—"everywhere." It seems fitting, in such a context, to reflect by way of a conclusion on the question of boundaries and their nature, which in some way connects all of the investigations in this collection as well as the activities of the organization that hosted their original presentation.

As Laetitia La Follette points out in her introduction, the collection emanates from a year-long seminar titled "Cultural Ownership" arranged by the Interdisciplinary Seminar in the Humanities and Fine Arts (ISHA) at the University of Massachusetts Amherst in 2006–7. ISHA was founded in 2001, and since that time has offered some fourteen seminars on such topics as "Reproduction," "Migrations," "Religious Politics," "Marriage and Its Alternatives," and "(Ir)rationality and Public Discourse," among others.[1] During that time, I have been privileged to participate in almost all of the discussions as our various fellows gave presentations on their work. Our fellows have been drawn from an unusually wide range of disciplines, not only in the humanities and arts but also in the social and even biological and natural sciences. Although there might be some perplexity as to what the concept of "interdisciplinarity" actually means, in the context of our seminars I have come to understand it not as a "thing" but as a practice. Semester after semester, interdisciplinarity is what we have come to construct as a practice around the conference table. Among other things, it has meant a willingness to learn and speak in one another's languages, to hear and absorb what at might at first sound alien. It has not meant—though this may come as a surprise—losing the insights and perspectives of one's own discipline. Indeed, interdisciplinary practice has come—in our particular form of it—to mean working in and across the boundaries of the disciplines, and not in some vacuous or abstract sense simply negating or transcending them. In other words, the interdisciplinary, or what we might more meaningfully call the transdisciplinary, is in a continuing dialogue with the disciplinary. From that point of view, the question of boundaries has been central to the history and practice of ISHA as a forum. The central insight of such a practice, that boundaries are not the limit to interaction but in some profound way their precondition, is the idea I would like to explore in my reflections here, because it may have some implications for the underlying preoccupations of this volume.

There is a natural tendency to think of the boundary as being synonymous with the "limit." That is what it appears to mean: the boundary is something one cannot get across. Yet boundaries are crossed all the time, whether they are fences, borders, rivers, oceans, the airways, or space; artifacts that come to us from the past have crossed the boundaries of time—they are, in some sense, time-travelers, as are we when we encounter them. Similarly, there is a natural tendency to think of ownership and boundaries as somehow co-dependent and co-defining. If I own this particular statue, then by definition you do not, and you cannot simply put it in the back of your truck and drive it away. If I have written a play, then by definition you will have to pay copyright fees if you perform it. The boundaries must be observed, and this is true whether ownership is personal and singular or collective. The question of boundaries then seems foundational, whether a single person claims ownership or it is a nation or ethnic grouping that does so. Whoever owns the object owns it in some absolute sense—the meaning of the term "inalienable" property.

Yet, as some of the examples just cited suggest, there is no intrinsic contradiction between the notions of ownership and distribution. Ownership can be distributed among a group of people, and the degree of relative ownership within such a grouping can also be distributed variably (one person has a 25 percent stake in a movie, another 17 percent). Even personal ownership can be understood as a special form of distribution: a distribution of "one." What matters in such cases then is not whether boundaries apply, but where we set the frame—where the boundaries come into force, and with what implications. For instance, a nation-state may claim ownership of a statue, but does that mean that everyone in the nation has a personal stake or claim in it, or even full rights of access to it, which is one of the usual implications of ownership? Nation-states may lock up statues for safekeeping; here ownership and distribution are mutually exclusive in practical terms, but not in the ways we normally think of when we model the concepts, because distribution might be limited *for* the nominal owners. We might complicate the issues in other ways. An ethnic group may claim "ownership" of their language, but this cannot mean that every native speaker has equal access to every last secret of the language. Nor can it mean that no one else on earth has the "right" to speak the language, at least in practical terms. Ownership and distribution in these various senses may be neither homologous nor mutually defining; nor are they completely exclusive.

Language is a good phenomenon to think about when it comes to questions of cultural ownership, because along with music and art it is one of the core expressions of human culture, in fact of what it means to be human. As such, it seems that at best we can talk of a spectrum of possibilities regarding language and ownership ranging from conceptions that are wholly open to those that are almost wholly closed. At one end of the spectrum is the question of how language operates as language. Here the essential insight, deriving in one massively influential form from Chomskyan linguistics, is that language as such is an innate property (in every sense) of all human beings, no matter which particular "language" they happen to speak. This is the generative grammar, syntactic and recursive in its intrinsic promptings, that (in Humboldt's famous formula) "provides for infinite use of finite means."[2] In the wider, more everyday sense, we can say that language is a medium that flows between us all, which we lay claim to from time to time, where every utterance may be distinct yet draws from the reservoir to which we varyingly have access and which, every time we speak, we replenish. In that regard, language is one resource that cannot be used up by being used. If we are talking of boundaries and ownership (who owns language?), then this is a version that is primarily porous, osmotic, nonexclusive; it is a model which may suggest that language is "loaned" to us for use, as we similarly loan it to others every time we read, write, or are in conversation. Yet somewhere in the middle of the spectrum is the idea that an ethnic group may (as Margaret Speas describes in her contribution to this volume) claim "ownership" of its language. And at the far end of the spectrum, when it comes to questions of ownership, are laws of copyright which suggest that in particular instances language may, after all, be quite exclusive and proprietary, to be bought and sold on the market—the opposite of the idea of the "commons" that David Bollier writes about.

This brings us to the question of money, another key marker in a theory of cultural ownership, because if anything defines ownership, it is money. This is the reality of the art and antiquities markets Laetitia La Follette engages with; it is increasingly a large part of the universe of genes that preoccupies Banu Subramaniam. (It is intriguing how, as Steven Pinker points out, there are ready analogies between genes and language, in the sense that DNA provides the generative grammar of our biological forms of expression;[3] but clearly genes are also alienable by pharmaceutical companies and others, as well as open to "claim" or rejection by ethnic or racial groupings.) From this point of view, it is clear how decisive money can be when it comes to ownership—not only because it defines ownership but because it, quite obviously, facilitates it. Money in this sense can be wholly destructive, as it is in the art market of looting and exchange, or even in the more regulated flow of artifacts from the global south to the north, a structure of imbalance.

Yet the intriguing thing—and here my argument begins to travel in a different direction—is that if we consider money *as* money (in the way we considered language as language), it also suggests a spectrum of possibilities. At one end is the way in which money defines property, becomes almost coterminous with it. This is money as the hoard, the bank, Fort Knox, the impregnable vault that defines wealth and power. And yet, at the other end, we might ask the question: what is money without the possibility of flow, of exchange, of transition in some form? As with language, we can ask who "owns" money in the abstract. Certain people may lay claim to it, or portions of it, for a certain time, but without circulation, or the potential for circulation, money is useless and indeed meaningless.[4] In other words, as much as money may be sealed away in vaults, it also has to cross boundaries, or have the *potential* of crossing boundaries, to take on significance. The origin of the word "currency" is the Latin *currere*—to run (or, in an extended sense, move about). Without that, money is indeed merely Midas's hoard, and as in the legend, when gold is the end in and of itself, it brings not life but a literal stifling of circulation, or death.

And so we come, even in this short account, to the question of meaning, also at the heart of cultural ownership, because issues of culture and meaning not only cannot but should not be divorced. Why do people, or nations, or cultures claim to "own" cultural objects or heritages? This has to do not only with money, authority, or power but quite centrally with meaning; primarily it concerns the meaning of the object for the owner, and often—where it is a group that claims ownership—it is connected with notions of cultural identity, also a kind of meaning. Yet here, as with questions of language or money, we need to recognize that there is a spectrum of possibilities when it comes to how meanings are constructed. In saying this I am not so much concerned with the problem of whether meaning (or value) inheres in the object itself (objectively, so to speak) or whether it is projected onto the object by those who find it meaningful (which seems very likely to be the case). In this I am more concerned with the question of meaning and boundaries, and the *kinds* of boundaries we construct in setting up our models of meaning.

At one end of the spectrum—if we adopt that idea again—we need to recognize that in some cases the meaning of particular objects will be so wrapped up in particular forms of experience that the boundaries need to be closed—or at least closed at this point in our history. This is the argument around meaning that underlies the NAGPRA legislation in the United States which Joe Watkins discusses, and it is essentially reclamatory and intended to restitute or make whole in some form.[5] So, where Native American remains have been abducted or stolen, they need to be returned for proper treatment, and the same may be true for aboriginal artifacts of various kinds for which a "closed" custodianship is argued. Where art belonging to Jews or others was seized or stolen by the Nazis, it should be returned, no matter who claims to "own" it at present. It should be clear: cases such as these concern not only property rights, because they also very much concern meaning—the two are fully entangled. The boundary in this form seems to be coterminous with a notion of *respect:* the rights of others which have been violated must be respected, and their claims should be recognized. Intriguingly, this strong form of the boundary, connected with a moral pull to restitution, occurs where previously those boundaries have been completely open to violation because of the dispositions of rampant power. The boundaries of the defenseless have been breached, and we now attempt to redeem that not only through the restitution of objects but also through the restitution of meaning. In that sense, the history of open boundaries—or boundaries that have been *forced* open (the distinction is important) is not a happy one, and may lead us to question the notion of open boundaries altogether.

At the other end of the spectrum, however, is the case argued compellingly in this volume by David Bollier that value is created not only by the originators of cultural works but also by their users. Here we should remember that "value" is itself a term whose range of reference operates along a spectrum, from questions of monetary value at one end to notions of worth at the other, which are more intangible but may be no less significant, including the meaning a work has for its creator *and* its audience. In this latter sense especially we might say that maximum circulation creates maximum value. Such a view might underpin an argument for boundaries that are wholly open—the kind that the Internet might propagate in its most decentralized forms. Yet as Bollier indicates, even in the "digital commons" form, which revolutionizes capitalized principles of value, the rights of creators must be acknowledged in the construction of boundaries—limiting, for instance, the right of third parties to use commons work for personal financial gain. In a more nuanced account we could then say that the recognition of boundaries might *add* to the value of a work in the course of its circulation, not least in terms of the overall cultural experience it invites, *including* some contemplation of what boundaries in culture mean. Both practically and morally, then, the boundaries even of the Internet cannot be completely open; at the least, new models of recognition, generation, and ownership need to be developed.

What all this means is that, whether in the most traditional and ancient or contemporary of forms, there are enormous areas of complication when it comes to questions of cultural ownership, often around the question of boundaries and value. Should the Elgin Marbles be returned to Greece? Should museums that can "take care" of objects more successfully than their countries of origin be allowed to keep them? What are the ratios of "ownership" in objects that belong both to particular cultures (or to more than one culture) and to our human heritage as a whole?[6] What of the rights of musicians or other cultural producers in an age of instant reproduction and dissemination? Who "owns" our common genetic heritage? But as much as there are complications, there are also opportunities for rethinking our philosophy of boundaries and how they might operate.

It is in this light that I would like to return to the question of meaning as meaning—in the same way we have thought about language "as" language, and money "as" money. Doing so will have the virtue of tying together some of my preoccupations around the question of boundaries and ownership. The simple observation or proposal I would like to offer is this: there is no meaning without boundaries.[7] The fact is, we often think of the boundary as the limit to meaning—the limit which it cannot cross—but the equal fact is that the boundary is the *precondition* to meaning. This may sound paradoxical, but again, let us think of this by way of considering language. In any given sentence, meaning is constituted in the *transition* between one word and another; in the word it comes in the transition between one sound and another; in the utterance, through the transition between speaker and listener; in the sound, between the mouth and the ear. In the neurology of the brain, even the smallest element of the message occurs across a gap—the gap of the synapse. From synapse to syntax, what is significant in language, what *signifies,* occurs in what I have called elsewhere "the space of crossing;" it is the boundary not as the limit but as a *space*.[8] We should then think of the boundary not like the impermeable walls of Fort Knox storing its gold, but as a space in which meaning occurs through its crossing. If there were no crossing there would be no meaning; but there would also be no meaning if there were no boundary to cross.

It seems to me that a perspective such as this has important implications for theories of cultural ownership and the various forms of meaning they help us sustain. The key question in this light is not whether we should have boundaries—since we always have them in one form or another—but *what kinds of boundaries* we construct. Such boundaries may indeed be variable, depending on circumstances. Here they might recognize the need for royalties—a need which through that very mechanism allows access, a crossing of boundaries. There they might recognize the need for restitution—rebuilding the boundaries of respect and recognition that have been willfully destroyed: another kind of crossing, even as the boundaries are restored. Primarily, what a perspective such as this should help recover is a sense of the *transitive* nature of culture—that it takes on meaning only through its circulations and crossings, whether across space or time. On the one hand an awareness of the boundary helps us recognize key things: the need for respect; for certain kinds of inviolability; for the pastness of the past; for the nature of loss as well as recovery. It also helps us recognize the boundary as a *complex* and challenging space, for people do not necessarily approach the boundary as equals: there are asymmetries of authority, resources and power—what Emmanuel Levinas calls a difference in "height."[9] Such considerations need always to be taken into account, legally, morally, philosophically. On the other hand, a sense of the transitive boundary will induce other recognitions: how culture is all about negotiation—negotiating boundaries, otherness, differences in space and time; how culture "travels" (to use James Clifford's term);[10] how the meaning of culture, and even the meaning of ownership, can be transformed through a notion of transitivity. In this sense no ownership is absolute or final; the object can "belong" to a person or culture, but there is a key sense in which it belongs to us all. The boundary should not limit or prevent that recognition but *enable* it: a boundary we can navigate certainly with respect but also with openness and awareness, a sense of the various "belongings" to which we belong. It is *because* of the complexity of the boundary that its navigation is so important, because the challenges of doing so are also what make us human.

In this, given my own disciplinary origins but also interdisciplinary wanderings, I draw inspiration yet again from language, and a particular linguistic account. Just over fifty years ago, the linguist Roman Jakobson undertook a study of aphasia in which he distinguished two axes of language.[11] The one, basically vertical, is the axis of selection or substitution, the kind that allows us to say "The cat sat on the mat" or "The dog sat on the mat." In the latter case "dog" is selected instead of "cat." This vertical axis Jakobson aligns with the metaphoric function in language, where one word may substitute for another. But in this model the horizontal axis is what Jakobson calls metonymic—and this is the capacity whereby we put those words together in sequence and make meaning out of them: "The-cat-sat-on-the-mat." In this sense the metonymic function is what underlies syntax, the capacity to generate meanings by putting words next to one another; it is a function not of selection but *contiguity*. There are some problems in Jakobson's model, not least that he offered too binary an opposition between the metaphoric and metonymic.[12] But there is still something that can be taken from it if we wish to think about culture, ownership, boundaries, and meaning. For the key issues in human culture are those of contiguity. We stand next to one another, but we don't know how to contact one another, how to generate meaning out of that contact. We think of ownership as absolute, not understanding that it can take on meaning only through connection and transitivity. We think of the boundary as the limit, not understanding that it is the precondition and space of crossing. Like the sentence, the words by themselves have a static kind of meaning, but it is when one puts them together through syntax, traversing the spaces between the words, between the speaker and listener, that a more meaningful and dynamic process results. That, it seems to me, is the way we need to think about culture and ownership. All of us have culture; we are like the separate "words" in the sentence. But it is by putting the words in contact with one another, by crossing the spaces between them as creatively and mindfully as possible, by doing our best to meet the challenge of the navigation that a different and more meaningful kind of human syntax might result.

NOTES

1. For further information on ISHA (which in the fall of 2012 became the Interdisciplinary Studies Institute), see www.umass.edu/isi.
2. Noam Chomsky, "Linguistics and Adjacent Fields: A Personal View," in *The Chomskyan Turn,* ed. Asa Kasher (Oxford: Blackwell, 1991), 7. For the original, see Wilhelm von Humboldt, *On Language,* ed. Michael Losonsky, trans. Peter Heath (Cambridge: Cambridge University Press, 1999), 91.
3. Steven Pinker, *The Language Instinct: How the Mind Creates Language* (New York: Perennial Classics, 2000), 76.
4. Marx has much to say on the character of money as a *perpetuum mobile* even as

he establishes its capacity to step outside of circulation as "treasure" or "wealth." Though because of this Marx is suspicious of any simple analogy between money and language, nonetheless, in terms of my argument here it is clear that cultural ownership can and does mediate the circulations of meaning, sometimes halting it altogether. See Karl Marx, *Grundrisse,* trans. Martin Nicolaus (Harmondsworth: Penguin, 1993), 186–218.

5. Besides Watkins's essay in this volume, see also his article "Cultural Nationalists, Internationalists, and 'Intra-nationalists': Who's Right and Whose Right?," *International Journal of Cultural Property* 12.1 (2005): 78–94.

6. On these and related questions, see some classic articles by John Henry Merryman: "Two Ways of Thinking about Cultural Property," *American Journal of International Law* 80 (1986): 831–53; "Cultural Property Internationalism," *International Journal of Cultural Property* 12.1 (2005): 11–39; and "Whither the Elgin Marbles," in *Imperialism, Art and Restitution,* ed. Merryman (Cambridge: Cambridge University Press, 2006), 98–113. It is worth saying that Merryman's accounts have come under criticism: see Nora Niedzielski-Eichner, "Art Historians and Cultural Property Internationalism," *International Journal of Cultural Property* 12.2 (2005): 183–200; and Lyndel V. Prott, "The International Movement of Cultural Objects," *International Journal of Cultural Property* 12.2 (2005): 225–48.

7. My discussion from this point on draws strongly from my book *The Grammar of Identity: Transnational Fiction and the Nature of the Boundary* (Oxford: Oxford University Press, 2009), especially the introduction and conclusion.

8. Ibid., 24–25.

9. Emmanuel Levinas, "Martin Buber and the Theory of Knowledge," in *The Levinas Reader,* ed. Seán Hand (Oxford: Blackwell, 1989), 72–73.

10. James Clifford, "Traveling Cultures," in *Cultural Studies,* ed. Lawrence Grossberg, Cary Nelson, and Paula A. Treichler (New York: Routledge, 1992), 96–112.

11. Roman Jakobson, "Two Aspects of Language and Two Types of Aphasic Disturbances" (1956) in *Selected Writings,* vol. 2 (The Hague: Mouton, 1971), 239–59.

12. This was something Jakobson himself later recognized: see Roman Jakobson, "Linguistics and Poetics," in *Selected Writings,* vol. 3, ed. Stephen Rudy (The Hague: Mouton, 1981), 42; see also Clingman, *Grammar,* 13–15.

ABOUT THE CONTRIBUTORS

DAVID BOLLIER, coeditor with Silke Helfrich of *The Wealth of the Commons: A World Beyond Market and State* (2012,) is an author and activist who studies the commons as a new paradigm of politics, culture, and economics.

STEPHEN CLINGMAN, professor of English and director of the Interdisciplinary Studies Institute at the University of Massachusetts Amherst, has written widely on South African as well as transnational fiction. His biography of Bram Fischer, the lawyer who defended Nelson Mandela, won the Sunday Times Alan Paton Award.

SUSAN M. DIGIACOMO is a cultural anthropologist. She teaches at the Universitat Rovira i Virgili in Tarragona (Catalonia), and holds an adjunct faculty appointment at the University of Massachusetts Amherst.

LAETITIA LA FOLLETTE is director of the Art History Program at the University of Massachusetts Amherst and Vice President for Professional Responsibilities of the Archaeological Institute of America.

ORIOL PI-SUNYER, professor emeritus of anthropology at the University of Massachusetts Amherst, works in Iberia and Mesoamerica. His publications explore different dimensions of political economy, including the relationship between structures of power and forms of representation.

MARGARET SPEAS is professor of linguistics at the University of Massachusetts Amherst and a founding member of the Navajo Language Academy, a nonprofit group that promotes the study and teaching of the Navajo language.

BANU SUBRAMANIAM, coeditor of *Feminist Science Studies: A New Generation* (2001) and *Making Threats: Biofears and Environmental Anxieties* (2005), teaches in the department of Women, Gender, Sexuality Studies at the University of Massachusetts Amherst.

JOE WATKINS, A member of the Choctaw Nation of Oklahoma, is Supervisory Anthropologist/Chief of the Tribal Relations and Amerian Cultures Program,

National Park Service. Since beginning fieldwork in 1968, he has wored to allevi-ate tension between archaeology and Indigenous communities globally.

H. MARTIN WOBST, professor emeritus of anthropology at the University of Massachusetts Amherst, studies how artifacts help to constitute individuals and societies, and how that varies across time and space.

INDEX

aesthetics, 39, 44–45, 53, 77–79, 81
African American Lives (Gates), 152
Albéniz, Isaac, 79
Alfonso XIII (of Spain), 80
Allen, Jennifer, 62n38
Amazon (company), 180
American Anthropological Association, 46
American Association of Museums, 46
American Declaration on the Rights of Indigenous People, 101
American Indian Movement, 21
American Indian Religious Freedom Act of 1978, 128
American Indians. *See* Indigenous peoples; Native Americans
American Philological Association, 46
amnesia. *See desmemoria;* memory
amnesty, 72–93
anthropology: linguistic culture and, 111–18, 122–40; methodological assumptions of, 1, 4, 15–18, 21–25, 27–31, 74–77, 112, 152–53, 155–58, 188–96; Native American remains and, 15, 23–33; violence and, 73–93
antiquarians, 123–24
antiquities, 5, 20, 38–57. *See also* art; Greece; museums; Rome
Antiquities Act of 1906, 20, 128
Aphrodite of Morgantina (statue), 41
Aplin, Graeme, 19
ARA (newspaper), 91
Aragay, Ignasi, 88
Archaeological Institute of America (AIA), 43, 46, 60n21
Archaeological Resources Protection Act of 1979, 22
archaeology: antiquities markets and, 40–41, 43–44, 47, 51–57; definitions

of, 33n2; descendant populations and, 23–33, 123–40; heritage concerns and, 18–25; Human Subjects Review and, 133–35, 144n34; language and, 122–40; methodological assumptions of, 1, 4, 15–16, 21–25, 32, 74–77, 123, 127–34, 141n10, 142n19, 188–96; postmodern-, 6–7, 130–34; scientific detachment and, 6, 16–18, 31–33, 122–34, 141n10, 142n19, 188–96
Archivo Histórico Nacional Sección Guerra Civil, 84. *See also* Salamanca Papers
art, 1, 3–4, 40, 43–50, 191. *See also* aesthetics; antiquities; museums; *specific artists and works*
Aryans, 16, 148–50, 161
Ash, Anna, 110, 118
Ashworth, Gregory, 18
Asociación para la Recuperación de la Memoria Histórica (ARMH), 83
Assembly of First Nations, 103
Association for State and Local History, 46
Association of Art Museum Directors, 46–48
Association of Science Museum Directors, 46
Australian Aborigines, 103, 122, 128, 144n36
AVUI (newspaper), 88

Baldwin, James, 150
Bamshad, Michael, 153, 156–57, 159–61, 164–65
Barcelona Masonic Lodge, 88
Barr, Antonio, 82
Beazley, J. D., 56
Becchina, Gianfranco, 41, 55